A Handbook of Problem Words & Phrases

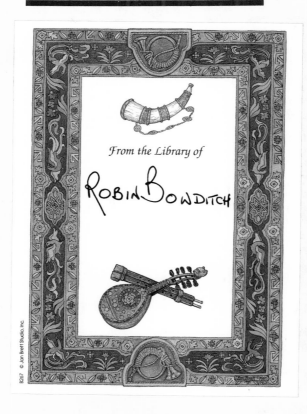

From the Library of

ROBIN BOWDITCH

The Professional Writing Series

This volume is one of a series published by ISI Press®. The series is designed to improve the communication skills of professional men and women, as well as students embarking upon professional careers.

Books published in this series:

A Handbook of Problem Words & Phrases

Morton S. Freeman
Foreword by Isaac Asimov

iSi PRESS®

Philadelphia

ISI PRESS®

3501 Market Street, Philadelphia, PA 19104 U.S.A.
(215) 386-0100, Cable: SCINFO

© 1987 Morton S. Freeman

Library of Congress Cataloging-in-Publication Data

Freeman, Morton S.
 A handbook of problem words and phrases.

 (The Professional writing series)
 1. English language—Usage—Dictionaries. I. Title.
II. Series.
PE1460.F654 1987   428′.00973   86-29906
ISBN 0-89495-080-0

Printed in the United States of America.
93 92 91 90 89 88 87   7 6 5 4 3 2 1

To my brother, Lester,
who was always there
when I needed him.

Foreword

Our Tool

What a tool the English language is! It has a vocabulary that is enormously large and that seems to be growing constantly. There is no word that doesn't seem to have a dozen synonyms, no two of which are exactly alike in meaning or implication.

Many of the frills common to most languages have dwindled, atrophied and nearly disappeared in English. We have no cases, except for pronouns; we have no arbitrary gender so that our masculines, feminines and neuters parallel the sexual situation almost everywhere.

But, lest things become too simple, we have a marvelously eccentric system of spelling and a grammatical pattern that only specialists can grasp.

The self-assurance of the English language is such that it borrows freely from every language and casually naturalizes whatever it appropriates. It uses foreign words with an approximation of the original pronunciation or with a carefree Anglicization. It twists every phrase to its own use and adds them to the native stock of idioms, which is already incredibly rich.

The English language is fortunate in having been for centuries the speech of a downtrodden peasantry so that by the time it became "literary" it was too late to fasten aristocratic chains upon it. There is no "Academie Anglais" to tell us in scholarly thunder what is right and what is wrong. The language has grown freely and happily.

Of course, there are penalties. How easy it is to misuse an enormous vocabulary and a wilderness of idioms. How readily one can go astray when there is a whirlwind growth with *no* set authority. How almost inevitable the confusion of words, the invention of foolish combinations, the loss of shades of meanings, and so on.

And yet though there is no absolute certainty in such things, there is a consensus among those with a feel for the language and those who have studied the language. Such people can serve as guides to the fine points of the incredibly rich English language.

Morton S. Freeman is such a guide, and this book on problem words and phrases will help guide you around the quicksands, boulders, and tree stumps, and place you on the peerless highway of the tongue that is now the nearest thing to a universal language for educated people of all countries.

ISAAC ASIMOV

Preface

Why *A Handbook of Problem Words and Phrases?* Is not almost every word a problem to someone—in usage, in spelling, in pronunciation?

For many years as a student of the English language, as an English teacher, and as the Director of Publications of the American Law Institute-American Bar Association (ALI-ABA), I made note of errors in grammar, word usage, punctuation, and related matters committed by my students as well as by the lawyers and college professors whose manuscripts I edited. With time, I observed that certain misusages appeared so frequently as to indicate a widespread pattern. This *Handbook,* basically, is concerned with those solecisms.

A question bound to be asked, and justifiably, is, Who determines the correct way to say or write something? Who is the arbiter? And what guidelines are there for one to follow? That's a stickler. For generations the advice given students and young writers was to speak and write the way the educated did. Emulate them, they were told, and your speech and writing, too, will be on the highest level. In recent years, however, a more practical scholarly approach (through studies, surveys, and usage panels) has made information available on specific points of concern, points that one could mull over, and then agree or disagree on, for there it was, all spelled out to be read and evaluated. (See *The American Heritage Dictionary,* with its prestigious panel, of which Edwin Newman served as chairman.)

These provocative studies—and some will be referred to shortly—unfortunately do not offer "the guidelines" mentioned in the previous paragraph. They indeed sometimes place the reader in a quandary because the authorities who compiled those studies and the usage critics to whom questions were addressed did not, in most cases, agree with one another. In fact, their diversity of opinion soon became the expectable. One may therefore wonder: If authorities (the elite among speakers and writers) lack unanimity, what can be expected of the layman, and where can he go to seek correct answers?

Morris Bishop points out that the 100 or more *American Heritage Dictionary* panelists agreed on only one reference—in disfavor of *simultaneous* as an adverb ("The referendum was conducted *simultaneous* with the election"). Even in such a supposedly clear case as the word *unique,* with its accepted sense of one of a kind, 6 percent approved of *rather unique* and *most unique.*

Margaret M. Bryant, in her scholarly compilation *Current American Usage,* noted that "usage levels are defined in terms of the educational and cultural background of the speaker or writer." But since usage is part of everyone's speaking and writing facility, that usage becomes established in the community where it is most often heard. Such localisms, or geographical variations, are effective in their locality and indeed impart a hearty regional flavor. But a basic set of standard English rules must be adhered to simply to ensure that words put together express thoughts clearly on a national level and that common agreement exists on the meaning of words and their connotations.

And so this *Handbook* (prescriptive where misusage is disastrous, *irregardless,* for example) presents prevailing points of view but with no autocracy. The reader is free to accept or reject the recommendations and to decide what to adopt when opinions differ.

Roy Copperud's *American Usage and Style: The Consensus* has hundreds of entries in which no consensus has been reached. Here is one taken at random: *dove.* "Bernstein . . . objects to *dove* as the past tense of *dive;* the *American Heritage* panel narrowly rejects it (51 percent) but as in other instances when the editors seemingly did not agree with the panel, they chose to state the minority acceptance. Four authorities consider *dove* standard. Two of the current desk dictionaries consider it informal, two consider it standard; both Random House and Webster accept it." Take another: *anxious, eager.* "Four authorities agree that *anxious* connotes foreboding, and should not be used for *eager* in such sentences as 'We are anxious to see the play.' Evans and Fowler say *anxious* for *eager* is fully established, and Webster and Random House call it standard. Opinion is thus divided."

The well-respected *Harper Dictionary of Contemporary Usage,* by William and Mary Morris, contains the opinions of a wide array of authorities. But here again, unanimity is a rarity. In fact, the questions posed to the panelists were sometimes answered in as many different ways as there were panelists.

And so I return to my very first sentence—why *A Handbook of Problem Words and Phrases?* This book is designed to present in concise and readable form a clear exposition of problems involving word usage, spelling, and pronunciation—and their suggested answers. It is not expected that everyone, even those with an aptitude for the English language, can take the time to pore over authoritative works, such as those just mentioned. This *Handbook* eliminates the need to do all that. It says, "Here it is. What you do with it is now up to you."

MORTON S. FREEMAN

Acknowledgments

I am grateful to many friends and colleagues who urged me to write this book and then made helpful suggestions that moved it along. In fact, many of the entries can be attributed directly to them. But I am particularly grateful to my daughter Janet (Mrs. Dennis Miller), who typed and retyped the manuscript and never grumbled when it all had to be done over again. I am pleased to acknowledge the copy reading by my friend Dr. C. Weil, of Briehen, Switzerland. I would not be comfortable going to print without the benefit of his editorial eye. One more doff of my hat. My work would not have been completed had it not been for the unwavering assistance and encouragement of my wife, Mildred, my most demanding (but cheerful) critic. To all of you, I say—thanks.

M.S.F.

a. See *the/a.*

a/an. The accepted practice is to use *a* before words that begin with a consonant sound (*a box*), even though their initial letter may be a vowel (*a eulogy, a unit*); otherwise, *an.* Whether *a* or *an* should be used before words beginning with *h* (a matter on which opinions differ), the preference is *a* when the *h* is sounded (*a hotel, a house, a historic* document) and *an* when the *h* is silent (*an honor, an heir, an hour*). (See *historic/historical.*) Numbers in a sentence are treated like other words (*a* seven-hour workday; *an* eighty-hour week).

ability/capacity. *Ability* is the power to do—to walk, to dance, to write, to meet obligations, to repair a vacuum cleaner. *Capacity* is the power to receive or contain—a tank may have a capacity of 15 gallons; a motel, of 200 guests. When applied to intellectual development, *capacity* is held by some authorities to be innate and *ability* to be acquired, but there is no consensus.

abjure/adjure. These uncommon words are best replaced by simple, everyday terms. But if you do use them, do not confuse them. To *abjure* is to renounce or repudiate. To *adjure* is to command or entreat earnestly.

-able. See *-ible/-able*; *spelling.*

able. Do not use with a passive construction. Not "It is *able to be done*" but "It *can* be done."

about, in "The play is *about* over," has the sense of "almost," which, although commonly used, is informal. (See *at about.*)

about/approximately. Because *about* is the shorter and crisper word, it ordinarily is to be favored. But *approximately* suggests an attempt at accuracy, an effort to get close to the correct count ("*Approximately* a hundred people attended"). *About* implies a mere guess.

about to. See *not about to.*

above. When wondering whether to use *above* as an adjective, as in "the *above* examples" or "the *above* figures," it is good to know that although it is acceptable, many writers prefer "the examples *above*" and "the figures *above*" or, better still, "the figures *given above*" or "the *preceding* examples." The expressions "above listed" and "above mentioned" sound stilted and should be avoided. *Above* is often unnecessary. If figures have just been cited, or an example set out, it can be called to the reader's attention by saying simply *in the figures cited* (no *above*) or *in the example* (no *above*).

abridgment. Unlike the English, Americans drop the *e* after *dg* if *ment* is to be added—not *abridgement,* but *abridgment.* (See *acknowledgment*; *judgment.*)

absolutely is frequently used as a needless intensifier. It is meaningless in "Dwight *is absolutely* the best mathematician in our class." Omit *absolutely.*

absolutes. Such words as *complete, dead, equal, fatal, indispensable, total,* and *unanimous* admit of no comparison or intensification because they have only one degree. Clearly something cannot be more equal than something else, nor can a stab wound be the most fatal of all. One object cannot be more round than another object, nor can a thing be more perfect than another thing (despite the Constitution's "more perfect union"). Careful speakers and writers do not use the comparative or superlative degrees to qualify words that are absolutes. To modify an absolute, they express a nearness to the absolute idea with adverbs that do not imply degree, like *almost* or *nearly.* Some authorities, nevertheless, do allow a comparison and sanction its use in such sentences as "I never saw *a more perfect* day" and "We found *a more direct* route than the one you suggested." Incidentally, the word *absolute* itself is an *absolute.* It, too, cannot be compared, but it may be qualified by *nearly* ("It was *nearly* an *absolute* agreement"). (See *complete*; *unique.*)

absolve takes the preposition *from; aversion* takes *to* ("He may have been *absolved from* all blame, but I still have an *aversion to* him").

abstruse. See *obscure/abstruse.*

accent marks. Some foreign words, although anglicized, have retained their diacritical marks. Using these marks is not essential, but many writers employ them to aid pronunciation; *fiancée, garçon, naiveté, papier mâché, señor.*

accident. See *mishap/accident.*

accidentally. See *incidentally/accidentally.*

acclimate has two acceptable pronunciations: uh-*klie*-muht and *ak*-lih-mayt.

accommodate is right up there when it comes to misspelling honors. Note the double *c* and the double *m.* (See *recommend.*)

accompanied takes *with* when a preposition is needed with *things* ("He *accompanied* his declaration *with* a challenge") but *by* with *persons* ("I was *accompanied by* my uncle").

accompanied by, when joined to the subject, does not affect the number of the subject ("The architect, *accompanied by* his associates, *is* surveying the land now"). (See *together with/along with.*)

according to, in some statements, reflects unfavorably on the speaker quoted, although no deprecation is meant. In *"According to* Stanley, the boss is giving us a party," an implication is that Stanley may not really know or that his information is dubious. Make it "Stanley said. . . ."

accost. A streetwalker who *accosts* a prospect sidles up to his ribs—perhaps a costly come-on. In Latin, *costa* means "rib" or "side."

accusation/recrimination. One gives birth to the other—an accusation breeds recrimination. An *accusation* charges someone with wrongdoing. *Recrimination* is a countercharge, an accusation brought against the accuser by the accused.

accused/alleged. "An *accused* murderer was arrested last night." Doubtful. A man is an accused murderer only if a formal charge has been lodged against him. Otherwise, he's only a suspect. To *allege* is to state without positive proof. It must concern a thing, not a person. There is no such thing as an *alleged* robber (only a suspected robber), although there may be an *alleged* robbery.

acknowledgment. The preferred spelling is as given, without the *e* after the *g* (not *acknowledgement*). But note that the final *e* is not dropped before the suffix -*able* (*acknowledgeable*). (See *abridgment; judgment.*)

acme. See *climax.*

acoustics. Sometimes misspelled *accoustics.* (See *-ics.*)

acquaint, meaning "to make familiar," is followed by *with* ("John will *acquaint* him *with* the details"). But since *acquaint* sounds quaint, prefer *tell* or *inform* or even idiomatic *give* ("John will *give* him the details").

acquaintance. See *personal friend.*

acquit. See *convict/acquit.*

active voice/passive voice. It is wise to favor the active voice of verbs, the voice in which the subject does the acting ("The Eagles *beat* the Dallas Cowboys") rather than the passive, the voice in which the subject is acted upon ("The Dallas Cowboys *were beaten* by the Eagles"). The active voice is vigorous, direct, dynamic. The passive is indirect and sounds mealy-mouthed. It also is wordy. Use the passive only when the recipient of the action is more important than the agent. "Our controller *was killed* yesterday by a truck" gets to the point more quickly than "Yesterday a truck *killed* our controller.")

actress. Despite the Women's Liberation Movement and a general feeling that words which designate sex may be prejudicial, certain feminine words are entrenched, and with good reason. One is *actress*. In this instance feminine charm and appearance make the designation desirable. (See *-ess endings.*)

actually. See *virtually/actually.*

acumen, which means "keenness of mind," is accented on the second syllable (a-*kyoo*-m'n).

acute/chronic. In medicine, the former means "coming quickly to a turning point." An acute disease needs immediate attention. *Chronic* means "lingering." It refers to a physical condition of long duration that refuses to improve despite constant medical care. *Chronic* and *severe* are not equivalents.

A.D./B.C. B.C. means "before Christ," but follows the year (Cicero was born in 106 B.C.). A.D., which stands for anno Domini, "in the year of the Lord," precedes the year ("Pompeii was destroyed A.D. 79"). B.C. is introduced by *in* (in 106 B.C.) but not A.D., which carries its own preposition—*anno* means "in the year" (destroyed A.D. 79). Although a century cannot be in the year of anything, A.D. may follow a century for the sake of brevity and clarity. ("Many ancient tombs were discovered in the fourth century A.D.") Not all authorities approve of this use of A.D.

ad. Do not use this abbreviated form for *advertisement* in formal discourse. Some writers deplore this restriction because *ad* is short and snappy; *advertisement,* long and drawn-out. Note that the shortened form *ad* is not followed with a period.

adage. In "We believe in the old *adage* that work never killed anyone," *old* does not belong. *Adage* means an old saying or proverb. Nothing is gained by calling something "old" if the sense of "old" is already there.

adapt may take the preposition *for* or *to.* A play is *adapted* (revised, expurgated) *for* television and *adapted to* the taste of the viewing public. (See *adapt/adopt.*)

adapt/adopt. To write these verbs right, think of *apt,* which means "suitable." To *adapt* means "to alter" or "to make suitable." *Adopt* means "to take and use as one's own" ("We will *adopt* the plan submitted by your architect").

add an additional, as in "If my father would *add an additional* $10 to my allowance, I could meet expenses," is an obvious, and clumsy, redundancy. The sense "an additional" is incorporated in *add.*

addicted to/subject to. Careless use of these words can lead to misunderstanding. The first means "habituated" or "strongly inclined," as is said of bad habits. The phrase is always followed by a noun ("Edward is *addicted to* alcohol"). The second means "liable to or to suffer from," as is a person subject to colds, or "conditional upon," as the purchase of a house is subject to the buyer's obtaining a mortgage.

address has two pronunciations. One is for the noun *add*-ress, a residence or business location ("My *address* is 419 Main Street"); the second is for the noun ad-*dress,* a lecture or speech ("The speaker's *address* lasted one hour"). The verb *address* is always stressed on the second syllable.

adept. When a preposition is needed, use *in.*

adequate seems to entice an unnecessary word—"enough." Not infrequently you will see a sentence such as "The number of firemen at the scene was not *adequate enough* to handle the blaze" or "The available amount of material was not *adequate enough* to make four shirts." The sense of "enough" is built into *ade-*

quate. It means "enough." And enough is enough. Note that *adequate* takes the preposition *to,* not *for* (*adequate to* her needs).

adhere/cohere. Both words mean "to stick fast or together," but the first refers to a holding by grasping or gluing, whereas the second refers to a sticking together of parts of the same thing, as molecules of iron cohere. When the attachment is to a cause or belief, the word to use is *adhere.*

adjacent/contiguous are interchangeable in general usage, but on a formal level *adjacent* has the more restricted sense of "lying near," "neighboring"; *contiguous* has the sense of "touching." If there is no actual contact, use *adjacent;* otherwise, *contiguous. Adjacent* takes *to,* not *of.*

adjudge. See *judge/adjudge.*

adjure. See *abjure/adjure.*

ad-lib. The phrase comes from Latin *ad libitum,* meaning "at pleasure." Its English sense is "without restraint," but it is often used to mean that a speech was improvised. As so used, *ad-lib* is synonymous with "off-the-cuff," an even more informal expression. (See *extemporaneous/impromptu.*)

admittance/admission. Discriminate carefully between these words. One gains *admittance* to the club's grounds with a valid ticket, but he gains *admission* to membership if favorably voted upon. Use *admittance* only in the sense of allowing entry, and *admission* to suggest accompanying privileges, obligations, and so on.

ad nauseam. If you have to refer to something that is sickening (*nausea*), be sure to spell it right, not *ad nauseum.*

adopt. See *adapt/adopt.*

adult may be stressed on the first or the second syllable. Stressing the second syllable—a-*dult*—is commoner and preferable.

advance planning. See *plan ahead/advance planning.*

advance reservation. See *advance warning.*

advance warning is as redundant (a warning is a notice in advance) as an *advance reservation* (an arrangement made in advance for accommodations).

advantage. You may have an advantage *over* other musicians if you have the advantage *of* superior talent. Use *over* when referring to people.

adverbs. The erroneous idea that an adverb should not be placed so as to separate a compound verb (*have gone, will be*) may be a carryover from the fear of splitting an infinitive. The fact is that the normal place for an adverb when modifying a compound verb is immediately before the verb, even though the placement splits the compound (are *unanimously* endorsed, was *wholeheartedly* approved, has been *fully* explored). In negative sentences the adverb *not* cannot logically be placed in any other position ("He *would not believe* what I told him").

adverse/averse. In "We decided that we were not *adverse* to acquiring a large apartment in Chicago," the required word is *averse. Adverse* means "unfavorable," "opposed." And it is not used of persons, only of statements or circumstances, like "adverse comments," "adverse publicity." *Averse,* which also means "opposed," refers to opposition by the person involved. Its sense is "unwilling," "reluctant," referring to a feeling of dislike.

advert/avert. Sometimes confused. To *advert* is to refer to ("The treasurer *adverted* to the increasing rate of costs"). To *avert* is to turn away ("She *averted* her eyes") and to prevent ("His absence *averted* a confrontation").

adviser/advisor. Either form is acceptable, but *adviser* (with an *er*) is commoner. The same latitude in spelling does not apply with *deviser* and *devisor*. A *deviser* is someone who devises; a *devisor,* one who devises property in a will.

a few. See *few.*

affect/effect. Sometimes these verbs are misused, one for the other, not because their meanings are confusing but because their pronunciation is similar. To *affect* is to influence or pretend ("The loss of his job *affected* him deeply, but he *affected* indifference"). To *effect* is to make happen or to accomplish ("The accountant *effected* changes and their *effect* was startling"). Note that in the example *effect* is also used as a noun, meaning "result."

affinity. The preposition that follows this word, which means "a natural liking for, or attraction to, another person or thing," is either *between* (there can be an affinity *between* two things or persons) or *with* (a person may have an affinity *with* another). In general usage *affinity* does not take *for* (it does in certain scientific matters) or *to*. Some critics adopt a lenient view toward the preposition that follows *affinity*. They would allow *for* or *to*, but many discriminating writers do not approve.

affirmative/negative. The verb with a compound subject made up of the following expressions agrees with the *affirmative* subject: "The foreman, not the laborers, *was* mistaken." "The laborers, not the foreman, *were* mistaken." (See *and/but*.)

aforementioned is a stodgy expression best replaced by one less obtrusive, such as *this point, that fact, these ideas,* or *those considerations.*

afraid/frightened. "I'm *afraid* I can't make it" is colloquial language for "I think I can't make it." Better English uses *think, believe, imagine,* or some other suitable word. To be *frightened* is to experience a sudden condition of fear or alarm. *Frightened* should not be followed by *of.* A person is frightened *by* something, not *of* something. (See *frightened/scared*.)

aftermath originally meant "a second mowing." Although it no longer is an agricultural term, it still refers to a second happening, as would be a gathering of hay for the second time. Figuratively it now suggests a result or consequence that is harmful or disastrous. An explosion might be an aftermath of a fire at the oil refinery and a disease an aftermath of unsanitary conditions.

afternoon. See *time.*

afterward/afterwards, adverbs meaning "at a later time," are acceptable on all levels of English. The shorter form, *afterward,* is favored by most writers.

again. See *re-.*

agenda, meaning "things to be done," is, as all Latin students know, a plural form; its singular is *agendum. Agendum* did not enter the English language, however; *agenda* did—as a singular noun. Its English plural is *agendas.* (See *data; phenomenon*.)

aggravate. "My uncle *aggravated* me beyond my point of endurance." This sense of *aggravate* ("to annoy," "to make angry," "to exasperate") has been widely used for centuries. In formal English, nevertheless, *aggravate* should be confined to its basic meaning of "to make worse" or "to intensify" ("The extreme cold *aggravated* Alma's arthritis"). Many other words express the idea of annoyance—*irritate, exasperate, displease, offend, vex,* and *provoke,* to cite a few, each having a shade of difference.

agnostic/atheist. Differentiate. An *agnostic* is "a thinker who disclaims any knowledge of God." His belief is that the existence and the nature of God cannot be known. An *atheist* denies that God exists. Such a person would probably spell God with a lowercase *g*.

ago/since. "It was twelve years *ago since* the building was dedicated" contains a not uncommon error. The element of time implied in *ago* makes the addition of *since,* which reckons time from a point in the past to the present, redundant. Either change *since* to *that*—"It was twelve years *ago that* . . ." or drop *ago* and recast, "It has been twelve years *since.* . . ." (See *since.*)

agree. One who agrees *to* a proposal agrees *with* the one who prepared it. *Agree to* means "consent," *agree with* means "concur."

agreement of verb and subject. See *affirmative/negative; collective elements; sentence structure.*

ahold. "The coach said that what he needed was to get *ahold* of a good pitcher." Make it *get hold of. Ahold* is substandard.

aid/aide. Loosely interchanged in the sense "assistant" or "helper." In "I am looking for my *aid,*" *aid* could be construed to mean either "assistant" or "assistance." Prefer the spelling *aide* for "assistant."

aim should be followed by *at* or an infinitive, and not by *at* and a gerund. A person takes *aim at* someone or *aims to do* a job right—but does not *aim at doing* the job right.

ain't has become a controversial word between prescriptive and descriptive grammarians. The best advice is to use it in informal speech, if so inclined, but not in writing. Some people still consider *ain't* an illiterate form.

à la carte. See *table d'hôte/à la carte.*

alibi colloquially means "excuse," as in "What's your *alibi* for not bringing home the newspaper?" To satisfy usage critics, *alibi* must be used only in its traditional sense of a plea of having been elsewhere at the time of the crime for which the defendant is charged.

"a little knowledge is a dangerous thing" is a misquotation of Alexander Pope's famous line "A little *learning*. . . ."

all might make some sentences more emphatic, but generally it serves no useful purpose. "*All* the students must leave now" says in direct language, "The students must leave now."

all around/all round.   See *round.*

all but one.   See *more than one.*

alleged.   See *accused/alleged.*

all of.   For those who wonder whether *of* must follow *all*, and for those who insist that it should not, as in "All (*of*) the employees protested," the answer is to take your choice. *All* is an adjective when it precedes a noun, and therefore *of* is unnecessary. But both constructions are permissible. If you wish to omit the slightly redundant *of*, fine. If the rhythm of the sentence with *of* sounds better to your ear, fine, too. Of course, *all of* must precede a pronoun (*all of us, all of you*).

allotment.   See *occurrence/allotment.*

all over the world is good idiom, but in formal writing, make it *over all the world.* And note that *all over* is not an acceptable substitute for *everywhere.* In "We looked for the book *all over*," replace *all over* with *everywhere.*

allow when used to mean "concede" or "admit" not only is informal but sounds bucolic ("Clem *allowed* that his idea was all wrong"). In standard usage *allow* means "to permit."

all ready/already.   "My son is *all ready* 50 inches tall" and "We are *already* to leave" reflect confusion in the use of the lead words. *All ready* means "prepared" or "completely ready" ("We are *all ready* to leave." "The dance will not begin until the musicians are *all ready*"). *Already* refers to time, suggesting that an action is now complete ("Sammy *already* looks exhausted") or, more commonly, has the sense of "previously" or "earlier," that an action was completed at a moment in the past ("My son is *already* 50 inches tall." "They have *already* gone"). Note that *all* in *all ready* is not necessary; it merely adds emphasis.

all right.   Spell it this way—two words, no hyphen, and no fancy shortening, not *alright.*

all-round.   To express versatility, *all-round,* as in an *all-round* athlete, is preferable to *all-around,* even though *all-around* is often heard. The *all* in *all-around,* which means "everywhere about," is usually unnecessary. Try using one word instead of two: "The water rose (*all*) *around* us." (See *round.*)

all that, as in "We don't consider Roy *all that* smart," is non-standard. Change *all that* to *especially* or *particularly.*

all the better to eat you up is correctly put. *All* with a comparative was standard English long before Little Red Riding Hood went to visit her grandmother. Which makes it all the easier to remember.

all the farther is a colloquialism for *as far as.* In formal writing do not say, "This is *all the farther* I can take you." Say "This is *as far as* I can take you."

all together/altogether. *All together* means "all in one place" or "at the same time" ("The legislators are *all together* in the rotunda"). *Altogether* means "completely," "entirely," "thoroughly" ("This coffee is *altogether* too strong." "We were *altogether* perplexed by his proposals"). (See *all ready/already.*)

allude/elude are sometimes confused, possibly because of their similar pronunciation. "We *alluded* to his professional standing," not *eluded.* To *allude* is to make an indirect reference; to *elude* is to escape or slip away from, to evade. Note the spelling of these words—*allude* has two *l*'s; *elude,* one.

allude/refer. "Andy *alluded* to Mr. Bluestone's age by saying he's now 82." Andy did not allude; he referred. To *allude* is to mention someone or something indirectly. To *refer* is to mention something directly, to make a specific statement, such as naming the title and author of a book—or someone's precise age.

allusion/illusion. The meanings of these words are entirely dissimilar. Yet occasionally we find them misused, one for the other. An *allusion* is a passing, unspecific reference ("The doctor made an *allusion* to the patient's habit of drumming the table with his fingers.") An *illusion* is a deceptive appearance, a false mental image or impression ("A mirage is an optical *illusion*").

almost. See *close to*; *modifiers*; *most.*

alone. "I think we'll win, not *alone* because we have proof, but because right is on our side." Do not use *alone,* which means "by itself" or "solitary," to displace *not only.* And note the difference in meaning between "For that, they *alone* will be fined" (no one else) and "For that *alone* they will be fined" (nothing else).

along, when used to mean "approximately," is dialectal ("*Along* about the middle of summer we decided to leave"). Drop *along*— "About the middle of summer. . . ."

along with. See *together with/along with.*

a lot of. See *lots of.*

aloud. See *out loud.*

already. See *all ready/already.*

alright. See *all right.*

also is an adverb, not a conjunction. In "He will be visiting three states, also one island," replace *also* with *and* or insert *and* before *also.* Be particularly careful not to begin a sentence with *also* serving as a conjunction. Not "We will be inviting the dean, the comptroller, and the faculty. Also the clerical staff will be invited." Use *furthermore, in addition,* or an equivalent. Or recast by shifting the position of *also*: "The clerical staff *also* will be invited." Some authorities disapprove of *also* at the beginning of a sentence even when used as an adverb.

altar/alter. Distinguish *altar,* a noun meaning "a sacred part of a church or synagogue, the central point of worship," from *alter,* a verb meaning "to change."

alter/change. If a person *alters* an interior decorator's plan, he keeps the basic design but modifies some detail; if he *changes* the plan, he makes it into something new. The preceding sentence exemplifies the distinction between the key words in their primary sense of "to make different." To *change* is to cause a complete turnabout. The result may bear no resemblance to the original. To *alter* is to retain the identity, which, despite the modification, is easily recognizable.

alternate(ly). See *alternative(ly)/alternate(ly).*

alternative(ly)/alternate(ly). If you are given an *alternative,* you have a choice between two things. (*Alternatively* means "choosing one of two.") To *alternate* is to occur in turns, first one, then the other. (*Alternately* applies to "two things following each other.") Today, except in the opinion of conservative writers, *alternative* (and *alternatively*) is no longer restricted to a choice between two but may be used of any number: "The *alternatives* are assaults by the military, encirclement by the navy, or sporadic landings by the marines." *Alternate* has become synonymous with *substitute,* as is commonly seen in highway signs (*alternate* route), a usage now entrenched and accepted. Likewise, a person may be selected as the *alternate* to a convention, to serve in case the delegate cannot attend.

although. See *though/although.*

altogether. See *all together/altogether.*

alumnus is the masculine form; the feminine is *alumna.* Their plurals are *alumni* (rhymes with *nigh*) and *alumnae* (rhymes with *knee*). The term *alumni* embraces both sexes of coeducational institutions ("My sister and brother are *alumni* of Albright"). Note that *alumni* are not only graduates but also those who left without diplomas.

a.m./p.m. See *time.*

am. See *shall be/am.*

amateur/dilettante. Both these words describe nonprofessionals. An *amateur* (from Latin *amare,* "to love") loves doing something as a pastime. (*Amateur* is preferably pronounced *am*-uh-tuhr.) A *dilettante* (from Italian *dilettarsi,* "to take pleasure in") is a dabbler, usually in the arts. He is superficial and affected. Note that *dilettante* takes one *l* followed by an *e,* which in turn is followed by a double *t.* Its plural has two forms— *dilettanti* and *dilettantes.* The first is preferred.

ambiguous/equivocal mean "susceptible of two or more interpretations." Although these words are generally interchanged in everyday speech, they should not be. *Ambiguous* is applied to a statement or term in which one meaning is intended but another is possible. It should be borne in mind that although an ambiguous statement usually comes from carelessness, there always exists the possibility of intent. *Equivocal,* defined as "ambiguous," "questionable," often refers to a statement that is deliberately evasive; the "ambiguity" is intentional. An ambiguous statement, it may be said, is made by a person who has failed to make himself clear; an equivocal statement is made by someone who is purposely deceptive. Note that whereas the word *ambiguous* may be applied only to statements, *equivocal* may be applied to either statements or actions that admit of two plausible interpretations.

ambivalence/vacillation have distinctive uses and are not to be interpreted as synonyms. *Ambivalence* is a psychological term, referring to two irreconcilable emotions—such as love and hate—possessed simultaneously. Unless this term can be used correctly, it is best avoided. *Vacillation* is merely a swaying from one opinion or emotion to another irresolutely. In current usage *ambivalence* is used synonymously, although erroneously, with *vacillation*. A person who is undecided, who goes from one idea to another, is said to be ambivalent. To repeat, and emphasize, that usage is incorrect.

among/between. *Between* is usually called for when a relationship involves two persons or things and *among* when it involves more than two. A cake is divided *between two* persons, but *among three* persons. This rule bears one exception—*between* is used of more than two when the relationship of a thing links it individually to others ("The Constitution regulates relations *between* the states").

amoral/immoral/unmoral. Do not use these words indiscriminately. That which is *amoral* has no moral standards. Animals fall into this category. But one who acts contrary to moral principles—knowing the difference—or is wicked or evil is said to be *immoral*. *Unmoral* is synonymous with *amoral*.

amount/number. Use *amount* when referring to quantity, things viewed in bulk, weight, or sums. We speak of a large amount of sand, a large amount of firewood. Use *number* for units, items that are countable, as in "The *number* of members here is small." Incidentally, rather than "Here's a check in the *amount* of $50," make it "*for* $50." Spend the $50 but save three words.

ampersand. For those who wonder whether they may use *ampersands* (&) to save time and space, the answer is that *ampersands* are properly used only in company names and then only if so used by the company. Otherwise, write *and*, even in informal letters.

analogous/analogy. *Analogous* takes the preposition *to*, but *analogy* takes the preposition *between* or *with*.

and/but. Two singular subjects connected by *and* or *but* that are sharply contrasted with each other are regarded as separate statements and therefore take a singular verb ("Good fortune, *and* not his fine appearance, *was* the key to his career." "Good management, *but* also financial resources, *makes* for a profitable operation.") Observe that commas set off the statements. (See *commas*; *sentence structure*; *word arrangements*.)

Either *and* or *but* may permissibly begin a sentence. (See *but*.)

and/or. Avoid this unsightly combination. If you mean "and," "or," or "both," say it. For instance, "a $50 fine and/or 5 days in jail" should be recast "a $50 fine, or 5 days in jail, or both."

and moreover. Omit *and*.

and so forth/and the like are English substitutes for Latin *etc.* Before using them, be sure they are needed—that other things could be added. Otherwise, omit.

and which/but which. "The education of minorities is a matter *which* (not *and which*) is of deep concern." "The community needs a larger library *which* (not *but which*) has been disapproved by city council." Use *and which* or *but which* to introduce a *which* clause that is the second of two *which* clauses ("The disease is one *which* is known, *but which* doctors have not yet found a cure for"). Likewise, do not join *and who* or *but who* unless they are coordinated with a previous *who* clause.

anglicize. See *roman letters/russian dressing*.

angry/annoyed. You are *annoyed with* a person, as you are *angry with* a person. But use *at* when the annoyance or anger is directed at a thing, event, or action. And note that one is *annoyed by* his neighbor's loud conversation. (See *aggravate*.)

anoint. Sometimes misspelled *annoint*. Note that *anoint* has only two *n*'s, and they are not adjacent.

another. "The report said that although only one thousand people attended the event, another five million watched it on television." The mathematics is wrong. There cannot be another five million unless there had been a previous five million. Drop *another*. (See *the other*.)

another couple. "We will be taking a vacation with *another* couple." What, one may ask, is the word *another* doing there? Why not use *a* instead? The answer is that *another* is superfluous, but it has attained idiomatic respectability in the opinion of most authorities.

antagonist. See *protagonist*.

ante-. Spell compounds as one word—no hyphen (*antedate, antechamber, antemeridian*) unless the second part begins with a capital letter (*ante-Elizabethan*).

anti-. Spell words beginning with *anti-* as one word (*antitrust, antisocial, antiaircraft*) unless the second element is capitalized (*anti-British*) or begins with an *i* (*anti-industrialization*).

anticipate. Rather than "I *anticipated* a younger ballplayer," make it "expected." *Expect* means "to look forward to." To *anticipate* is to foresee and take action against, to forestall ("We *anticipated* the move of our enemy").

anxious/eager. *Anxious* is widely used to mean "eager" ("I am *anxious* to get tickets for tonight's baseball game"). But in serious writing, *anxious* should be used to express only its basic meaning, "distressed in mind," "ill at ease," "full of anxiety." At least a bit of apprehension should filter into every use of *anxious,* as is evident in "We're *anxious* to leave before it starts snowing." To be *eager* is to be intensely desirous. But note that although the word *eager* may be followed by an infinitive (*eager* to dance), *desirous* may not be (*desirous* of dancing).

any should be followed by *other* (*any other*) when a member of a group is being compared to the group itself. For example, *other* should follow *any* in "Holland is cleaner than *any* country in the world," since Holland is part of the group; it is a country in the world.

any and all is not only a trite expression but also a redundancy at best and a misusage of the language at worst. What is meant by the phrase is hard to tell. A grandmother who says, "Send me the kids, any *or* all," makes sense. She'll take some or all. But she could not have *any* (which means "some") *and all,* at least not at the same time. In "*Any and all* payments to the terrorists will be scrutinized," choose either *any* or *all,* or drop both.

anybody. See *any time/anyone/anybody.*

anybody else's. See *somebody else's.*

anymore. The answer to the question whether this word should be written as one word (*anymore*) or two (*any more*) is that the current trend is to write it as one word. In any case it is used only in negative contexts ("We don't go there *anymore*").

any old port in a storm is a common idiom. It would be more accurately stated "any old harbor in a storm." A *port* is a place where ships are loaded and unloaded or, more loosely put, a city where steamers come to discharge passengers or unload cargo. Ports are in a *harbor,* which means "haven," an area protected against the weather. It is "any old harbor" that one should seek when a storm breaks. But *port* has come, for this purpose, to be the equivalent of harbor—a place of comfort and security. (See *port/harbor.*)

anyone. (See *any time/anyone/anybody.*)

anyone else. "Hubert is a better accountant than anyone in Raleigh's office" implies that Hubert is not employed by Raleigh. If Hubert is so employed, say "Hubert is a better accountant than *anyone else* in Raleigh's office." It's the *else* that brings Hubert into the group.

anyplace is nonstandard for *anywhere.* (See *noplace/someplace/ anyplace/everyplace.*)

any time/anyone/anybody. *Any time* is preferably spelled as two words, even though some traffic signs write it as one ("No parking *anytime*"). Pronouns *anyone* and *anybody,* in the sense of "any person," are always written as one word ("*Anyone* [*Anybody*] who wishes may come"). When a particular person or item is being emphasized, as in "My teacher said we may select *any one* of these three books for home reading," two words are required.

anyway means "nevertheless"—that is, regardless of what else is true. *Anyways* is a substandard form of *anyway.* (See *at*; *someway.*)

anywhere is the correct form, not *anywheres.* (See *somewheres.*)

a period of time. See *period of time.*

apostrophe. That an apostrophe indicates possession needs no explaining (the *boy's* coat, *Roger's* hat). Be careful, however, when joint possession is indicated to apostrophize only the final element (John, James, and David's radio). The one radio is owned by three boys. When there is separate possession, each possessor gets an apostrophe (John's, James's and David's radios) and the object possessed is in the plural form. Each boy owns a radio.

apparent. "It is *apparent* that it's going to rain." "His *apparent* lassitude made us all wonder." The word *apparent* in those sentences has different, if not somewhat contradictory, meanings. In the first sentence *apparent* means "obvious"; in the second, "seeming." Certainly what only seems to be is not obvious. Be sure that the context leaves no room for ambiguity, or else use *obvious* if that is what you mean, or *seeming* when you mean "seeming." One should not say that a person died of an *apparent* heart attack. An apparent heart attack never killed anyone. Make it "It *seemed* that he died of a heart attack" or "He died, *apparently* of a heart attack."

appear, followed by an infinitive, may be unclear in such a sentence as "At the bake-show, Madeline displayed her cookies but no judges *appeared* to enjoy them." One may wonder whether no judges appeared at the show or whether none seemed to enjoy what they tasted.

appointed. See *elected/appointed.*

appositives. "Us men will meet tonight," or is it "We men will meet tonight"? The latter is correct. This conclusion can be reached by omitting the noun. Without *men,* obviously "We will meet tonight" is the way to say it. The rule is that a noun or pronoun in apposition must be in the same case as the noun or pronoun it explains or identifies; hence "We men." Note that the word *apposition* takes *to* (in apposition *to*), not *with.* (See *let's.*)

appraise/apprise. "I will apprise him (not *appraise* him) of conditions as I see them." To *appraise* is to evaluate. To *apprise* is to inform.

appreciate. The question that troubles some writers is whether *appreciate* may properly be used to mean "understand," as in "I *appreciate* what you're saying, but I can't agree with you." Some usage critics disapprove of this sense, yet more find nothing wrong with it. But be careful of such a sentence as "The Club will *appreciate* it if you come early." *It* has no antecedent, which makes the sentence unacceptable. Change to "The Club will *appreciate* your coming early."

apprehend/comprehend. Despite the overlapping of their meanings in the sense of "understand," these words are distinguishable by their usage. To *apprehend* is to grasp the meaning of something; to *comprehend* is to understand it fully.

apprise. See *appraise/apprise.*

approve. In "The controller refuses to *approve* the voucher," the sense of *approve* is "give consent to." And so in "The order *has been approved* by the board" (*approve* is more commonly used in the passive). In "The President did not *approve of* the Ambassador's behavior," the sense of *approve of* is "to regard favorably" (*approve of* is found in the active voice).

approximately. See *about/approximately*.

apropos is both an adjective, meaning "fitting," "suitable," and an adverb, meaning "fittingly," "suitably." Sometimes followed by *to*—"His remark is *apropos to* what was being discussed"—but more often by *of*—"This is *apropos of* what the chairman was saying." In "*Apropos of* the meeting, how many items are on the agenda?" the sense of *apropos of* is "with regard to."

apt. See *liable/likely/apt*.

arabic figures. See *roman letters/russian dressing*.

arbitrate/mediate are often used loosely for each other even though their functions are different. To *arbitrate* is to hear evidence and to reach a decision. The *arbitrator* (selected by the disputants) serves as a judge to conduct the matter. To *mediate* is to reconcile the differences between opposing parties. A *mediator* consults the disputants in an effort to get them to agree. Mediators do not make judgments or awards. Arbitrators do.

arctic needs its middle *c* sounded—*ahrk*-tic.

arise. See *rise/arise/get up*.

aroma. See *smell/stench/scent*.

around. Best not used to mean "about." "I will be home *about* six o'clock," rather than "*around* six o'clock."

as. The subordinate conjunction *as* in the sense of *because* or *since* is sometimes ambiguous. "*As* he left, his wife began to cry" may mean "while he was leaving" or "because he was leaving." For the sake of clarity avoid *as* in this kind of construction. A common question is, What pronoun follows *as* in such a sentence as "Robin likes Mike *as* much *as* (*I* or *me*)"? The answer depends on the meaning intended. *I* is correct if the sense is as much as *I do; me* if Robin likes *me* as much as she likes Mike. In "*As* much as I dislike Arthur, I admire his artistic ability," omit the initial *as*. A comparison is not being made; the sense is concessive—in effect, "Although I dislike Arthur. . . ." (See *as/like*; *like*; *than*; *the way/just as*.)

as (omission of). Be careful to use the second *as* in an *as . . . as* construction. "Thomas plays as well and in certain areas better than Roger" needs correcting—"Thomas plays as well *as*. . . ." Some writers would restructure this kind of sentence as follows: "Thomas plays as well as Roger, if not better" (*than Roger* being understood).

as/like. In the sentence "Like present-day Russia, communism is the form of government in China," change *like* to *as in.* The error here is that "Russia" is being compared with "communism," and they are not comparable things. But be sure not to overbend and misuse *as* for *like. As* is a conjunction; *like,* a preposition. Just as one should not say "Pickles taste good *like* (needs *as*) good cucumbers should," so *as* does not belong where *like* does ("Writers make mistakes in grammar *as* (needs *like*) anyone else"). Bear in mind that *like,* if no verb is expressed (as in the last example), is the proper word. If a verb is found in the following group of words, use *as.* (See *like/as.*)

as . . . as/so . . . as. Traditional grammarians prefer *as . . . as* in positive comparisons ("My sister is *as* old *as* yours") and *so . . . as* when they are negative ("My sister is not *so* tall *as* yours"). But many respected writers use *as . . . as* in negative constructions as well. (See *so as.*)

ascent/assent. Be sure to spell these sound-alikes correctly. The first, a noun, is an upward slope or incline ("The *ascent* of the mountain was arduous"). The second is both a noun, meaning "consent" ("Charles gave his *assent* to his friend's idea"), and a verb (used with *to*), meaning "to express agreement" or "to concur" ("The school principal said he would *assent to* the students' demands").

as far as often leads to verbiage with no gain in clarity. The sentence "Sales of pone *as far as* Kentuckians are concerned have reached an all-time high" if reworded "Sales of pone *among* Kentuckians . . ." becomes more economical—and improved.

as follows. The question raised is whether *follows,* the singular form, or *follow,* the plural, is properly used when a plural noun precedes and a list of items follows. "The students absent yesterday are *as follow* (or *as follows*): Raymond, John, Anne, and Sammy." Idiom prescribes the use of *as follows* in this construction, even though *students* and *are* are plural.

as good as. A colloquialism that serves no useful purpose. Instead of "Mary *as good as* told me to stay home," make it "Mary *practically* told me. . . ."

as good or better needs a second *as*—as good *as* or better. Or, instead of "He's *as good as or better* than his uncle," vary it and say "He's *as* good *as* his uncle, *or better.*"

as if/as though. Both are acceptable. *As though* enjoys a slight shade of preference in formal texts. Follow it with a subjunctive form of the verb in a statement contrary to fact ("Although it was the first day of the baseball season, the men played *as if* [or *as though*] it *were* the last").

as per. Commercialese that belongs in no writing, not even commercial. Rather than saying "Your goods were sent *as per* your instructions," make it, "Your goods were sent according to your orders."

assay/essay. Exercise care when using these words as verbs. To *assay* is to test, to analyze. To *essay* is to attempt. A chemist may essay to assay a strange mineral.

assemble together, as in "Let's *assemble together* in the rotunda," is redundant. Omit *together.*

asset. If the question is whether *asset* is a suitable word in "This tool is an *asset* to remove a tire," the answer is no. Replace it with a *useful thing* or recast, "This is a useful tool with which to remove a tire."

assuage idiomatically takes *with* in the active voice ("*Assuage* pain *with* cold compresses") and *by* in the passive ("Pain is *assuaged by* cold compresses"). Pronounce as-*swhage.*

assume/presume. To distinguish the use of these words, one might recall that sometimes, for the sake of argument, a premise is assumed. Obviously, it has no supporting evidence. One might therefore remember that *assume,* rather than *presume,* is used when a matter is supposed or inferred without proof. To *presume,* on the other hand, is to believe that something is true because some evidence or the circumstances could lead to that conclusion. There is a likelihood for belief. Hence the famous "Dr. Livingstone, I presume." *Presume* also means "to take too much for granted," but that sense is not being considered here.

assurance. See *insurance/assurance.*

asterisk. A little star that calls the reader's attention to information apart from the text. Frequently used in footnotes. Note its spelling; it's not *asterick*. Pronounce the *isk*.

as though. See *as if/as though*.

as to. Often superfluous. In "We didn't stop to think *as to* who came next," delete *as to*. As a substitute for a precise preposition, *as to* is clumsy; for example, in "There was some doubt *as to* the nature of the contract," *about* would be better. "They established rules *as to* conduct" (*of*). "They disagreed *as to* the meaning" (*on*). *As to* is properly used at the beginning of a sentence to introduce a subject that would otherwise be delayed ("*As to* Ellis, his grades will assure him a scholarship"). (See *as to whether*.)

as to whether, a wordy and useless phrase, is preferably rendered with *as to* omitted. "The question *as to whether* we should buy mutual funds is on the agenda" is reducible to "The question *whether* we should buy mutual funds is on the agenda." Except in an introductory position, *as to* should be used only as a last resort—when no other preposition will do.

as well as. This phrase makes ambiguous a sentence such as the following: "Robert plays a violin *as well as* Tom." Does this mean that Robert's playing is as good as Tom's or that Robert also plays a violin? Change to reflect the intended sense: "Tom and Robert play a violin equally well" or "Both Tom and Robert play a violin."

As a connective, *as well as* does not create a grammatical plural. "Roberto, *as well as* his parents, *were* seen in the shopping center" needs *was*. (See *in addition to*; *together with/along with*.)

as yet. See *yet*.

at. "Father is home now," "Nine o'clock I'll be leaving," "Come any time you wish"—all standard everyday speech. Noticeably absent in these examples is the preposition *at*, which is becoming more and more confined to formal English. There one would say, "Father is *at* home now," "*At* nine o'clock I'll be leaving" (or "I'll be leaving *at* nine o'clock"), "Come *at* any time you wish."

At (which like all prepositions requires an object) is frequently misplaced in such a sentence as "Where are you staying *at*?" Make it "*At* what hotel are you staying?" or, if you're brave enough to end a sentence with a preposition, make it "What hotel are you staying *at*?" In this last example, as in the previous one, the noun *hotel* serves as the object of *at*.

at/in. The authorities have quarreled among themselves regarding the correct use of *at* and *in*. The generally accepted guideline, although many critics object to it, is that *in* is used for large areas (*in* Montana, *in* China) and *at* for small places (*at* Wilkes-Barre, *at* Birchrunville). The objectors use *in* for a residence in a place of any size. Those who follow the "accepted guidelines" have to decide whether something is large enough to merit *in* or small enough to be denigrated with *at*. To a good extent, they must rely on what their ear tells them. One rule with a larger following is to use *at* with geographical locations ("We conferred *at* City Hall") and *in* to denote the interior of a place ("We conferred *in* City Hall"), which means "not outside."

at about. Never use this combination ("I'll see you *at about* three o'clock"). The words are contradictory in that context—*at* points to something specific; *about*, to an approximation. In informal usage *at about* may be acceptable in some constructions, but not in references to time. Using *by about* is no improvement. In "We plan to meet *by about* 12 noon," drop *by*.

atheist. See *agnostic/atheist*.

at present is as effective as, and more economical than, *at the present time*. And if *now* would serve, it would be still better.

at the back of. See *back of*.

at the present time. See *at present*.

at the rear of. See *back of*.

at the same time. Wordy for *while*.

at this (that) point in time is a vogue expression. Prefer *now* or *then*.

attorney. See *lawyer*.

audience. It has been a losing battle to restrict the use of the word *audience* to persons who are only listeners, even though *audience* was sired by Latin *audio*, "to hear." Almost everyone has come to agree that the word may be applied to spectators who look as well as listen—even to spectators who have nothing to hear (those attending a silent movie or an art show). Nowadays authorities approve of the application of *audience* to watchers or even readers, which means that the word applies to any group to whom a form of communication is addressed, no matter what the medium.

aught. See *naught/aught.*

aunt/uncle. See *father/mother/aunt/uncle.*

author/host. Although sometimes heard or read ("Hackett *authored* a new book and his publishers *hosted* a Launching Party"), these words as verbs are disapproved of by most critics. (See *gift.*)

authoritative is a word that should be written carefully because sometimes it is misspelled *authoritive* or *authorative.*

autograph. See *signature/autograph.*

auxiliary should be spelled as given, not *auxilary.* Be careful not to omit the second *i.*

avenge/revenge. Occasionally confused, and understandably so. The distinctions between these words are not always clear. *Avenge* is to mete out punishment for a wrong inflicted upon another person. It connotes the redressing of an injustice. *Revenge* is a retaliation, a seeking of personal satisfaction, for a wrong done to the revenger. *Vengeance* and *revenge* are the corresponding nouns.

averse. See *adverse/averse.*

aversion. See *absolve.*

avoid/evade. Although both these words refer to an effort to stay away from someone or something, their implications are quite different. *Avoid,* a general word, indicates a desire to keep from meeting someone or something that might be unpleasant. We speak of avoiding the boss or avoiding trouble. *Evade* connotes trickiness. The word suggests an avoidance by cleverness, by deception, or by stratagem, an evading of the issue.

awake/wake refer to a rousing from sleep. *Awake* is used of yourself (one *awakes*). *Wake* (often followed by *up*) is used of another (one *wakes up* someone else). (See *rise/arise/get up.*)

aware. See *conscious/aware.*

away. See *way/ways/away.*

awful. This word, one might say, is an awful one to use. Not really. *Awful* means "that which inspires awe." However, since almost no one uses *awful* in that sense, the word is best avoided in formal discourse, perhaps in any form of writing. Colloquially *awful* refers to the disagreeable, the annoying, the excessive, the great, the bad—a use that covers almost any notion. Hence you may hear that someone is awfully rich or awfully poor. The day may be awfully hot or awfully cold. A play may be awfully bad or awfully good. And so on ad nauseam.

awhile. "I'll study for *awhile*" should be rendered "I'll study *awhile*" (*awhile* is an adverb) or "I'll study *for a while*" (*while* is a noun, the object of the preposition *for*). (See *while.*)

back of. *"Back of* the school yard is a baseball diamond." Although some usage critics maintain that *back of* and *in back of* are idiomatically correct, most prefer *at the back of* to either of those phrases. A less wordy, and more formal, substitute is *behind* ("A baseball diamond is *behind* the school yard"). Avoid "at the rear of." It sounds clumsy.

backward/backwards. For those who wonder which of these is the preferred form, the answer is that, when serving as adverbs, meaning "in reverse order or direction," they are equally acceptable (he looked *backward* or *backwards*), although the shorter form, *backward*, is preferable. Note that *backward*, meaning "progressing slowly," "bashful," "facing the rear," is also an adjective (a *backward* glance, a *backward* boy). (See *downward*.)

bad/badly. A person whose arm pains *badly* feels *bad*. *Badly* is an adverb, *bad* an adjective, and *feels* a linking verb. Adjectives, not adverbs, modify linking verbs; hence *feels bad*, not *badly*. (See *feel bad/feel badly*.) *Badly* is colloquial for *very much*. An actress wants a part in a play *very much* (not *badly*).

bade, pronounced *bad*, is a past tense of *bid*, meaning "greet," "invite," "instruct," "say goodby." An alternative past tense is *bid*, which has several idiomatic uses (an offer to buy, an amount declared in a card game).

badly. See *bad/badly*.

baited/bated. Those who use the cliché *bated breath* should at least spell it correctly—*bated*, not *baited*. *Baited* is said of a fishhook that has a worm on it.

balance of the day is an unacceptable formulation in better writing. Make it "the rest" or "the remainder" of the day, preferably "the rest."

baleful/baneful. Do not confuse. The first means "lugubrious" or "dismal" and is often used in the expression "a baleful look," the kind one sees on the face of an old elevator operator.

The second means "poisonous," like the baneful effect of narcotics. The current sense of *bane* ("My girl friend is the *bane* of my life") is much milder; it suggests mere annoyance.

bank on, meaning "count on" or "rely on," as in "Don't *bank on* your neighbor," does not have the sanction of formal language.

barbecue/barbeque. Both spellings are acceptable, but the first is more widely used.

barely carries a concealed negative connotation and should therefore not be used with another negative. Not "We have *barely no* oatmeal left," but *barely any*. (See *double negatives*; *hardly/scarcely*.)

Barmecide feast. An empty pretense of generosity. The expression derives from an *Arabian Nights* tale in which a wealthy Persian, a member of the Barmecides, pretended to serve a beggar a feast on empty plates.

barrister. See *lawyer*.

based on. If *based on* were an absolute phrase, this sentence would be correct: "*Based on* her information, I am approving the application." As it is, it means that I am based on her information, since *I* is the subject of the independent clause. Amend by using *on the basis of* or the absolute participles *considering* or *given*. (See *dangling participles*.)

basically. A vague, overworked word which often serves no purpose, as in "*Basically*, he prefers butter pecan."

basis is an open door to circumlocution. "He hired a secretary *on a* temporary *basis* before deciding whether to rent an office" is reducible to "He hired a secretary temporarily before. . . ."

basis of. See *on the basis of*.

bated. See *baited/bated*.

bazaar/bizarre. Be sure to spell these words right. A *bazaar* is a place where many goods are sold. It may be an Oriental marketplace or a church fair. *Bizarre*, an adjective, means "strikingly odd," "strange," "grotesque" ("Some of our local discotheques attract *bizarre*-looking creatures").

B.C. See *A.D./B.C.*

be advised. See *please be advised*.

because. When *because* follows "the reason is," it is redundant because *because* means "for the reason that." Instead of "The *reason* I went home early *is because* I was feeling ill," say "I went home early *because*. . . ." Or substitute *that* for *because* ("The *reason* I went home early is *that*. . . ."). (See *not . . . because*; *on account of*.)

because of. See *due to*.

become to be. "If he keeps practicing long enough, he will *become to be* a star like his father." Amend to *come to be* or *will become* a star.

before/first. In "*Before* the suggestion is acted upon, it must *first* be sent to the committee," *first* is unnecessary, since *before* contains the sense of "first."

before/prior to. *Prior to* is wordy and usually sounds pretentious. Prefer *before*. Another wordy phrase for *before* is *in advance of*, as in "The parade took place *in advance of* the unveiling." Avoid it.

begging the question does not mean being evasive by talking around the subject or by ignoring it. The expression means that one assumes as true the point of the discussion, the truth of which is the issue. Or, as defined by Webster, "to employ an argument that assumes as valid the very same argument that one is trying to prove."

begin/commence/start. Prefer *begin* to *commence* wherever possible. *Begin* is an everyday word; *commence,* a formal word, too heavy for ordinary use. *Begin* and *start* are usually interchangeable, but in certain contexts custom prescribes which to use. *Start* implies a quicker, perhaps a more unexpected, beginning than *begin*. We start a race or a motor, for example. But we begin a letter, and we begin a meal—and we begin to look old.

beg to advise is as old-fashioned as the complimentary closing "your obedient servant." Although the latter expression has disappeared, the former is still sometimes seen in correspondence. It should be omitted. Instead of "I *beg to advise* that we will be arriving at 3," say directly, and more economically, "We will be arriving at 3." (See *please be advised*.)

behalf. Some careful speakers and writers are troubled by the expressions *on behalf* and *in behalf*, not because of their meanings—*on behalf* means "on the part of" or "acting as the agent of" and *in behalf* means "for the benefit of"—but because they are interchanged by educated people, and some dictionaries ascribe to both the same meaning. The problem is that no one now feels free to criticize the blurring of the distinctions that have traditionally existed between these expressions. Examples of correct use follow: "The controller thanked the shipping department *on behalf* of the president" (the controller was representing the president). "The Police Athletic League was established *in behalf* of fatherless boys" (the sense here is "for the sake of").

behave, meaning "to conduct oneself in a particular way," needs no accompanying reflexive pronoun, but the inclusion of one makes the expression more forceful ("We expect you to *behave yourself*"). Formal English prefers it.

behind. See *back of*.

being as. The phrase *being as* is dialectal and therefore unacceptable in formal discourse. In "*Being as* we had never played the game, we asked for instructions," substitute *since* or *because* or simply delete *being*. Equally to be deplored are *being that*, *being as how*, and *seeing as how*.

belabor. Even if you refuse to accept as a meaning of *belabor* "to beat," "to attack with blows," and insist that it means only to make "a big to-do about something," you are still better off to use *labor*, as in "to labor a point." All you get from *belabor* is an extra syllable, and an unnecessary one to boot. Nevertheless, authorities regard these words as synonyms.

believe/feel/think, although used interchangeably in general speech, have distinguishable meanings. Their precise senses should be considered in serious writings. *Believe* means "to accept as true or real." One believes when he has a settled conviction that something is true. To *feel* is to experience an emotion, not to reason. To *think* is to have a thought, an idea, or an opinion. Not "I *believe* I was never there"; "I *think*. . . ." Not "I *feel* that capital punishment is wrong"; "I *think*. . . ." But "I *feel* sorry for a man who doesn't *believe* his wife loves him."

believes that. See *is of the opinion that.*

belles-lettres does not refer to love letters written by the leading belles of the day but to literature for art's sake. Pronounce it bell-*leht'r.*

below, when used to refer to material that follows, as in *the material below,* is stilted but nevertheless standard. (See *above.*)

beneficence/benevolence. Easily confused. *Beneficence* is the act of doing good, the quality of being charitable. *Benevolence* is the desire to do good, a kindly feeling. It costs less to be benevolent than beneficent. *Benevolence* is now loosely used to mean "a generous gift," but originally it did not. Its Latin ancestors *bene,* "well," and *volens* from *velle,* "to wish," prove that.

benefit. Spelling its past tense is a problem to some writers. Should it be "benefited" or "benefitted"? The answer is *benefited.*

benevolence. See *beneficence/benevolence.*

beseech means "to beg," "to implore." Its past tense and present participle is *besought.* But it is not unusual to hear someone say, "I was *beseeched* for free tickets by my entire class." Prefer *besought.*

beside/besides. In "His aunt came to sit *beside* me at the wedding," *beside* is a preposition meaning "next to," "by the side of." *Besides* is an adverb meaning "in addition to" ("He is tall and handsome; *besides,* he is wealthy"), but it may also serve as a preposition when it means "except" ("No one in the world loves him *besides* his mother"). (See *in addition to.*)

besiege, like its smaller cousin *siege,* is often misspelled. Note the middle *ie,* a combination reversed in *seize.*

be sure and. The conjunction *and* is not an acceptable substitute for *to* in "*be sure and* go today." The correct combination to express the desired idea is "be sure *to* go today." (See *try and.*)

be that as it may is an old-fashioned expression. Where suitable, use *but* instead.

better. Not a satisfactory substitute for *more* in a sentence such as "I like tennis *better* than golf." (See *better/best.*)

better/best. "Here are the two nominees for class president—Tom and Jack. We will vote now, and may the *best* man win." Amend to *better*. The superlative refers to three or more; the comparative to two only. Be equally careful of the *worst of two* and the *finest of two*.

better/well. If you have been ill and say, "I'm *better* now," do you mean that you're fully recovered or that your condition has improved? In ordinary usage it would mean that you are now completely well, even though, strictly speaking, that is not what *better* means.

better had, as in "You *better had* get to school on time or face suspension," is dialectal and should be avoided. Make it "You *had better.* . . ." The idiom *had better* is less formal than *ought* or *should*.

better than. Often used to replace "more than," sometimes with ludicrous results. "Johnnie had *better than* five accidents last year." Avoid the expression in formal writing.

between. See *among/between*; *-self/-selves*.

between/from. These prepositions govern the number of a following noun. A single noun that follows *between* is plural ("I judge this building has *between* 60 and 65 *stories*"); a single noun that follows *from* is singular ("Franklin has been moved *from* the ninth to the tenth *floor*").

between each (every). "*Between each* (*every*) house is a grassy plot." Some respected literary figures have used this expression, but many grammarians frown on it. They point out that *each* and *every*, being singular in meaning, cannot logically follow *between* (which implies *two*). The safest course to take, and the one recommended here, is to say "*Between* the houses . . ." or "*Between* one house and the next. . . ."

between you and I is a noticeably common error. To avoid this blunder, simply remember that *between*, like all prepositions, takes pronouns (or nouns) in the objective case. Make it "between you and *me*," for *me* is in the objective case; *I*, in the nominative. (See *-self/-selves*.)

bi-. Compounds are written as one word (*bivalve, biweekly*).

bi-/semi-. Use *bi-* to mean "two"—*bimonthly* is every two months. Use *semi-* to mean "half"—*semimonthly* is twice a month. (See *bimonthly/biweekly*.)

biannual/biennial. *Biannual* refers to a happening twice a year; *biennial*, to a happening every other year.

big/great. Exercise care when using these words. In "Roger is a *big* architect in the field of industrial building," probably the word intended was *great*. Although *big* and *great* are synonymous in some cases, *big* generally refers to size, emphasizing bulk or weight; *great* suggests mental ability, implying a high degree of distinction. If Roger is a big architect—that is, a big man—he is physically big; but it would be more refined to say he is a *large* man.

bilk. Not "Their scheme was to *bilk* $10,000 from the insurance company" but "to defraud the insurance company of $10,000." A victim is bilked, not the money.

bimonthly/biweekly. Dictionaries give *bimonthly* and *biweekly* two irreconcilable meanings—"every two months" and "twice a month," "every two weeks" and "twice a week"—certainly a rich source of confusion. For the sake of clarity, use every two months, twice a month (or *semimonthly*), and so forth. (See *bi-/semi-*.)

bisect/dissect are not interchangeable words, even though each refers to a division of something. *Bisect*, with its prefix *bi-*, which means "two," is a cutting or dividing into two parts. To *bisect* a turkey is to cut it into two nearly equal parts. To *dissect* a turkey is to cut it into many segments. Note that "bisect in two" is redundant.

bite. Although the past participle of this verb is *bitten* or *bit*, in the passive voice only *bitten* is correct ("Scott was *bitten* [not *bit*] by a mosquito").

biweekly. See *bimonthly/biweekly*.

blame. In everyday usage *blame* is placed on people, animals, or things ("He *blamed* his scraped knee on that swinging barn door"). Although this informal style now appears in some well-edited writing, in formal English *blame* should not be attributed to inanimate objects. And if a preposition is needed, it must be *for*, not *on*, as in the example. Thus "They *blamed* me *for* the accident" and not "They *blamed* the accident *on* me." In sum, blame someone or put the blame on someone for something. One caution: Some usage critics say this rule is obsolescent and that nowadays it is correct "to blame something *or* someone."

blatant/flagrant. "One of the most *blatant* cases of perjury in the Watergate matter . . ." points up a common misuse of *blatant* for *flagrant*. *Blatant* means "offensively loud or noisy." A blatant person is loudmouthed. By extension *blatant* has come to mean "showy," especially in dress or manner. *Flagrant* (Latin *flagare,* "to burn") means "glaringly offensive," "outrageous." Antisocial conduct, that which is beyond the proprieties of acceptable social standards, is said to be *flagrant.*

blond/blonde. Many careful writers distinguish these words by using *blonde* as a noun when referring to a woman ("She is a pretty *blonde*") but *blond* of a man. Generally the adjective form for either sex is *blond*—a blond girl, a blond boy. But note the word *generally*. Some authorities use *blonde* both as a noun and as an adjective when referring to women.

boat. See *ship/boat.*

boatswain. Unless you're a petty officer in charge of a ship's deck crew, which is what a *boatswain* is, you would hardly believe that his title is pronounced *boh-*s'n.

bombastic. See *turbid/turgid.*

bona fide, meaning "in good faith," is not pronounced *boh-*nuh-*fide,* but *boh-*nuh-*fie-*dee.

boor/bore. "He was such a first class *boor,* I could have gone to sleep right in front of him." Probably the word wanted was *bore,* a tiresome, tedious person. A *boor* is a disgustingly ill-mannered person.

born/borne. Note the difference in spelling of these homophones. "Mrs. Johnstone has *borne* six children; two of them were *born* at home." *Born* is always used in the passive; *borne,* although usually active, may be found in the passive with the preposition *by* ("The burdens *borne by* Job seemed endless"). *Borne* means "carried" or "endured."

both. See *either.*

both/each. "*Both* children wore a new hat" should be recast "*Each* child wore a new hat" unless they had found a hat large enough for both to slip under at the same time. *Both* means two together ("*Both* women cried"). *Each* is used for two or more but taken one at a time ("*Each* horse had a white spot on its forehead"—there might have been five horses).

both alike. "The brothers are *both alike*" is pleonastic. Delete *both*.

both/. . . and. This combination is immutable. In "*Both* Thomas *as well as* his mother will attend," remove *both* or replace *as well as* with *and*.

both were not. *Both* may cause misunderstanding when used in a negative sentence. For example, "*Both* boys were *not* happy" does not make clear whether both boys were unhappy or whether one was unhappy and the other happy. Avoid confusion by wording in the positive—"One of the boys was unhappy but not the other" if this is so; otherwise, "The two boys were unhappy."

bourgeois/proletariat. Do not use these words if you are not acquainted with their meaning. Generally speaking, *bourgeois* refers to a member of the middle class, shopkeepers and the like; *proletariat*, to a member of the working class, those who own no property and depend on employment for their livelihood.

boyfriend. See *girlfriend/boyfriend.*

braggadocio, which means "vain boasting," is spelled with two *g*'s and one *c*.

brag on, as in "He likes to *brag on* his brother" is dialectal. Change to *brag about*.

brand. See *group*.

brand-new. Informally *bran-new* is spelled as given because it is pronounced that way, without a *d*. In serious writing, prefer *brand-new*.

breach/breech. One who writes "There has been a *breech* in our pact" is confusing *breach*, "a breaking" or "neglect," with *breech*, "the part of the gun behind the barrel."

breath/breathe/breadth. There is hardly a risk of confusing the meaning of *breath*, "an exhalation of air," and *breathe*, "to inhale and exhale," "to respire," with the meaning of *breadth*, "distance across," "width." The care to be exercised is in their spelling.

breed. See *group*.

brevity is the soul of wit, a quotation from *Hamlet,* does not refer to the soul of humor, which it is commonly taken to mean. In Shakespeare's time *wit* meant "intelligent discussion."

bridegroom/groom. In formal English a man about to be married is called a *bridegroom*; in everyday usage simply a *groom*, despite the objection of critics that a *groom* is a horsetender. In this machine age few people, especially among the very young, are aware of that fact anyhow. To them, a *groom* is a man who says "I do." Nowadays it is safe to call a *bridegroom* a *groom* without fear of being misunderstood.

brief/short. According to the ads, girls wear briefs, meaning "short garments." In formal language *brief* is used of time and is not a synonym for *short*. One may speak of a brief visit, but not a brief skirt. It is a short skirt. *Short* may serve in almost any situation: a short story, a short man, a short visit. Although *brief* is used most often to refer to duration of time, it is also used to mean "concise" or "curt."

brief outline/little sip. Since an outline by definition is a brief compilation, and since a sip is a very small drink, the adjectives create tautologies that, although often heard in casual speech, are blunders in better writing.

brilliant has an *i* after the double *ll*, not *brillant*. Watch it.

bring/take. It is simply a matter of direction. *Bring* implies motion toward a person or place; *take*, motion away from a person or place. The direction of *bring*, therefore, is toward the speaker; the direction of *take*, away from him. If the direction is confusing, use either *carry* or *fetch*.

Britain. See *Great Britain/United Kingdom.*

broach/brooch. Exercise care in spelling these words. Although they are derived from the same ancestor (Latin *broca*, "spike"), their meanings are far apart. *Broach* means "to tap a cask" or "to begin to talk about," the way one broaches a subject. A *brooch* is an ornamental breastpin. These words are pronounced identically (*brohch*).

brother-in-law is made plural by pluralizing *brother—brothers-in-law*. (See *possessive case forms*.)

bulk of, as in "The *bulk of* the job has been finished," meaning the "greater part," and in "The *bulk of* the people have left," meaning "most of" or "the majority," has been decried by many grammarians, but to no avail. Except in scholarly texts *bulk of* has established itself. But it should not displace *majority* where a count is possible ("The *majority of* [not *the bulk of*] the delegates voted against the proposal"). The use of *bulk* is best confined to references of mass, volume, and size, as in "The *bulk* of the grain has already been shipped to Russia."

burgeon. The sense behind this verb is to sprout, to appear suddenly, like a new growth in the spring. When translated into general speech, it should apply to something that is just beginning, budding, so to speak, not to something well established that is now expanding or to something long continuing, such as the population growth in Shanghai with its twelve million inhabitants. That city's population is not beginning to sprout; its number has been tremendous since the days of Marco Polo.

burglar. See *robber/thief/burglar*.

burglarize/burgle. A robber robs. A thief steals. What does a burglar do? Unfortunately, no verb describes this felon's unlawful activities. In formal English you must expend a few words and say the burglar entered the premises to rob or to commit some other felony. Two verb forms have risen to fulfill this need for a single word to say all that. One is *burgle*, which has not caught on; the other, which is more widely accepted, is *burglarize*. Both terms are regarded as colloquialisms, however, but *burglarize* has been making marked inroads among some respected writers. Watch it.

burned/burnt. Either form may be used as the past tense or participle of *burn*. Let euphony be the deciding factor. But avoid such trite phrases as "all burned up," meaning "angry" or "frustrated."

burros. See *-o*.

burst. Note that the principal parts of the verb *burst*, "to break open," are *burst, burst, burst*.

bus. See *shortened words*.

business. Rather than "My brother had *no business* being there," say "My brother had no right being there." In the sense used *no business* is colloquial.

but. There is no valid reason why *but* should not begin a sentence. But avoid using it after *cannot help*. Use a gerund instead ("I *can't help thinking*," not "I *can't help but* think"). (See *and/but*; *cannot help but*.)

but him (he). For those who are stumped by such a construction as "No one but *him* will do it" versus "No one but *he* will do it," the advice is to heed your own inclination. Both are correct. Those who treat *but* as a preposition, regarding it as the equivalent of *except*, follow it with the objective case—*but him*. Those who regard it as a conjunction follow it with the nominative (*but he*), assuming an ellipticized clause ("No one [did it] but he will do it").

but that/but what are informal expressions. In "He didn't doubt *but that* the defendant would confess," *but* is unnecessary. And in "We never schedule a round of golf *but what* it rains," *what* serves no purpose. Omit it. However, *but what* may permissibly replace *except what*: "He drank everything *but what* tasted sour."

but which/but who. See *and which/but which*.

by about. See *at about*.

by and large is a popular expression borrowed from a nautical term meaning "to the wind and off it." In everyday usage it means "generally speaking," "on the whole," or "for the most part" and implies that what the speaker is about to say should be regarded as a generalization. It is tiresomely overused.

by a score of is frequently misused by sportscasters who, since they report the scores of games, ought to know better. The Eagles didn't beat the Cowboys by a score of 37 to 21. They beat the Cowboys 37–21, which was the final score.

by the same token is a cliché beloved by many writers. It has a pleasing rhythm and sets the right tone for the coming sentence. But for a change try *likewise*, *similarly*, or *besides*.

C

cacography.   See *calligraphy*.

Caesarean.   In "The young woman's baby was delivered by *caesarean section*," the name of the operation is variantly spelled *Caesarean section*, with its initial letter capitalized or in lowercase, or *caesarian* or *cesarean*. The preferred spelling is *Caesarean*.

calculate in the sense *guess, intend, think* is dialectal and should be avoided both in speech and in writing.

calligraphy.   Because this word means "beautiful writing," saying "Her *beautiful calligraphy* was highly praised" is redundant. Omit *beautiful*. And of course saying someone's calligraphy is poor is a contradiction in terms. The antonym of *calligraphy* is *cacography*.

callus/callous.   When referring to hard, thickened skin, spell the noun *callus* and the adjective *callous*.

call your attention to.   See *fact*.

can/may.   "He *can* leave if he wishes." "He *may* leave if he wishes." Both sentences are correct, but their meanings are different. *Can* denotes "ability to do." One who *can* is able to. *May* means "to have permission to." This distinction between *can* and *may* is preserved in formal English and by some careful writers, but in common language it has become almost completely blurred by the regular use of *can* for *may* ("*Can* I go out and play, Mom?").

cancel.   See *l* endings.

cancel out.   Delete *out*; it adds nothing useful. Be sure to spell *cancel* and its participial forms with only one *l*: *canceling, canceled*.

candelabra is not spelled *candleabra*. Although it is a large candlestick, the word *candle* is not in it. Actually *candelabra* is a Latin plural; its singular is *candelabrum*.

canine. Wrongly used in "His *canine* is vicious." *Canine* is not an approved variant for "dog"; it is an adjective meaning "doglike," just as *feline* means "catlike."

cannot/can not. Which form to use is the writer's choice. Both are standard. The predominant spelling is one word.

cannot hardly. See *can't hardly*.

cannot help but. Those who wonder why this expression is best avoided in formal discourse may note that it contains a double negative (*cannot . . . but*). Correct by using a gerund— "I *cannot help thinking* that I should have gone," and drop *but*, not "I cannot help *but think*." The double negative by itself (without *help*) is acceptable to some good writers in such a sentence as "The Prime Minister sadly said that we *cannot but* regret this violation of international law."

can't hardly, as in "He *can't hardly* lift his right arm," is substandard. (See *hardly/scarcely*.)

can't seem to. "He *can't seem to* find the baseball" in polished English should be rendered simply "He *can't* find" or "He *is unable* to find. . . ." Opinions of experts are almost evenly divided on whether *can't seem to* may be admitted into formal writing. To avoid any criticism, avoid the expression.

canvas/canvass. Only the spelling is confusing. The first is a material. The second as a verb means "to solicit" and as a noun, "a detailed examination."

capacity. See *ability/capacity*.

capital/capitol. Although the word *capital* is used in many senses, it is being compared here to *capitol*. A *capital*, a city, is the seat of government ("The *capital* of the United States is Washington, D.C."). A *capitol* is a statehouse, the building where the legislature holds its sessions. When spelled *Capitol*, with a capital *C*, it refers to the building in which Congress assembles to conduct its business.

capitalization. See *father/mother/aunt/uncle*; *seasons, capitalization of*; *titles*.

capitol. See *capital/capitol*.

captious/carping. Both words refer to "criticism," but *carping* is said of a person whose criticism is continual and ill-tempered. That which is *captious* is fault-finding; it reflects peevishness.

The difference in sense between these words is a hairline, and that sometimes requires a magnifying glass to see.

car is standard English for *automobile*, but in scholarly texts the word *automobile* is preferable.

carat/karat/caret. So as not to mix the reporting of gems and gold, bear in mind that gems are measured in *carats* and gold in *karats*. A *carat* is a unit of weight; a *karat*, a unit of fineness. A *caret* is an editor's mark to indicate an insertion.

careless needs proper "prepositioning." A person is careless *about* the appearance of his dress or his desk; *in* the way he trims his lawn or ties his shoelaces; *of* the feelings of others.

caret. See *carat/karat/caret*.

carping. See *captious/carping*.

case lends itself to several redundant expressions. Replace *in most cases* with "usually" and *in case*, as in "*In case* we go," with "if." Change "It is *not the case*" to "It is not so." *Case* is best used when it stands for "in the event" ("*In case* of a power shortage, pull this switch").

catalog. This spelling is general and is fast becoming universal. But *monologue* has not been divested of its *-ue* by many particular spellers.

catholic, an adjective derived from Greek *katholikos*, meaning "worldwide," is written in lower case. Capitalize only when referring to an adherent of the Catholic church.

catsup. See *ketchup/catsup*.

cause. See *on account of*.

cause is due to. Redundant, since *caused by*, *attributed to*, and *due to* mean the same. In "The *cause* of the accident was *due to* a faulty brake lining," delete *due to* or make it "The accident was *due to*. . . ." (See *due to*.)

cavalier. A tricky word because it has two disparate meanings. Be sure the context makes clear whether *cavalier* is being used to mean "arrogantly haughty" or "carefree and gay."

-cede/-ceed/-sede. Often confused because these endings all sound alike. In the English language only one word ends in *-sede* ("supersede"); three in *-ceed* ("exceed," "proceed," "succeed"). All the others with endings that have this sound are spelled *-cede*—"accede," "concede," "recede," "secede," and so on. (See *supersede/consensus*.)

Celsius. See *centigrade/Celsius*.

cement/concrete. These words are not interchangeable; the first is an ingredient of the second. *Cement* is a paste formed from clay, rock, and water and is the adhesive element in concrete. *Concrete* is a construction material that, when poured into a mold, makes sidewalks, structural columns, and the like. A sidewalk is commonly called a cement sidewalk, even though it is made, not of cement, but of concrete.

censor/censure. Note that to *censor* is not necessarily to *censure*. To *censor* is "to remove objectionable material"; to *censure* is "to reprimand" or "to condemn."

censure. See *censor/censure*.

center/centre. See *theater/theatre*.

center around. A common idiom that everyone understands ("The team's offense is *centered around* Honigman's throwing arm"). Strictly speaking, however, what should have been said is *centered on* because a *center* cannot be "around" anything. If the word *around* improves the sentence rhythm, or is important for any other reason, try "rotate around"—although a little stuffy—or "revolve around."

centigrade/Celsius. These terms mean the same. Both refer to the 100-degree temperature scale in which zero is the freezing point and 100 the boiling point.

ceremonial/ceremonious pertain to a ceremony, "a special form of acts performed on special occasions," such as a wedding, funeral, or graduation. *Ceremonial* is applied to occasions performed with rituals or formalities ("Weddings are important *ceremonial* occasions"). *Ceremonious* means "formal, punctilious, precise" and is commonly applied to persons ("Dr. Waldron in dress and demeanor is *ceremonious*"). It may be said that *ceremonial* is associated with the ceremonies themselves ("The Queen's duties are chiefly *ceremonial*") and *ceremonious* with the person involved ("The Vice President is *ceremonious*; he enjoys the pageantry of the events over which he presides").

chaise longue is French for long chair. Furniture ads sometimes spell it *chaise lounge*, a misusage far from uncommon in everyday speech. Pronounce it *shez-lounhg*.

change. See *alter/change*.

changeable is a word that causes a spelling problem to some people. Note it is not *changable*; the middle *e* is retained before the suffix *-able*—*changeable*.

chaos is disorder. *Complete chaos* is grammatical disorder. The expression, though often heard, is redundant.

character/reputation. Discriminate carefully between these words. *Character* is what you are. *Reputation* is what people think you are.

chassis/chasm. Although the first (a framework of a vehicle) is pronounced *shass*-ee, the second (a deep gorge) is pronounced *kaz*-um, as though it began with a *k*.

chauffeur is sometimes misspelled *chauffur*. Note the final *eur*. Preferably accent the second syllable.

chic, meaning "elegant," "stylish," is pronounced *sheek*, not *shick*.

Chief Justice of the United States, not Chief Justice of the Supreme Court of the United States, is the correct title of the Chief Justice.

childish/childlike, although suggesting the behavior of children, have different connotations when applied to adults. *Childish* points to the undesirable, the unpleasant or immature characteristics (*childish* temper, *childish* demands); *childlike*, to appealing qualities, to the better aspects of childhood (*childlike* faith, *childlike* trust).

Chinese/Chinaman. When reaching for a word to refer to a Chinese person, or to the Chinese people, choose the former, *Chinese*. The term *Chinaman* is considered disrespectful. And note the spelling. *Chinese* has only one *e* before the *s*.

cholera/choleric. A person who has *cholera* is suffering from a disease. A person who is *choleric* is quick-tempered.

choose. See *pick/choose*.

chords. See *cords*.

Christian name. See *given name*.

chronic is not to be construed to mean "severe," as in "She is so *chronically* ill we can't be sure when she'll recover." *Chronic* (from Greek *chronos*, "time") means "of longstanding duration," "constant." It may refer to a mild affliction. (See *acute/chronic.*)

cigarette. If you wish to ignore the Surgeon General's warning, at least spell *cigarette* this way rather than *cigaret.*

Cincinnati/Pittsburgh. Be careful of these spellings. In the first, note the two *n*'s in the middle; in the second, the *h* at the end.

cipher. See *naught/aught.*

circum-. Solid as a prefix (*circumnavigate, circumscribe*).

Civil War. If you're writing for a Southern audience, use *War Between the States.* That is the term preferred below the Mason-Dixon line.

claim is one of the most popular words in the English language, perhaps because of its vigorous ring. Used properly, a *claim* is a demand as a matter of right or title. But when used as a verb, it often merely replaces *assert, declare, maintain, profess, protest, remark,* and ordinary *say*—any of which might be more suitable.

classic/classical. To avoid misuse of these words, use *classic* to connote "outstandingly important" or "of the first class" ("Shylock is a *classic* example of bigotry") and *classical* as a term that refers to ancient art and culture, especially Greek and Roman ("We took a course in *classical* studies").

clauses. A sometimes perturbing construction. In "All we want is balls and bats," the singular verb *is* must be used because its subject is the clause *all we want* (and all clauses are singular). The plural form *balls and bats* are predicate nouns and do not, therefore, govern the number of the verb.

clean/clear. These words are colloquial in a sentence such as "The water rose *clean* (or *clear*) up to the first step."

cleave. Note that this word has opposite meanings—"to split" and "to adhere."

climactic/climatic. That which pertains to a climax is *climactic. Climatic* refers to climate. The words are adjectives.

climax is the culmination, the high point of interest or intensity in a series or progression of events. It should not be used to indicate the lowest point in a series ("In the morning Joe's car wouldn't start; in the afternoon he got a parking ticket; and his troubles reached their *climax* when he had a flat tire en route home.") *Acme* seems synonymous, but it is not entirely so; it means "summit" or "highest point," implying the point of perfection. No continuity is suggested. *Epitome* (which see) is not a synonym of *climax*.

climb up/climb down. Even though *up* in *climb up* seems redundant and *down* in *climb down* contradictory, both expressions are in good English usage.

close/near mean "at a short distance." When nearness—immediate proximity—is to be emphasized, *close* is preferred to *near*. *Close* seems closer than *near*. We use *close* in such idioms as "a close shave" or "a close call." Many people may be *near* the President, but few are *close* to him.

close/shut. There is no difference in sense between "Close the door" and "Shut the door." They both mean "to make not open." But in other uses, *close* means "to block" (*close* the opening, *close* the tunnel). *Shut*, on the other hand, may mean to close so as to bar ingress and egress ("The outside cellar door has been *shut* tight").

close proximity is tautological. Anything in proximity to something is close to it.

close to, meaning "almost" or "nearly," as in "*Close to* 2,000 teachers attended the convention," is an expression not recommended for formal writing.

co-. The best rule to follow, when using this prefix, is to judge whether it looks better if written solid or open. *Coordinate* is usually spelled as shown, but *co-owner* and *co-worker* take a hyphen. *Copilot* is seen as a solid word but not *co-star*. Whether *coauthor* and *codefendant* are preferable to *co-author* and *co-defendant* has partisans supporting each side. The trend is to make it *coauthor* and *codefendant*.

coed. An all-female school has female students, not *coeds*. Calling them *coeds* is a technical misusage. A school that has both male and female students is said to be *coeducational*.

coequal is defined in dictionaries as "a person or thing equal to another." *Equal* is defined as "evenly matched." Which makes *coequal* and *equal* equivalents. But someone might rightly ask, What advantage has *coequal* over *equal* in a sentence such as "In gymnastics the two boys are considered *coequal*"? The answer:

none. In fact *coequal* is a liability. The added *co-* makes the word uneconomical.

cohere. See *adhere/cohere*.

cohort. "The robber's *cohort* escaped in the crowd." The equating of *cohort* with "accomplice" or "confederate" has been laid at the doorstep of newspaper reporters. In general usage the term has acquired the additional sense of "colleague," "associate," "assistant," and "companion." However, linguists deplore these extensions. They say that a *cohort* cannot be an individual; it must be a group united in a struggle, hearkening back to the days of the Roman legions when a cohort was a company of soldiers.

coiffeur/coiffure. To be chic in spelling as well as hair style, use *coiffeur* for the hair dresser and *coiffure* for the hairdo.

coincidence, the chance occurrence of two or more events at the same time, may not, by definition, refer to a single event. Therefore, saying "His arrival at my house was a *coincidence*" is incorrectly put, although his arrival at my house at the same time my brother arrived might be a coincidence.

collaborate together. The only way to collaborate is by getting together with someone. Delete *together* and avoid a tautology.

collectible. See *includable*.

collective elements. Although the rule is clear that a verb must agree with its subject in number and person, a subject consisting of two or more elements joined by *and* is not always to be treated as a plural. This is so when obviously only one thing or idea is meant. Then the elements combine to make a collective thought, and the subject is singular. The often heard "Ham and eggs *is* my favorite" is a case in point. The subjects do not consist of two distinct items; they have been compounded into a oneness. And so we say, "A horse and buggy *is* a pleasant means of traveling." "Hail and brimstone *is* a favorite topic of a Sunday sermon." (See *sentence structure*.)

collective nouns. The failure of a verb to agree with its collective-noun subject is probably the most common error in English grammar. The problem lies with those nouns known as nouns of multitude because they may take either a singular or plural verb, depending on whether the emphasis is on the individual or on the group. Take the noun *jury*. It is correct to say, "The jury *is* in the jury room." It is also correct to say, "The jury *are* disagreeing among themselves." In the first example the jury is considered a unit, a collective. In the second, the members of the jury are acting individually; they are not disagreeing collectively. And so, "My family *has* arrived"; "My family *are* all ill"; "That couple *was* engaged yesterday"; "The older couple on your left *live* far away." One other point. Whether the collective is considered a singular or a plural, it should be treated consistently throughout the sentence. In "Pitt has paid their coach a large bonus," either make it *have* or change *their* to *its*. "The company has announced that they are not moving." Here again, change *has* to *have* or *they are* to *it is*.

college. See *university/college*.

collide. Strictly speaking, a *collision* is a coming together of two moving objects. An accident involving a moving and a stationary vehicle is not properly called a collision. And it certainly should not be in formal English. But in everyday speech a truck that rams the side of a barn is said to be in a collision. This loose usage is so widespread that it may be considered standard English. If an actual collision does occur—that is, two moving vehicles strike each other—saying they *collided together* is redundant. Inherent in the word *collide* is a coming together.

colloquial English. See *English, levels of*.

colon. Two questions that often arise are whether a capital letter should follow a colon and whether a colon is properly placed after the verb that precedes a series. The answer to the first is that it is simply a writer's choice. If the statement introduced by a colon is very important, a capital letter makes it more emphatic. Regarding the second, it is a mistake to place a colon in this construction after the verb. In "The delegates from Louisiana are: Johnson, Greenstein, McCaulley, and Browne," omit the colon. Or convert the statement into an appositive—for example, "All the delegates from Louisiana are senior citizens: Johnson. . . ."

color. Not "My wife abhors that *color* of purple," but "That *shade* of purple."

comely. See *homely/comely*.

comma. See *comma splice*; *nevertheless*; *of course*; *serial comma*; *suspended modifiers*; *which/that*.

comma/parenthesis. If a sentence requires a comma where a parenthesis is also needed, insert the comma after the closing parenthesis, as in "We believe that Tom Smyth (that six-foot man), our captain, will lead our team to victory."

comma splice. Occurs in a compound sentence in which no coordinating conjunction joins the clauses ("He picked up his belongings and packed the car, his brother did not join him"). Either insert *but* after *car* or replace the comma with a semicolon.

commas with dates and places. Note that in "September 10, 1947, was a memorable day" a comma follows the year. In "The convention was held in New Hope, Bucks County, Pennsylvania, three years ago," each element of place takes a comma. Do not omit the last comma.

commence. See *begin/commence/start*.

comment on. See *critique*.

commitment. Although *committed* and *committing* have two *t*'s, *commitment* has only one.

common/mutual. *Common* refers to something belonging equally to, or shared by, two or more persons. *Mutual* means "interchanged"; it connotes reciprocity, referring to something experienced by two or more persons for the benefit of all. These words, however, are often loosely used one for the other, despite the protests of purists. A mutual friend, really a common friend, will continue to be called in common usage "a mutual friend."

commonly/generally/frequently/usually. Be careful to distinguish these terms. What is *commonly* so or done is common to all. What is *generally* so or done is true of the larger number. *Frequently* means "often" and *usually* means "customarily."

communication is pretentious when used for *letter* or *memorandum*.

compact. See *pact/compact*.

comparatively. See *relatively*.

compare. This word is bothersome primarily because it may take either of two prepositions, *to* or *with*, depending on the context. When a comparison is made of things or persons of the same kind—an actual comparison—citing both similarities and differences, *compare with* is the preferred combination ("We are *comparing* our current figures *with* last year's"). When the comparison is metaphorical—a figurative one, citing only the similarities—*compare to* must be your choice ("His swimming antics were *compared to* the tricks of a dolphin." "Shakespeare *compared* the world *to* a stage"). In most instances, since a real comparison is being made, the preposition that gets the bigger play is *with*.

comparisons. When comparisons are made with *like* as a preposition, the result may be absurd if a *that* or *those* is omitted or a possessive case does not follow. "He has ears like a donkey," compares his ears to a donkey. The intention was to compare two sets of ears. Make it "He has ears like *those* of a donkey" or "He has ears like a *donkey's*."

compass directions. Write *north, south, east,* and *west* in lower case when referring to direction ("Camden lies *east* of Philadelphia"). Capitalize if a region is meant ("We like the deep *South*." "Our children would like to live in the *West*").

compendious. Do not confuse with *comprehensive*. *Compendious* refers to a brief compilation; *comprehensive*, to one that covers the entire field.

compendium. Those who believe that *compendium* refers to a massive, comprehensive work are mistaken. A *compendium* is an abstract or outline. Obviously, it must be brief and concise.

compile. See *compose/compile*.

complacent/complaisant. The first is often used when the second is required. A complacent person is smug, pleased with himself ("We thought his manner was decidedly *complacent*"). A *complaisant* person is agreeable, eager to please others ("The director's *complaisant* manner has attracted many friends"). This latter term is gradually disappearing in favor of *complacent*, which more and more is coming to represent both meanings. Nonetheless, careful writers preserve the traditional distinction between these words. The corresponding nouns are *complacency* and *complaisance*.

complected. "He was tall and dark *complected*" would read better *tall and dark complexioned* or *of dark complexion*. Although widely used, *complected* is regarded as a dialectal form.

complement/compliment. One way to keep these words straight is to remember that *complement* means "to complete" ("Wine *complements* a meal") and that both words have two *e*'s or that *compliment*, which means "to praise," has an *i* because *I* like compliments. (See *supplement/complement*.)

complete. An absolute term, not to be modified by *more* or *most*. But "most nearly complete" is acceptable. (See *absolutes*.)

complete and unabridged. See *tautology*.

completely destroyed. See *destroyed*.

complete master. Omit *complete* and avoid a redundancy.

compliment. See *complement/compliment*.

compose/compile. To *compose* is to arrange into a single finished work—a poem, a sonata, a document. To *compile* is to acquire and put in order all material that forms a book or other literary product. In some cases the meanings of the words overlap, but handbooks, like this one, are said to be compiled. (See *comprise*.)

compound nouns, plurals of. See *teeth*.

compound subjects. See *affirmative/negative*; *collective elements*; *sentence structure*.

comprehend. See *apprehend/comprehend*.

comprehensive. See *compendious*.

comprise. The common use of *comprise*, as in "These three divisions *comprise* our best fighting corps," implies that it is synonymous with "compose" and "make up." It is not. The whole *comprises* the parts; the parts *compose* or make up the whole ("Our best fighting corps *comprises* three divisions"). Use *comprise* to mean only "consist of" and "be made up of." And note that it takes a direct object. Note further that it is always incorrect to say *comprised of*. (See *include/including*.)

compulsive/impulsive. Regard *compulsive*—referring to an irrational, uncontrollable urge—as a psychological term. A compulsive gambler gambles as long as his money holds out. A compulsive eater continues to eat as long as food is available. *Impulsive*—a sudden driving force or influence—is a more ordinary term. Suggesting spontaneity, it implies that premeditation has played little or no part in what was done. For example, one might impulsively kiss his wife—or his secretary—or make an unexpectedly generous gift to charity.

conceived. A woman can conceive many times, but an idea or notion can be conceived only once. Do not, therefore, say "After the idea was first *conceived*, we decided. . . ." Drop *first*.

concerning. See *dangling participles*; *regarding/concerning/respecting*.

concise. See *succinct/concise*.

concur in/concur with. A person concurs *in* an action or decision ("The judges all *concurred in* giving him the prize"). But a person concurs *with* another person when he is in agreement ("The priest *concurred with* the minister").

condign. Often misused in the sense of "severe." *Condign* means "deserved" or "adequate." If condign punishment happens to be severe, it is nonetheless deserved.

confidant/confidante. You may call your wife a *confidant* or a *confidante*. But she must refer to you as a *confidant*. *Confidant* applies to either sex; *confidante* is only feminine.

confine/contain. Do not confuse. Something *confined* is restricted, kept within limits, like a toddler or an invalid confined to his room. Of course, a laconic person will confine his thoughts to a few words. Something *contained* is restrained or kept within reasonable or normal bounds. The bounds may be physical, a vessel capable of holding (this pot *contains* a quart of soup), or abstract, referring to one's feelings (a person *contains* his temper, his emotions).

conjunctive adverbs. *Accordingly, consequently, furthermore, however, likewise, nevertheless, therefore*, etc., serving as conjunctions between independent clauses are preceded by a semicolon. They may be followed by a comma, but the modern trend is to omit it ("We will leave soon; therefore let's prepare." "His survey was finished; consequently he decided to deliver it today"). But note that many good writers have not as yet joined this trend.

connected with can usually be omitted without affecting the sense of the sentence. Rather than "They agreed on several matters *connected with* geography," make it "They agreed on several geographical matters." "Jeff is *connected with* the Burroughs Corporation" is reducible to "Jeff is *with* the Burroughs Corporation."

connive/conspire. To *connive* is simply to ignore wrongdoing by pretending it doesn't exist. Conniving at someone's thievery is not to conspire with that person to steal, but merely a willingness to assist by not speaking or acting. *Connive* and *conspire*, therefore, are not synonymous. To *conspire* is to plan with others to do something wrong, usually a criminal act.

connoisseur, "an expert in a given field," is misspelled by those who fail to note the double *n* and the double *s*. Pronounce it kahn-uh-*seur*.

connote. See *denote/connote*.

conscious/aware. Although used synonymously, with the blessing of some dictionaries, the distinction in meaning between these words should be preserved for the sake of precision. *Conscious* refers to our physical or mental being, that which we feel within ourselves. We are conscious of a pain in the toe, of fear of the dark. *Aware* implies a cognizance of what goes on about us, a knowing or a realization of something either by perception or through information ("The waving flagman made us *aware* of the danger ahead").

consecutive/successive. Although these words imply that something follows one upon the other, they are not exact synonyms. *Consecutive* denotes an uninterrupted happening, like three days in a row, such as Friday, Saturday, Sunday, or three months in a row, such as January, February, March. *Successive* points to things in relation to each other that follow in a regular order but not necessarily without interruption. Monday, Wednesday, and Friday are successive days. June, August, and October are successive months. But note that that which follows normally may be not only consecutive but also successive—for example, the days that correspond to the weekly order are both consecutive and successive.

consensus. See *supersede/consensus*.

consensus of opinion. It is best to avoid the snares of those who would give this expression linguistic credentials. *Consensus* means "agreement or unanimous agreement of opinion." Since "opinion" is implied in the word *consensus*, all that "of opinion" accomplishes is to create a redundancy. Note the spelling of *consensus*. It has three *s*'s.

consequent.   See *subsequent/consequent*.

consequent result.   See *tautology*.

consider/regard.   When *consider* means "to judge" or, more loosely, "to think," unlike *regard* it does not idiomatically take *as* ("We *regard* him *as* a fool" but "We *consider* him a fool"). Although *consider* may be followed by an infinitive, particularly a perfect infinitive, it is better not to follow it with *to be*, not "We *consider* him *to be* an enemy" but "We *consider* him an enemy."

considerable is used as an adjective in standard English ("He made *considerable* advances in his job"). It is colloquial when used to mean "much" ("They made *considerable* during the past two years").

considering.   See *dangling participles*.

consist in/consist of.   The first means "to be contained in"; the second, "to be composed of." *Consist in* identifies a quality and is used in an abstract sense ("The importance of his advice *consists in* its directness and conciseness"). *Consist of* suggests parts of a whole ("The chef's featured dish *consists of* many ingredients, some of which he keeps secret").

conspire.   See *connive/conspire*.

consume entirely is a tautology.

contact.   One who prefers the brevity of verb *contact* to "get in touch with" or some similar phrase has some authoritative support, even though many critics object to that usage on the ground that it is pure commercialese. But prejudice against it is fast disappearing. Perhaps what accounts for the word's popularity is its all-embracing meaning—"You can telephone, you can write, you can wire, etc., but be sure to reach me in some way." Noun *contact* ("He has made some interesting *contacts*") is accepted on all levels.

contagious.   See *infectious/contagious*.

contain.   See *confine/contain*.

contemporary.   This word can confuse the present with the past and vice versa. The reason is that unless one fixes the time to which *contemporary* applies, it is difficult to tell the frame of its reference. The context must clarify it. A Shakespearean play advertised as using contemporary props and scenes may be construed as having either equipment and backdrops contemporary with Shakespeare or with that of modern times. If *contemporary* means "modern," it is wise, unless the intended period is made clear, to use *modern* or some other unambiguous expression.

contemptible/contemptuous are not to be equated. A person who feels or shows contempt is contemptuous (a scornful look is *contemptuous*). A person who is deserving of contempt is contemptible (cheats and liars are *contemptible*).

contiguous. See *adjacent/contiguous.*

continual. See *continuous/continual.*

continue. See *resume/continue.*

continue on. In "We want to finish, so let's *continue on,*" drop *on*; it's unnecessary.

continue to remain. "We hope they will *continue to remain* on their jobs" is redundant because if they continue, they will remain; if they remain, they will continue.

continuous/continual. Frequently misunderstood. *Continuous* means "without interruption" ("When the faucet is turned on, water runs *continuously.*" "The Delaware River flows *continuously*"). *Continual* means "recurring periodically," in the way a telephone rings. Ships ply a busy river continually. You may say it rained *continuously* for two hours if it rained steadily, or *continually* for two hours if it occasionally stopped during the two-hour period.

contra. See *pro and con.*

contractual. Sometimes misspelled *contractural.* Be careful.

contrary to fact. See *was/were.*

contrast as a verb is usually followed by *with* ("The lecturer *contrasted* the use of oil *with* that of coal"); as a noun by *with,* *to,* or *between* ("The present administration presents a startling *contrast to* (or *with*) the last one." "The *contrast between* the economies of today and fifty years ago is incredible"). In any of its uses *contrast* connotes an examination to find differences rather than similarities. (See *compare.*)

contributing factor. A redundancy. A factor would not be a factor if it didn't contribute. (See *element/factor/feature/phase.*)

contumacy/contumely. Easily confused. *Contumacy* is stubbornness, defiance of authority. *Contumely* is insolence, haughtiness, as in *Hamlet*'s "The proud man's contumely."

convict/acquit. Whatever the outcome of the trial, these verbs take preposition *of*—*convicted of* or *acquitted of* the crime.

convince/persuade. The easiest way to discriminate between their uses is to remember that *to convince* means to cause someone to believe; *to persuade* is to cause someone to act. A mother can convince her daughter that the floor needs washing, for example, but be unable to persuade her to wash it. And note that although *persuade* may be followed by a *to* infinitive ("They *persuaded* him *to* run for office"), *convince* may not. Use *that* instead ("They *convinced* him *that* he should run for office") or an *of* clause ("They *convinced* him *of* the advisability of running for office").

cooperate/coordinate. Spell as given, no hyphen (not *co-operate*, not *co-ordinate*) and no dieresis (not *coöperate*, not *coördinate*).

cooperation. See *mutual cooperation.*

coordinate. See *cooperate/coordinate.*

cope is followed by *with* ("He could not *cope with* conditions at the office"). Saying "He simply could not cope" is an impermissible curtailment of a thought. Add a *with* phrase, such as "*with* conditions at the office."

copulative verbs. The linking verb that ties subject and predicate. The most common copulas are verbs pertaining to the senses (*feel, look, smell, touch, taste*) and the verb *be*. Others are *seem, become, grow*, and *appear*. (See *bad/badly; feel bad/feel badly; good/well; look; wax/wane.*)

cords. A choir may sound its chords but not through vocal chords. The vibrators in the throat that make sounds are *cords*, not *chords*.

corespondent/correspondent. A person who, when writing to a *correspondent*, mistakenly spells the word *corespondent* may lose a pen pal. A *correspondent*, of course, is one who writes letters. A *corespondent* is one charged with adultery in a divorce proceeding in which he has been named as the third party.

corps, "an organized body or group," is both a singular and a plural. The singular ends in a silent *s* (*kor*); the plural is pronounced *korz*.

corpus delicti. Do not confuse this legal term with its popular conception, the body of the victim of a murder. Although in Latin this expression means "the body of a crime," it does not necessarily suggest a corpse. It refers to evidence that establishes that a crime was committed—which may or may not involve a dead body.

correlative conjunctions. See *either . . . or*; *neither . . . nor*; *not only . . . but also*.

correspondent. See *corespondent/correspondent*.

corroborate. See *verify/corroborate*.

could, when used as a subjunctive, need not be preceded by *if* ("*Could* Simon have jumped another two inches, he would have made the varsity" rather than "*If* Simon *could* have jumped . . .").

could of. See *should of*.

countenance/physiognomy. These synonyms, both referring to one's face, are distinguishable. *Countenance* means *face* as a part of one's body. It may also refer to an expression of the face (an angry *countenance*). *Physiognomy* points to features or to the type of face that reflects character (a kindly *physiognomy*).

counter-. Spell compounds as one word (*counterattack, counterclaim, counterterrorism*).

counterpart. Something that runs counter to, say, a trend, runs in an opposite direction. But a *counterpart* is not an opposite; it is a similar or complementary thing (President Reagan will meet with Gorbachev, his Russian *counterpart*).

countries/nations. "Rivers in the Scandinavian *nations* are frozen solid during the winter." Replace with *countries*. *Nation* denotes the people and suggests their political and economic organization; *country* refers to the territory of a nation.

coup. Pronounced *koo*; plural *coups* pronounced *koos*.

coup de grâce. Grâce (note the accent mark) is pronounced *grahss*.

coupe/coupé. *Coupe* (pronounced *koop*) is a dessert dish and has one syllable. Coupé (pronounced koo-*pay*) is a four-wheel vehicle with two seats inside and one outside. The accent mark is not essential, but either way pronounce it with two syllables.

couple. In precise English, *couple* is used to refer to two persons or things joined or related in some way. A couple is a pair, like two leashed golden retrievers or a married couple. Avoid "I bought a *couple* of books." Say "two books." But if *couple* is used, do not forget *of*, not "I bought a *couple* books." (See *collective nouns*.)

credible/creditable. Often confused because they sound so much alike. *Credible* means "believable"; *creditable*, "deserving of credit," "praiseworthy." "The jury found the testimony *credible* and the lawyer's summation *creditable*." But it is hard to say what accounts for a sentence such as "It reflected *credibly* on the image of the School Board." Possibly poor enunciation. *Credibly* means "in a believable or trustworthy manner." The word required was *creditably*.

creek, "a brook," is pronounced *kreek*, not *krihk*. The latter pronunciation is for *crick*, a muscle spasm.

crepuscular. For those reaching for a word to describe insects that appear at night, a good word is *crepuscular*, which also means "resembling twilight."

crick. See *creek*.

crisis implies a critical event. Therefore, do not modify with *acute* or *grave*.

criterion, which is a standard of judgment, has only one acceptable plural: *criteria*. One may occasionally see *criterias*; however, this variant spelling, like *mediums* for *media*, is not recommended. Of course *mediums*, referring to spiritualists, is not involved here. (See *medium/media*.)

criticism, like *odor* (which see), is a neutral word—that is, it implies nothing pleasant or unpleasant, favorable or unfavorable. But since the idea of faultfinding is generally imputed to the word *criticism*, it must be taken in that sense. Its connotation today is one of disfavor.

critique/criticize. *Critique* is a noun meaning "a critical essay or review." It also is a verb meaning "to criticize." Verb *critique*, however, sounds pompous ("He *critiqued* his daughter's composition"), which is reason enough to avoid it. Try *criticized* or *commented on*.

crucial. Do not intensify or deemphasize the degree of finality or decisiveness inherent in *crucial.* Avoid using with *more, less,* or *rather. Crucial* is an "absolute" and should be treated accordingly. The situation it describes must deserve such a strong word.

crumple/rumple. It matters not which of these words is used to suggest a crush into an unpatterned fold or mass. But it is better to use *crumple* to mean "crush together" and *rumple* to mean "wrinkle." The word *crumple* implies wrinkles made deliberately by crushing; *rumple,* wrinkles due to carelessness. We speak of a crumpled piece of paper, for example, but a rumpled suit of clothing. A rag may be crumpled but a bed sheet is rumpled.

culminate. "Injuries to the pitching staff *culminated* in the longest string of losses the team has ever had." *Culminate* does not imply a result or outcome, as in the example, but means "to reach its highest point or climax." Change "Injuries to the pitching staff resulted. . . ." or "caused the longest. . . ." One may properly say, "The romance between the Prince and the movie star *culminated* in marriage."

cupfuls. See *-ful.*

curiously enough/peculiarly enough/oddly enough. If you drop *enough,* you will not harm the sentence in the least.

custom. See *habit/custom.*

customary practice. Redundant. *Practice* means "customary action."

cute. Widely employed to mean "pretty or attractive" or "clever" ("What a cute idea!"). But its use should be restricted to informal English.

cut in half. The query whether "cut in half" is a correct expression or whether it should be "cut in halves" or "cut in two" is answered by idiom. Logically an apple cannot be cut in half, but idiom, which is concerned not with logic but with natural speech patterns, holds differently. Feel free, therefore, to say or write "cut in half," but the pedant, who is always overcorrect, may make it "in halves." It is a writer's choice. (See *half.*)

dais/podium/lectern. Sometimes confused and misused by lecturers who, since they use these facilities, should certainly know better. A *dais* (the first syllable is pronounced as though spelled *day*—*day*-ihs) is a speaker's platform, usually large enough to accommodate several people. A *podium*, which sits on a dais, is a raised platform on which a lecturer or conductor stands. A *lectern* is a raised, slanted speaker's table on which the lecturer places his notes. A reporter who said the lecturer kept striking the *podium* with his fist meant *lectern*, and a report that the nervous lecturer grasped the *podium* to steady himself was obviously inaccurate unless the lecturer had fallen.

dangling participles. To avoid this omnipresent problem, bear in mind that every participle—and they usually appear at the beginning of a sentence—must have a noun or pronoun to modify, and it should be the first word after the modifying phrase or clause. In "Running through the woods, three boulders were seen on top of a ridge," the boulders were not running. Make it *"we* saw three boulders." "While crossing the highway, a truck knocked him down." Here again, the truck was not crossing the highway; the man was. Change to, *"he* was knocked down by a truck."

Anyone wishing to dangle with no grammatical fault may do so with a select group of participial phrases that idiom has decreed need not relate to a particular noun or pronoun. This group consists of *generally speaking, considering, concerning, judging, owing to, speaking of, providing, excepting,* and many others. (See *based on.*)

dash. Most writers employ the *dash*—typed with two hyphens with no space before, between, or after—primarily to set off a parenthetical element or to summarize what has just been said. Although dashes may usually be replaced by commas or parentheses, these latter marks are not so distinctive, nor do they supply the emphasis to a preceding statement that dashes do ("He confessed—and everyone remained silent").

dastardly. Dictionaries define *dastardly* as "cowardly and mean-spirited." The problem in current usage is that the word seldom contains an element of cowardice but refers solely to that which is reprehensible.

data, although considered a singular noun by some respected authorities, their theory being that *data* represents the whole rather than its parts ("Such *data supplies* the information we need"), is best treated as a plural, especially in formal discourse ("Such *data supply* the information we need"). The singular form of *data* is *datum*, a word seldom used. (See *agenda*; *phenomenon*.)

dates. The best stylists say that a number following a month should be a cardinal ("We'll meet on *October 1*") and that a number preceding a month should be an ordinal (*the second of March*). Ordinal numbers should be spelled out, not the 6th of September, but *the sixth of September*.

dates from. A span of time beginning with a particular date *dates from*. "His tenure *dates from* 1967," not *dates back to* 1967.

daughter-in-law. Its plural form is not *daughter-in-laws*, but *daughters-in-law*. (See *possessive case forms*.)

daylight saving time. See *save*.

de-. Write compounds as one word (*decentralize, desegregate*), even if the second part begins with *e* (*deemphasize*).

dead. See *absolutes*.

deal, as in "Triester completed a big *deal* in New York," is a colloquialism for "transaction." It is likewise colloquial when used to mean "underhanded arrangement" ("The casino operator, you can be sure, made a *deal* with the commissioners") or "treatment" ("What an unfair *deal* that kid got").

death/demise. *Death* is the general term to signify the end of life. *Demise*, originally associated with the transfer of title to real estate as a consequence of death, has become a fancy synonym for *death*, especially when one wishes to avoid the latter word. *Demise* should be used sparingly.

debar/disbar are alike in that both words mean "to exclude." The sense of *debar* is "to prevent," as in "Those whose dues are in arrears are *debarred* from voting" and in "Improperly dressed members will be *debarred* from admittance to the premises." *Disbar* is a technical legal term used to indicate that a lawyer has been "excluded" from practicing in that jurisdiction. Found guilty of violating a canon of the American Bar Association, he has been expelled from the bar.

debut. Just because noun *debut*, meaning "the first public appearance" or "the formal appearance of a young woman in society," is well established is no reason to convert it into a verb, either transitive or intransitive. Neither form should be encouraged. Most respected writers would not approve of "General Motors will *debut* its new models" (transitive) or "Arthur Sporkin *debuts* as an actor tomorrow" (intransitive).

decided/decisive have distinctive usages. The first means "definite" or "unmistakable" and the second, "conclusive." "There is a *decided* difference between communism and capitalism." "The defeat of Rommel was a *decisive* victory for the Allied forces."

decidedly. See *emphatically/decidedly.*

decimate originally meant "to kill one in ten" (to quell mutinous troops, the Romans executed one man chosen by lot out of ten), but its meaning has been extended to cover any killing or destruction—of people, animals, crops—short of annihilation. Do not use, however, where a percentage is indicated. In "The hurricane *decimated* 60% of the town," change to *destroyed.* And to avoid redundancy, do not modify *decimate* with either *totally* or *completely.*

decisive/incisive. *Decisive* means "conclusive," "settling a matter beyond question or doubt." Its effect could put an end to something, an argument, for example. An *incisive* remark could have that effect, too. *Incisive* means "keen," "penetrating." It goes right to the point. (See *decided/decisive.*)

deduce/deduct. Occasionally confused because their spelling is similar. *Deduce* means "to draw a conclusion," "to infer." *Deduct* means "to take away," "to subtract." Both words form the same noun: *deduction.*

deduction/induction. Sometimes confused and little understood. One who reasons by *deduction* (*a priori*) moves from general laws to particular cases. He draws a conclusion by establishing its conformity to general truths or principles ("All men shave their faces; this person shaves his face; therefore this person is a man"). *Inductive* reasoning (*a posteriori*) draws a general conclusion from observation of various phenomena. By observing and studying many similar situations, one establishes a principle or reaches a conclusion. Scientists employ this method. It is said that deduction goes from cause to effect; induction goes from effect to cause.

defendant. See *plaintiff/defendant.*

defensible/defensive. That is defensible which is capable of being defended ("The French considered the Maginot Line *defensible*"). Figuratively *defensible* means "justifiable, proper, or capable of being defended in argument." *Defensive* means "ready or intended to defend" ("The high walls were a *defensive* barrier against intruders").

definite/definitive. Often confused. *Definite* means "clear," "explicit," "concrete," as does *definitive* except that the latter also connotes finality. A *definite* answer is precisely defined and unmistakable. A *definitive* answer is conclusive; it brooks no argument and leaves no room for appeal.

degradation. Sometimes misspelled *degredation.* Be careful.

degree/extent. Specificity is not the hallmark of these words. They both point to an unascertained point in a scale or to an indefinite extension of space. Yet everyone understands what "to a degree" or "to an extent" implies—an unspecified limitation.

deism/theism. These theological terms have distinctive meanings. Although both *isms* espouse a belief in the existence of God, *deism* bases its belief on the evidence of reason and nature. God is not considered the ruler of the universe. After creating the world God abandoned it so that He does not influence natural phenomena, nor does He control life. *Theism* is the belief that God created the world and is its ruler. Furthermore, He is the source of supernatural revelations.

delusion/illusion. Both words suggest an impression of something that is not. The first is a false belief; the second, a deceptive appearance. A scarecrow that looks alive when blown by the wind creates an *illusion*, but anyone who thinks it's alive is suffering from a *delusion*. The unreal image of an *illusion* is understood to be unreal ("The sun is sinking into the ocean but we know better"), whereas the false belief of a *delusion* deceives; it is accepted without question ("Agnes is sure that, although her son died today, he'll return to life tomorrow").

demean. The argument of purists that *demean* relates only to behavior has little influence on today's speech. Although it may still refer to conduct ("Officers must *demean* themselves like gentlemen")—*demeanor* means "behavior," the way a person acts—*demean* is generally taken to mean "to debase, degrade, or disparage oneself." Of course, the context should clarify the sense intended. With either meaning, *demean* is used reflexively—*demean himself, demean yourself, demean ourselves*.

demise. See *death/demise.*

demolished. See *totally.*

denote/connote are sometimes loosely interchanged. Although both refer to "a meaning," to *denote* is to express explicitly (as does a definition in a dictionary); to *connote* is to suggest or imply. *Connote* is a broader word. It goes beyond the exact meaning to the word's associations. For example, the *denotation* of *home* is "a place where a person or family lives; a dwelling place," but the *connotation* of *home* is warmth, comfort, and security.

deny. See *refute/deny.*

deprecate/depreciate. To *deprecate* is to protest against or to disapprove of ("The faculty *deprecated* the dean's latest decision"). To *depreciate* is to lower in value or to lower the price ("The value of his art objects has *depreciated*"). A man may modestly depreciate his accomplishments or speak in a self-depreciating manner. But in general usage few use *depreciate* in that sense—self-belittlement—particularly with compound adjectives. It is almost always *self-deprecating* or *self-deprecatory*. Nowadays when *belittlement* is meant, no one expects to hear *depreciate* rather than *deprecate*. Trying to preserve the distinctive meaning of *depreciate* as opposed to its popular usage is waging a losing battle.

depredation. Sometimes misspelled *depradation.* Watch it.

de rigueur. This French phrase, meaning "required by current etiquette," "socially obligatory," is often misspelled. Note the two *u*'s, one before the *e* and one after.

derrière, a fancy synonym for fanny or rump, is a borrowing from the French word for "behind." Spell it as given, with an accent mark over the second *e*. (See *accent marks*.)

desert/dessert. A *dessert* is a course of sweets at the end of a meal. But one's just *deserts* (spelled with one internal *s*) is not an edible but something "deserved"—usually something unexpected and unwelcome. The word *desert*, a barren waste, is also spelled with one *s*, but is accented on the first syllable, unlike the other two words.

desirous. See *anxious/eager*.

despair/desperation are not synonyms, even though they are frequently interchanged in general language. *Despair* is a state of hopelessness ("*Despair* seized us when we saw our guide hit by a truck"). *Desperation* is a hopeless feeling that makes one willing to run any risk, which means that desperation is a form of despair ("Since the fire blocked all exits, in *desperation* the hotel guests jumped out of the window").

despicable, meaning "contemptible," preferably stresses the first syllable rather than the second—*dehs*-pih-kuh-bul.

despite/in spite of. Since these words have the same meaning, some writers prefer the single word for the sake of brevity. Introducing either one with *but* ("*But despite* what he did" or "*But in spite of* what . . .") is poor style; the *but* is superfluous. *Despite* is more formal, but *in spite of* is more forceful. (See *to the contrary*.)

dessert. See *desert/dessert*.

destroyed. Is it correct to say "completely destroyed"? To destroy means "to make useless," "to break into pieces." But since the verb alone does not necessarily suggest an entirety (something may be partially destroyed), *completely destroyed* makes clear the intended meaning. Of course, if a living thing is destroyed, adding *completely* would be redundant. And bear in mind that according to some authorities *completely* or *totally destroyed* is redundant when it means "demolished."

deter. Strictly speaking, in the light of the original meaning of *deter*, "to frighten," only people and animals can be deterred, not things. But by loose extension, *deter* has acquired the sense of that which prevents the happening of anything undesirable— paint that deters rust, jetties that deter beach erosion. No longer is fear a necessary ingredient. However, its negative form, *undeterred*, may not apply to things, since only a person or animal can be undeterred—that is, undaunted, not to be scared away.

develop is a poor replacement for *happen, occur,* or *take place.* It should not be so used in better writing. *Develop* connotes a gradual unfolding. Rather than "We look for something pleasant to *develop*," say *happen.*

deviate. See *digress/deviate.*

devil's advocate, although a popular phrase, has different meanings for different people. Originally a person designated to ferret out derogatory history of a person being considered for canonization, a *devil's advocate* nowadays is more likely taken to be one who espouses questionable, controversial, or even evil causes. He is the upholder of the wrong side. Be sure the context makes clear the meaning intended.

deviser/devisor. See *adviser/advisor.*

devoted/devout. Both words reflect a sense of dedication. *Devoted* suggests a positive sense of loyalty, a giving of oneself to some person, purpose, or service, as with a devoted mother, wife, or friend. *Devout* is mainly used in religious contexts. A devout person is active in worship and other religious affairs and may sometimes border on the fanatic.

devout. See *devoted/devout.*

diagnose. "The patient was *diagnosed* as suffering from leukemia." Ailments are diagnosed, not people. And if the patient dies, he dies *of* leukemia, not *from* leukemia. (See *enthuse; from.*)

diagram/program/kidnap. Except when spelling the lead words, preferably double the final consonant in all other forms—*diagramming, programmed, kidnapper,* even though ordinarily the consonant in two- or three-syllable words is not doubled if the stress does not fall on the last syllable (*rebound, rebounding; bisect, bisected; develop, developer*). Some authorities do not approve of this doubling, but most do. Note that *kidnapper* if spelled with one *p* is apt to be mispronounced with a long *a*: *kidnāper.*

dialect/idiom/jargon/vernacular. *Dialect* is regional language; *idiom* is speech form characteristic of native speakers. *Jargon* is gibberish, meaningless talk or writing or, completely unrelated, the language of a particular group, profession, or activity, such as the jargon of lawyers, doctors, or architects. *Vernacular* is standard local or native language.

dialogue is preferably spelled as given rather than *dialog*, even though *catalog* (which see) has had its rear *ue* clipped by most of today's writers.

diamond. See *jewelry*.

dichotomy when used as a synonym for *division* or *split* is incorrect. Its precise meaning is quite different, "a division into two usually contradictory parts or opinions." Unless the word fits, it is best omitted.

diction. If a radio announcer's diction is being discussed, one might wonder whether the issue concerns his choice of words or his enunciation. Originally the former—skillful use of words—was the only meaning of *diction*. But today, in general usage, it has come to signify the manner of pronouncing words. Be careful, therefore, to make certain that the context clarifies the meaning.

did. See *do/did*.

die from. See *diagnose*; *from*.

different is often used unnecessarily, as in "The dean wrote three *different* books" and in "Ronald was approached by three *different* men." The books certainly were different from each other, and the men could not be the same man. Excise *different* and lose nothing except a superfluous word.

different from/different than. *Different* is idiomatically followed by *from*. In "Of those things in Lexington that are *different to* what we have in Baltimore, the City Hall is most outstanding," make it *different from*. *Different than* is acceptable in condensed clauses—"His lifestyle in Florida is *different than* it was back home," rather than *from what it was*, but all authorities do not agree. Conservatives insist on *from* in all cases. Of course, the sentence may be restructured using "other than" or "not the same as."

differ from/differ with. *Differ from* suggests a contrast, pointing to something that is unlike something else ("A shawl *differs from* a scarf"). *Differ with* means "to disagree with" ("My teenager always *differs with* me about her bedtime").

digress/deviate suggest a turning aside. To *digress* is to drift from the main subject when talking or writing. To *deviate* is to drift from the course, rule, or standard, but only slightly or temporarily.

dilapidated. The use of this word troubles only those who have been transfixed by its Latin origin. *Lapis* in Latin means "stone"; hence the belief that the word applies only to what is made of stone. That belief is discountenanced by current usage, however. *Dilapidated* is now properly employed to describe any run-down structure, whether made of wood, tin, or stone. *Dilapidated* has come to mean "in disrepair," "deteriorated."

dilemma in "My mother's *dilemma* every Thanksgiving is whether to invite her uncle" is used inaccurately. *Dilemma* is not the equivalent of "problem, difficulty, or predicament," but a choice between two undesirable alternatives, such as having to choose between communism and fascism.

dilettante. See *amateur/dilettante.*

diminish/minimize. *Diminish* means "to make smaller, lessen, or reduce" ("Lubricating the cogs can help *diminish* wear"). To *minimize* is to reduce to the smallest amount or number. It does not mean "lessen" or "belittle." The thought expressed in "The problems experienced by the elderly should not be *minimized*" is sheer nonsense. The word required is *underestimated.* The fact is it would be well if the problems of the aged were minimized. Since *minimize* is an absolute term—it does not come in degrees—it is not to be modified by *partially, greatly, considerably,* or any other such adverb.

diminution. Sometimes misspelled *dimunition.* Think of *diminish*; it will put you on the right road.

diphtheria. Note the *hth.* Pronounce with an *f* sound, not a *dip.*

direct/directly. As adverbs these words may be used interchangeably. They both suggest a movement in a straight line. One may go *direct* (or *directly*) to the airport. But note that *directly* also means "immediately." Therefore, "I will go to the airport *directly*" may mean "by the shortest route" or "at once." Avoid using *directly* where its sense is ambiguous. Although *direct* is an absolute term, and should therefore not be qualified, most authorities would approve of this sentence: "He took a *more direct* route." Conservative grammarians would insist on "a *more nearly* direct route."

directions. See *compass directions.*

direct quotations (sequence of tenses). To avoid confusion, follow these guidelines. As a general proposition, if the main clause is in the past tense, the dependent clause should likewise be in the past tense ("Thomas *said* he *went* to Vermont last week"). But be careful of these exceptions in which the dependent clause is put in the present tense: expressions showing habit or custom ("He *said* he *goes* to work early every day." "He *said* that there *is* always a parade before Thanksgiving Day") and general or permanent truths ("He *said* honesty *is* the best policy." "The teacher *said* that water *freezes* at 32 degrees Fahrenheit").

disability. See *inability/disability.*

disappointed takes various prepositions. Which one to use depends on the meaning to be conveyed. A person is *disappointed in* his interior decorator but *disappointed by* the decorator's lack of imagination. And he may also be *disappointed with* the final rendering. In sum, a person is disappointed *in* or *by* someone, but when a thing causes disappointment, the preposition changes to *with*.

disassociate/dissociate. Either implies the severing of relations, but the latter term quickens it. It's simpler and shorter.

disbeliever/unbeliever. Both words indicate that a person does not believe. A *disbeliever* is a person who refuses to believe. An *unbeliever* is one who has concluded that he ought not or need not believe.

disclose. See *divulge/disclose.*

disclose/reveal. *Disclose* means "to make known" or "to open to view." To *reveal* is to disclose suddenly, as a magician does who lifts a veil to reveal a rabbit where a young lady had been sitting only seconds before. *Disclose* and *reveal* are dramatic words, appropriately used when an important secret is being reported or something exposed that had never been previously seen. But those words are inappropriate in ordinary language, where *said* and *tell* sound more normal. One doesn't *disclose* to a friend that the price of gasoline just rose; he *tells* him. And a man *says* what he means; he doesn't *reveal* it.

discomfit/discomfort. "Matilda always *discomfited* her guests by her lack of manners" needs correcting. The guests were not *discomfited*; they were *discomforted*. To *discomfit*, at least tradition-ally, is to rout, overwhelm, or defeat utterly ("The enemy troops were sorely discomfited"). In its modern sense it means "to confuse," "to make uneasy," "to frustrate," and "to humiliate." Its noun form, *discomfiture*, is more common. *Discomfort*, which is lack of comfort, is, in all likelihood, a concomitant of *discomfiture*—that is, a person frustrated or humiliated is certain to feel uncomfortable.

discover/invent. Sometimes misused for each other. To *discover* is to see or learn of something for the first time. Whatever it was, was already there, but previously unknown to man ("Balboa *discovered* the Pacific Ocean"). To *invent* is "to make up for the first time." That which is invented had not previously existed; it's new ("Alexander Graham Bell *invented* the telephone").

discreet/discrete. Not to be confused, especially since their pronunciation is identical and their spelling almost so. *Discreet* means "prudent," "tactful," as is a person who exercises good judgment. *Discrete*, which is used of things, means "separate," "distinct," "unrelated" ("A book and a pear are *discrete* objects"). Where possible, avoid *discrete*; it sounds bookish.

discriminate/distinguish. The latter term is more general as to perceiving and making distinctions. To *distinguish* is to recognize those qualities and features of a thing that make it different from others ("The upright horn of a rhinoceros *distinguishes* it from other animals"). To *discriminate* is not merely to perceive differences but to evaluate them in terms of their significance. Unfortunately, although discrimination can have positive aspects, it seldom does. Discrimination usually is against, not in favor of.

disgruntled. See *unsatisfied/dissatisfied*.

disinterested/uninterested. "My closest friend is *disinterested* in my new project" is wrongly put. He is uninterested. *Disinterested* means "impartial, influenced by no self-interest" ("A *disinterested* third party was called in to settle the argument"). *Uninterested* means "having no interest," "indifferent," "bored." In everyday parlance *disinterested* has acquired all the senses of *uninterested*. Nevertheless, in careful usage the distinctive meanings of these words should be observed. If concerned that *dis-*

interested might be misunderstood, replace it with *unbiased* or *neutral*.

dislike. See *hate/dislike.*

disorganized. See *unorganized/disorganized.*

dispel, meaning "to rid of by scattering" or "to dispense with," on the analogy of *misspell* is sometimes mistakenly spelled with a double *s*, sometimes with a double *l*, and sometimes with both those letters doubled. Be careful.

disregardless is an illiteracy. Do not use it in any form of speaking or writing. It consists of a double negative—*dis* plus *less*. Use *regardless* instead. (See *irregardless.*)

dissatisfied. See *unsatisfied/dissatisfied.*

dissect. See *bisect/dissect.*

dissimulate. See *simulate/dissimulate.*

dissipated has two unrelated meanings—"dissolute" (a *dissipated* appearance) and "scattered" (clouds *dissipated* by wind). The first is an adjective; the second, a verb.

dissociate. See *disassociate/dissociate.*

distasteful/tasteless. *Distasteful* means "disagreeable or unpleasant" (*distasteful* medicine) or "offensive or disgusting" (the *distasteful* smell of escaping gas). *Tasteless* means "lacking flavor" (a dish of *tasteless* asparagus) or, by extension, "exhibiting poor taste" (an uncalled-for social remark or a living room in crazy quilt colors).

distinct/distinctive. That which is *distinct* may be *distinctive*, but that does not make the words synonymous. *Distinct* means "clearly perceivable" or "characteristic." Something distinct is unmistakable, definite, different in quality or kind (the *distinct* smell of rotting oranges). *Distinctive* means "characteristic of a particular thing so that it is distinguished from others." Its attributes are special, peculiar to it ("Creole cooking has a *distinctive* flavor").

distinguish. See *discriminate/distinguish.*

distrust. See *mistrust/distrust.*

disturb. See *perturb/disturb.*

dived. The past tense of *dive.* In popular, but not in formal English, *dove* is acceptable ("The quarterback *dove* for the loose ball").

divers/diverse. The first means "many"; the second, "completely unlike." "The *divers* essays on the professor's desk covered *diverse* subjects." Stay away from *divers*; it sounds pedantic. Try *various* instead.

divulge/disclose. These words share the meaning "to make known what originally was intended to be kept secret." *Divulge* is preferably used when the information is revealed to only a few people; *disclose* when the information is disseminated widely. Remember, you can *tell* something to a few people or to many. You don't need *divulge* or *disclose*.

do is colloquial in such expressions as "It will *do* for now" (suffice); "*Do* your lessons" (study); and "We don't want to *do* him out of his money" (cheat).

do/did. These verbs when used as principal verbs ("He *does* well," "He *did* it yesterday," "He *has done* it") raise no problems. But writers sometimes hesitate to use *do* as an auxiliary in the belief that its addition is uneconomical. True, it adds a word but it also makes for emphasis. Certainly "I *do* believe it" and "I *did* believe it" are stronger than saying merely "I believe it" and "I believed it." However, with questions this is not always applicable. In educated writing "*Has* he any stamps to sell?" is preferable to "*Does* he *have* any stamps to sell?"

do/have. In serious writing the colloquial use of a form of *do* for the more formal *have* is best avoided. For example, to the statement "He has a fellowship at Yale," the interrogative response should be "*Has he?*" not "*Does he?*" Likewise, to "The Buten Museum has the world's largest private Wedgewood collection," the response should be "*Has it?*" not "*Does it?*" Although "*Does* Brenner *have* the ability to do it?" is idiomatically acceptable, conservative writers object to a form of *do* and *have* in the same sentence. They would correct the example to read: "Has Brenner the. . . ."

doctor. See *physician/doctor.*

doff/don. You will use these words correctly if you remember that *doff* is a coalescing of "do off" and *don* of "do on."

dollars. See *figures.*

dollar sign. It is proper, with large numbers, to use the dollar sign—$496 million. If you wish, you may use the word *dollars*—496 million *dollars*—but remember to omit the dollar sign. You can't use both the sign and the word *dollars* without being charged with a redundancy. (See *money*.)

dominant/dominate. See *predominate/dominate*.

domineering. See *officious/domineering*.

don. See *doff/don*.

donate is a back formation from *donation*. Purists have railed for years against it, taking every opportunity to spoof those who dared use it. Nevertheless, the battle by self-appointed guardians of English has been lost. *Donate* is employed today in every kind of English, even by formalists, who solicit their friends to donate generously to the school fund. All this does not mean, however, that *donate* is to be preferred to the simpler word *give* or even to the longer word *contribute*. It is not. Most careful writers, if given a choice, would shun *donate* in favor of a more suitable substitute. (See *enthuse*.) And so with its noun form, *donation*. It is preferably not used when *gift* will do.

done is an undesirable colloquialism in "We're *done* with dinner" (finished). (See *through*.)

don'ts. See *dos, don'ts, and maybes*.

don't think. Some orthodox grammarians insist that "I *don't think* I will go" implies an unthinking mind. But more realistic authorities take a different view. They hold that the adverb *not*, which expresses negation or denial, negates the phrase *I will go* and not just the verb *think*. The idiomatic sense then is "I am not going to go" rather than "I do not think." Of course, using the positive form—"*I think* I will not go"—obviates the problem and this discussion.

dos, don'ts, and maybes. Spelled as given in the title of Theodore Bernstein's book. Note that there is no pluralizing apostrophe. The apostrophe in *don'ts* indicates a contraction. But the plural of words-as-words in texts should be italicized and end in *'s* ("Mac used too many *do*'s and not enough *maybe*'s in his first paragraph").

double entendre. A nonexistent French phrase. Since 1670 those delighting in this Frenchified sound have used it with great relish. But the proper expression for a double meaning, one of which is indelicate, is *double entente*. Attempts to revert to the correct French have been futile; *double entendre* has become firmly established. Use it, therefore, and fear no criticism, but why not substitute an ordinary English phrase like "double meaning"?

double negatives. The best advice is not to use them, even though in the past some literary giants employed them advantageously. In modern usage, double negatives ("I *didn't* say *nothing*") are confusing and sound illiterate. They are used occasionally to make an indirect affirmative ("It is *not* that I do *not* want to go"). Also to be avoided is a combination of *hardly*, *scarcely*, or *barely* and another negative, since those adverbs convey a negative idea. ("Fulton has *not* been here for *hardly* five minutes"). Omit *not*. In "*Without hardly* any funds, he engaged a chauffeur," change *without* to *with* or delete *hardly*. (See *hardly/scarcely*.)

double possessive. This formulation, technically known as the double genitive, combines *of* followed by a noun expressed in the possessive case: "Dan is a friend *of* my father's," which means that among my father's friends, Dan is one. Purists decry this construction, labeling it informal. But the validity of their criticism is questionable. Many reputable writers use it to good effect—and achieve clarity; for example, "This is a painting of *Picasso*" says that Picasso is the subject of the painting, whereas "This is a painting of *Picasso's*" says that among the paintings Picasso owns, this is one.

double superlative. Sometimes used by those who are so enthusiastic that they cannot intensify enough to prove their point. "This is the *most cheapest* auto that one can buy" is nonstandard because the *-est* ending makes *cheap* a superlative as does *most* when placed before an adjective or adverb. One designation is enough.

doubt/doubtful. Idiom has fixed the conjunction to use in negative and interrogative constructions: *that* (I do not *doubt that* . . . It was never *doubtful that* . . . Does anyone doubt *that* . . . ? Is it doubtful *that* . . . ?). In affirmative statements use *whether* or *if* ("I doubt *whether* [or *if*] he'll come"). Formalists shade toward *whether*.

doubtlessly. Prefer *doubtless*, which is both an adjective and an adverb. Better yet is the stronger word *undoubtedly*, which connotes a sense of conviction. (See *undoubtedly/doubtlessly*.)

dove. See *dived.*

downward is preferred to *downwards.* (See *backward/backwards.*)

dozen/dozens. "Two *dozen* eggs" is the correct way of putting it because a number precedes *dozen.* Otherwise, make it *dozens of* ("Several *dozens of* eggs are on the shelf").

drank/drunk. "He *drank* the wine." "He has *drunk* the wine." But not "He *drunk* the wine." *Drunk* is a past participle, a variant of *drunken,* and needs an auxiliary. Idiomatically, a person who has imbibed too much is *drunk,* not *drunken.* However, he is, when properly put, a *drunken* man, not a *drunk* man. Use *drunk* predicatively after the verb and *drunken* in an attributive position before a noun.

drastic is an adjective meaning "acting with force or violence." Colloquially it is often used to mean "exceeding," "excessive," or "very great," as in "There was a *drastic* change in our vacation plans" or in "We have had *drastic* improvement in our machinery since the new mechanic arrived." In formal discourse use *drastic* only in accordance with its traditional meaning ("The police adopted *drastic* measures to control the rioters").

drop to drink. See *nor any drop to drink.*

drought/drouth, meaning "lack of rain," are variant spellings. The first, more commonly used, is pronounced *drowt.* The second is pronounced *drowth.*

drowned. In "He *was drowned* during that last thunderstorm," *was* should preferably be excised. Saying *was drowned* implies he was murdered.

drunk. See *drank/drunk.*

due to is best used predicatively, where it means, and is replaceable by, *caused by* or *attributable to* ("His delusions are *due to* [*attributable to* or *caused by*] a mental breakdown"). In fact, some writers, to avoid possible misuse, never employ *due to* in any other position, although it may permissibly be used after a noun (an accident *due to* carelessness). Strictly speaking, *due to* is a compound adjectival preposition and must modify a noun or pronoun. It is therefore wrongly used in "The game was postponed *due to* rain" because the adjective *due* has nothing to modify. It is not the game but its postponement—a word not present in the sentence—that was due to rain. The sentence needs an adverbial phrase like "because of" or "owing to"

("The game was postponed because of rain"). Although the distinctions between adjective *due* and those prepositional phrases are blurred in most people's minds and are fast disappearing, grammarians still look askance when *due to* qualifies a verb.

due to the fact that is no more effective than the single word *because*. (See *due to*; *fact*.)

dumb, meaning "stupid," is a common term, one probably used by almost everyone. But in formal discourse, the use of *dumb* should be confined to its traditional sense of "mute" or "speechless."

dumbbell/numskull/nincompoop. A dull and stupid person—a dummy—is often called a *dumbbell* or a *numskull*. Although in this sense the words mean the same, note that *numskull* is preferably spelled with no *b*; *dumbbell* must have two. While on the subject of dolts, note also that *nincompoop* is spelled *nin*- not *nim*-.

during. Often used redundantly, as in "during the time that," a phrase economically replaced by *while*, and "during the course of," in which, "the course of" is superfluous. It should be dropped in "It rained *during the course of* the picnic."

E

e before *-able* or *-ible*. (See *spelling*.)

each. Treat *each* as a singular when it is the subject of a sentence ("*Each* is . . .") or when it modifies the subject ("*Each* man pays . . ."). Referents that follow are also singular ("*Each* of them has to work by *himself*," not by *themselves*). When *each* follows a plural subject to which it refers, it takes plural verbs and referents ("They *each are* swimming in *their* racing suits"). (See *between each* (*every*); *both/each*.)

each and every is an effort to emphasize at the cost of redundancy. Make it one or the other. But if the wordy phrase is used, note that it is the equivalent of *each* (the *and* is ignored), and it therefore takes a singular verb ("*Each and every* man *has* to shoulder his responsibilities").

each other/one another. Use *each other* when referring to two persons and *one another* when referring to three or more. Instead of "The members of Congress vied with *each other* in congratulating the speaker," amend to *one another*. Instead of "Randy and I see *one another* almost daily," make it *each other*.

eager. See *anxious/eager*.

earnest. See *sergeant/earnest*.

east. See *compass directions*.

easy is an adjective (an *easy* job) and, informally, an adverb (take it *easy*). In standard discourse prefer *easily* as the adverbial form. "So easy," "Easy does it," "Slow and easy," and other expressions like them are colloquial and trite. (See *take it easy*.)

eatable. See *uneatable/inedible*.

economic/economical. Do not interchange. Use the first to mean "pertaining to economics and finance" and the second to mean "thrifty." Other words ending in *ic* and *ical*, however, may be synonymous—*electric, electrical; fanatic, fanatical*. Prefer the shorter form. (See *-ics*.)

edible. See *uneatable/inedible*.

effect. See *affect/effect*.

effective. The word *effective* is an adjective and can modify only a noun, not a verb. Change "The price will be increased *effective* May 1" to "The price increase will become *effective* (on) May 1" or "The price will be increased on May 1" (no *effective*).

effete, a favorite term of disparagement, particularly by questionable politicians, means "decadent." Its sense is "lack of vigor." But bear in mind that the word originally, and still properly, applies to women. It means "no longer able to produce" because exhausted from bearing too many children. *Effete* has acquired the further sense of "not manly," "effeminate."

e.g. See *i.e./e.g.*

egoism/egotism. *Egoism* refers to a philosophical belief based on self-interest. *Egotism* is boastfulness, conceit. Unless the implications of *egoism* are fully understood, it is best to reserve this word for philosophers.

egregious, Latin for "standing out from the flock," had the sense of "conspicuous," which, early on, connoted something admirable. But the word developed a pejorative slant so that nowadays *egregious* refers only to a person's bad qualities ("He's an *egregious* liar"), meaning "flagrant" or "outrageous."

either means "one or the other of two" ("You may order *either* chocolate *or* vanilla, but not both"). When more than two are involved, use *any* or *anyone*; it would be wrong to use *either*. Note that in "*Either* of us *is* available" the verb is singular.

either . . . or. A correlative conjunction indicating an alternative, it takes a singular verb if both elements are singular and a plural verb if the correlated terms are plural. When the two subjects differ in number, the verb follows the form of the second element ("*Either* he or they *are* to leave." "*Either* they or he *is* to leave"). In combinations of different grammatical persons ("*Either* Martha or I [*am, are, is*] wrong"), let your ear be your guide. Most authorities will not commit themselves. They recommend recasting: "*Either* Martha is wrong, or I am."

Either . . . or sentences should be balanced. "The story should *either* be revised *or* forgotten" needs a repositioning of *either* after *be*. (See *neither . . . nor*.)

eke. "After being thrown for two losses at the line of scrimmage, Floyd finally *eked out* a gain." The sportswriter meant squeezed out. *Eke* (always expressed *eke out*) means "to make something, of which there is an insufficient supply, go further by supplementing it with something else." It is not a substitute for "use frugally" or "stretch" as though the result were eked out. Only the original supply, if added to, is eked out ("James *eked out* his meager income as a teacher by playing piano at night in a saloon").

elapse/lapse. The verb *elapse*, meaning "to slip away," "to pass," and noun *lapse*, meaning "an interval of time," may be interchanged if the sentence is reconstructed. The sense of the sentence will remain the same ("Fifteen minutes have *elapsed* since the manager was summoned." "There has been a *lapse* of fifteen minutes between the summoning of the manager and his arrival").

elder/older. *Elder* is used only of persons who are members of the same family. An elder brother need not be particularly old, even though the word *elder* suggests advanced age (the six-year-old is an *elder* brother of the three-year-old). *Elder* compares only two; *eldest*, more than two. *Elder* is commonly used in a few honorific expressions such as *elder statesman* and *one's elders*. *Older* and *oldest*, the comparative and superlative forms of *old*, may be used of persons or of things.

-elect refers to a person who has been elected but not yet installed in office. Used as a suffix *-elect* is always hyphened. Therefore, not "Lauren Rose is the president *elect*," but the *president-elect*.

elected/appointed. Do not follow these verbs with *as* in such sentences as "Charles was *elected* treasurer" and "Johnnie R. was *appointed* counsel"—not *elected as*, not *appointed as*.

element/factor/feature/phase. An *element* is a component part. A *factor* is "one of the elements that contribute to a given result or have a certain effect." *Feature* means "a particular and very evident characteristic." *Phase* suggests one of the changing stages of development of a person or thing (as in the *phases* of the moon).

The word *factor* has become a hackneyed substitute for *element* or *feature*. The elements of a plan are not the factors to consider, and the features—the outstanding characteristics—of a promotional scheme are not its factors. *Factor* serves best as a mathematical or business term. (See *contributing factor*.)

elemental/elementary. Originally synonymous, these words now have distinct meanings of their own. *Elemental* relates to the force and power of nature's phenomena, the four elements. It is often used of weather (the *elemental* fury of a typhoon). In ordinary usage it connotes basic power (*elemental* human rights). *Elementary* means "introductory," pertaining to the simple ("*Elementary*, my dear Watson"), the first principles of anything ("*Elementary* arithmetic is taught in primary schools").

elicit/illicit. In "He *illicited* all kinds of information from his nephew," change *illicited* to *elicited*. Be careful with these soundalikes. *Illicit*, an adjective, means "unlawful or improper" (an *illicit* relationship). *Elicit*, a verb, means "to draw out or extract," "to evoke" ("The minister could not *elicit* the truth from his parishioner").

eliminate means "to get rid of," "to remove." Clearly this cannot be done unless something is already there. In "Our upholstery protection will *eliminate* soil," the word needed is *prevent*.

ellipsis. Writing becomes more concise and tighter if unnecessary words are omitted. In "We're building a house *that is* on the edge of town," *that is* can be excised. In "The machine *that* Larry built works perfectly," *that* is unnecessary, as *whom* is in "He is the man *whom* we saw last night."

else. Superfluous in "Nobody [or Anyone] *else but* Jim." Although *nothing else but* is popularly accepted, some authorities frown on it, preferring *than* to *but*. They would change "*Nothing else but* a touchdown can win the game for us" to "*Nothing else than*." *Else* is an adverb, not a conjunction, in a sentence such as "We have to take parasols, *else* we might become sunburned." Make it *or else* (or simply *or*). (See *other*; *somebody else's*.)

elude. See *allude/elude*.

elusive/illusive. Often confused, possibly because they are pronounced almost alike. *Elusive* means "hard to understand or express" ("The song had an *elusive* melody"). *Illusive* means "lacking reality, misleading" ("The setting sun created an *illusive* look of gold on the Empire State Building"). In sum, *elusive* is equated with baffling; *illusive*, with deceptive.

embarrass is an embarrassing word to misspell. Note its two *r*'s and two *s*'s. (See *harass*.)

emerge/immerge. These words are opposites. To *emerge* is to rise out of, like a diver who emerges from the water. To *immerge* is to plunge into or to disappear, like the star that immerged into the light of the sun.

emigrant/immigrant take different prepositions. A Frenchman may emigrate *from* France and immigrate, say, *to* Mexico, which means that an *emigrant* arrives at his new country as an *immigrant*.

eminent/imminent. The report that said the commonwealth is taking over the Waldron Estate under its right of *imminent domain,* in which *imminent* was erroneously used for *eminent*, contained a ludicrous mistake. *Imminent* means "impending" ("A storm seemed *imminent*"). *Eminent* means "prominent," "distinguished" ("Chagall was an *eminent* artist"). When *eminent* is linked with *domain*, it refers to the power of a state to acquire property for public use.

emphatically/decidedly. Occasionally confused. The first means "forcefully"; the second, "clearly." "He *emphatically* claimed sole ownership." "The judgment was *decidedly* fair."

empty. See *vacant/empty*.

enamored. One is enamored *of* a person but *with* an object.

enclose/inclose. These synonymous words mean "to shut in on all sides," "to surround." When the sense is to close a piece of ground on all sides, *inclose* is commonly used ("The corral was *inclosed* by a chain fence"). Otherwise, *enclose* predominates ("I *enclose* my picture").

endorse. "To *endorse* on the back" is etymologically redundant, but it is an accepted expression on all levels of usage. At one time employing *endorse*, meaning "to recommend or give approval of," was deplored by conservative writers. But no longer. Those uses now have the approval of the strictest linguists—and they are so listed in many dictionaries.

end result is such a common phrase that it seems that almost everyone must occasionally use it. However, the expression is tautological, since the idea of *end* is conveyed in *result*. Omit the word *end*. Of course, a result may be intermediate, thus justifying *end result* to distinguish it, but that case is a rarity.

English, levels of. *Standard English*, which is of the highest level, is usually called *formal English* (some writers capitalize *formal*). The level below is *informal English*, sometimes called *colloquial English*. Below that is *slang* and *vulgar English*. The demarcations in many instances are arbitrary and may be called by different names by different authorities. Some words, with time, are elevated from one level to another; other words may sink to a lower level.

enhance. The problem with this handy word does not lie in its meaning but in its application. *Enhance*, which means "improve," "make greater," or "add to"—all to the advantage of the thing enhanced—must refer to something that already possesses some of the qualities that are being improved, made greater, or added to. It must, however, be used only of abstract matters, like beauty and reputation; a person may not be its direct object. One may correctly say "His lectures *enhanced* his prestige in the community," but not "The prestige of his lectures *enhanced him* in the community."

enjoy may properly be followed by a gerund, a verbal noun ("Brian *enjoys* fishing"), but not by an infinitive. Not "Brian *enjoys* to fish."

ennui, meaning "boredom," is pronounced ahn-*wee*.

enormity/enormousness. "The *enormity* of the new stadium left us breathless" would be more accurately stated "The *enormousness*." *Enormity* does not refer to great size; *enormousness* does. Its synonym is *hugeness*. *Enormity* means "wickedness, outrageousness."

enough. In "Julie was happy *enough* when she received her roster" and in "The university was fortunate *enough* to have a Nobel Laureate," *enough* is too much. Delete. (See *sufficient/ enough*.)

ensure/insure. We take precautions to *ensure*—make certain of—our safety. We *insure* our lives and property in case our precautions fail. For most uses *ensure* is the preferred word.

enthuse. In "Some members are not at all *enthused* by the prospects," *enthuse* is a created word, a back-formation from the noun *enthusiasm*. Back-formations are not all bad—many have been accepted into literary usage—*diagnose, donate, orate*, for example. But others have been disapproved, of which *enthuse* is one, despite its frequent use in common language. Properly amended, the example would read "enthusiastic about the prospects."

entirely completed. Omit *entirely*. Since *completion* means "the state of being completed," the phrase *entirely completed* is redundant.

entitled/titled. Either word is acceptable when referring to the title of a book, but *entitled* is more formal. Those writers who prefer *titled* ("The book is titled *Poland*"), reserve *entitled* to signify a right ("You are *entitled* to a refund"). *Entitle to* should not be followed by an infinitive but by a noun. "Audrey is entitled *to receive* a larger paycheck" should be amended to read "Audrey is *entitled to* a larger paycheck."

entomology. See *etymology/entomology*.

entrée, the main course of a meal, is not pronounced *entray* as in "entrance," but *ahn*-trae.

entrust. Idiomatically one entrusts something *to* someone but *entrusts* someone *with* something. Stated differently, to give over to another for care is *to entrust*; to commit something trustfully is to *entrust with* ("Mac *entrusted* the task *to* his assistant." "He was pleased that he could *entrust* his assistant *with* the task").

envelop/envelope. The verb *envelop* (pronounced ehn-*vehl*-uhp) means "to surround," "to wrap or cover." The noun *envelope* (pronounced *ehn*-veh-lohp or *ahn*-veh-lohp) refers to a paper wrapper in which a letter is sent. Note the final *e*.

envy/jealousy, although often used interchangeably, are not exact synonyms. You *envy* or are envious of another's belongings or accomplishments ("The way she trilled her voice was the *envy* of everyone in the chorus"). You are *jealous* of what you possess. A jealous person resents rivalry and is suspicious of attention paid to his wife or what appears to be an encroachment on his reputation. But if *envy* of another's possessions or position involves deep resentment (and here is where the words overlap in meaning), then *jealousy* becomes the more accurate term.

epigraph/epitaph/epigram. An *epigraph* is an inscription, especially on a building or a statue. An *epitaph* is a commemorative inscription on a tomb. Neither term is associated with the word *epigram*, which may be either a short poem that ends in a witty turn of thought or a short witty saying, like Oscar Wilde's "The only way to get rid of a temptation is to yield to it."

epithet is a word that needs watching. Construed strictly, it means "a descriptive expression; a word or phrase expressing some quality or attribute" (Honest Abe, Richard the Lion-Hearted—the epithets are "Honest" and "Lion-Hearted"). Time has changed the meaning of *epithet* to "a disparaging term." It is now generally used as the equivalent of a term of abuse ("They hurled *epithets* at each other").

epitome. In the sentence "He is the very *epitome* of grace," *epitome* was intended to mean the ultimate or the ideal. But that is not what it means. *Epitome* is not the best, or the highest of anything. It is, from a Greek word meaning "a cutting short," an abbreviation, a summary, or a condensed account. Quality is not an ingredient of *epitome*. In general parlance, however, in fact in the discourse of many people, *epitome* is now equated with "embodiment," the ultimate representative of an entire class. No longer, because of this widespread usage, may *epitome* be rightly criticized if employed in this sense. (See *climax*.)

equable/equitable. Restrict the first to its meaning of "pleasant," as an *equable* disposition or an *equable* climate. Use *equitable* as a synonym for *just* or *fair*, as an *equitable* decision or an *equitable* distribution.

equal. See *absolutes*; *coequal*.

equally as. *As* is redundant in "equally as good" and in "equally as cheap." Delete *as*—"equally *good*" (*cheap*)—or make it "*just* as *good*" (*cheap*). The rule is to use *as* when comparing two things ("Her plan was *as* foolish *as* his") and *equally* when only one is named ("Her plan was equally foolish").

equitable. See *equable/equitable*.

equivalent. Noun *equivalent* takes *of* ("This is the *equivalent of* that"). Adjective *equivalent* takes *to* ("This was *equivalent to* that").

equivocal. See *ambiguous/equivocal*.

eradicate often leads to redundancy, as in "to *eradicate* the root of the problem." The root (*radix*) is embedded in *eradicate*. Be careful.

ergo. Latin for "therefore." Best avoided in serious writing unless used humorously.

erstwhile is a fancy synonym for *former* ("We are going to restore him to his *erstwhile* position of "Keeper of the Keys"). Prefer *former.*

erudite/recondite. Don't confuse these words. The former means "learned"; the latter, "abstruse, concealed."

eruption/irruption. These words are sometimes misapplied. An *eruption* is a violent breaking out (a volcanic *eruption*). An *irruption* is a violent breaking in (an enemy invasion).

escape. A person escapes observation, escapes harm, escapes detection, or escapes punishment, but escapes *from* a prison.

especial/special. Although used interchangeably, *especial* is preferred when the reference is to something outstanding or exceptional and *special,* to something distinctive or particular. "This course is of *especial* importance to me." "Walter is a *special* friend." Be careful not to use *special* needlessly. Not "I have two *special* ideas where to vacation," which just means that there are two ideas. The ideas are not special.

esquire is usually used when addressing letters to lawyers. A common error is to use both *Mr.* and *Esquire* (or *Esq.*). Address as follows: Arthur H. Jackson, Esquire, no *Mr.,* or Mr. Arthur H. Jackson, no *Esquire.* But note that *esquire* traditionally applied only to members of the male sex. Perhaps it is now becoming a sex-neutralized word, so that women lawyers will also be known as *esquires.*

-ess endings, to designate feminine nouns, should be avoided except for those nouns whose relevancy to sex is pertinent, such as *actress, waitress,* or *hostess.* But be sure to avoid appending the suffix *-ess* where the emphasis on sex might be considered derogatory or prejudicial. For example, use *poet,* not *poetess; author,* not *authoress; sculptor,* not *sculptress.* (See *actress.*)

essay. See *assay/essay.*

essential. Restrict the use of this word to mean "needed to make a thing what it is"—that is, necessary for its existence. A stove is an essential part of a kitchen, just as a heart is an essential organ in a human body. Saying "My wife's vibrant personality is *essential* to our social life" is therefore erroneous. It may be important, but that is all; *essential* connotes indispensability. Although some dictionaries consider *essential* the equivalent of "very important," that denotation does not go far enough. It is better to use *essential* to suggest an absolutely vital element. And note that since *essential* is an uncomparable adjective, it may not be limited by "more."

estimate/estimation. These nouns, meaning "opinion" or "judgment," are often used interchangeably. *Estimate* is more usually applied to things in which questions are raised of how much, how good, and so on ("The *estimate* to drain the pool was $1,000"), and *estimation*, of an appraisal of persons ("In my estimation, John Le Carré is the best of the current mystery writers").

estimated to be about, as in "The silver was *estimated* to be worth *about* $4,000," is redundant. *Estimated* carries the idea of approximation. Drop *about*. One guess is enough.

et al., a Latin abbreviation meaning "other people," is appropriately used only in footnotes. It may not be used to mean "and other things."

etc. In "John, Bill, Russell, and *etc*. will all be there," two corrections suggest themselves. *Etc.* stands for two Latin words: *et*, which means "and," and *cetera*, which means "other things." *Etc.*, therefore, should not be used of persons and, since *et* means "and," the word is already built in. A comma belongs before *etc.* and, unless it ends a sentence, a comma after the period. In literary works, rather than *etc.*, use *and so forth* or *and the like*. When the reference is to a list of people, use *and others*.

eternal/everlasting should be distinguished carefully in serious writing, even though used interchangeably in general speech. *Eternal* is that which has no beginning or end; *everlasting* usually means going on without end.

etymology/entomology. Be sure to use the word that describes the science correctly. *Etymology* embraces the study of the origin and history of words. *Entomology* is the study of insects.

euphemism/euphuism are similar-sounding terms that have distinctive meanings. *Euphemism* is genteelism, a mild term substituted for a disagreeable one (*passed on* for *died*). *Euphuism* is an affected literary style, characterized by extended comparisons, alliteration, and elaborate antitheses, invented by Lyly in sixteenth-century England.

evacuate means "to cause to be empty by removing the contents." Hence the sentence "As soon as the alarm was sounded, the tenants were *evacuated,*" strictly speaking, should be reworded. The building was evacuated, not the tenants. However, idiom has transferred the evacuation from the building or place to the people forced to leave. It is now standard to say, "The tenants were *evacuated.*"

evade. See *avoid/evade.*

even creates the same kind of problem of placement as *only* does. For the sake of clarity, it should be placed next to the word it limits. If misplaced, the sense of the sentence may be different from the one intended. "*Even* Dennis did not call me on Sunday." (And he was the one person bound to call.) "Dennis did not call *even* me on Sunday." (If he failed to call me, he undoubtedly called no one.) "Dennis did not call me *even* on Sunday." (It is hard to believe he would miss that day.) (See *modifiers*; *only.*)

eventuate is a pompous equivalent for *happen, take place, occur, come about,* or *have as a consequence.* Any of these substitutes would be preferable.

-ever. What is confusing, especially since a consensus among authorities is lacking, is whether *-ever* words (*whoever, whatever, whenever, wherever*) should be written as one or two words. The best approach to take is to write them as one word if *-ever* is generalizing ("*Whoever* comes is welcome"), but as two words if part of an interrogative form ("*Who ever* would say that?" "*What ever* could have been in his mind?" "*When ever* will it come to pass?" "*Where ever* have you been?").

ever. Rather than saying "This year's sale will be the biggest *ever,*" say "This year's sale will be the biggest *ever held.*" (See *misplaced modifiers*; *only.*)

everlasting. See *eternal/everlasting.*

ever so often is good idiom, illogical though it be. It means "frequently," as in "*Ever so often* my granddaughter comes by to raid the cookie jar." (See *every so often.*)

every. See *between each* (*every*).

every . . . and every is a compound that ignores *and* and takes a singular verb ("*Every* man *and every* woman *has* to stand up and be counted"). (See *no . . . and no.*)

everybody/everyone, although meaning "all," are singular words and take singular verbs and referents ("*Everyone is* to report with a pack on *his* back"). However, some strange constructions may follow these pronouns ("If *everybody* is leaving, let *him* not forget *his* coat." "If *everyone* has a good appetite, send *him* to the dining room"). These absurdities, occasioned by the singular agreement, are rectified only by recasting: "If *all* the guests are leaving, let *them* not forget their coats." "If *they all* have good appetites, send *them* to the dining room." *Every one* is written as two words when "everybody" cannot be substituted for *everyone*, as here, "*Every one* of those seniors will be graduated." (See *they*.)

every day/everyday. The spelling of these words is sometimes confused. "We saw it *everyday* of the week" is a case in point. One-word *everyday* means "common" or "not unusual," as in "It is an *everyday* occurrence." In this sense the word is an adjective and precedes a noun. Written as two words—*every day*—it means "daily" ("We see them *every day*." "*Every day* someone is born").

every now and then. See *every so often*.

every once in a while. See *every so often*.

everyone. See *everybody/everyone*.

everyone else's. See *somebody else's*.

every other. "Lou is busy today, but *every other* day you'll find him at the office." The question is, Will Lou be at the office every day or every second day? Undoubtedly what was meant was every day. If so, why not say so? Or, if it should turn out to mean alternate days, make it every second day. Now everyone will know when to find Lou at his office.

everyplace, in the sense "everywhere" (and whether spelled as one word or two), is informal for *everywhere*. (See *noplace/someplace/anyplace/everyplace*.)

every so often, like its cousins *every once in a while* and *every now and then*, is colloquial and should be avoided in careful speech or writing. Simply say "once in a while" or, if appropriate, "at intervals" or "occasionally." This will also help avoid any confusions with *ever so often* (which see), which, quite oppositely, means "very frequently."

everything is not, as in "*Everything is not* the way it should be," is preferably worded *not everything is.*

every way. Spell it as given in "*Every way* we looked, we faced a blank wall," but make it one word when used as an adverb meaning "in every way" ("We tried *everyway* possible").

everywhere. "We looked and looked *everywhere* with no success," not *everywheres* or *everyplace* (*every place*). *Everywheres* is a dialect form of *everywhere,* and *everyplace* (*every place*) is colloquial when used to mean *everywhere.*

every which way means "in every direction," as in "We looked for it *every which way,*" and "in great disorder," as in "The gang split up and ran *every which way.*" In better writing use one of the definitions rather than the colloquial expression.

evidence/testimony. These terms are not interchangeable, since they are not synonyms. *Evidence* includes all the information produced to establish a contention. It may consist of business records, fingerprints, physical objects, laboratory reports, testimony, and so on. *Testimony* is evidence, under oath, of a witness to a cause. Note that *evidence* is proof; *testimony* may be worthless.

ex-/former. For those who wonder whether one may or should refer to the preceding president as *ex-* or *former,* be assured that either form is acceptable. *Former,* however, sounds more formal, and on that score is preferable. A thin line of authorities maintain that the president who held that office immediately before the current president is the ex-president and that all those who preceded the *ex-* are former presidents.

exact is an adjective and should therefore not qualify another adjective. In a sentence such as "The incoming chancellor said he would adopt the *exact* same policy as his predecessor," amend to *exactly*—"would adopt *exactly* the same policy."

exactly. See *only.*

exactly identical. See *tautology.*

exaggerate is spelled with a double *g,* not *exagerate.*

exasperate. See *aggravate.*

exceed/excel share the sense of "surpass" but have different applications. To *exceed* is to go beyond a given limit of time, quantity, quality, or extent, as is a delivery of more than is needed or material of a quality better than ordered. A person who exceeds the others in a race is superior to them. In this respect he excels; he is better than the others in that he outdid them. (See *-cede/-ceed/-sede*.)

exceedingly/excessively are not synonyms and are not interchangeable. Reserve *exceedingly* to mean "very much," "to a great extent" ("I was *exceedingly* delighted with your comments." "My daughter is studying *exceedingly* hard"). *Excessively* has the meaning of "too much," referring to that which is beyond proper limits ("He became bankrupt because he spent *excessively*." "It is *excessively* hot, considering the season of the year"). At one time the word *excessively* was frowned upon if used of the weather. This is no longer so.

excel. See *exceed/excel*.

except/excepting have the same meaning of excluding, but whereas *except* is followed by a noun, pronoun, or adverbial phrase, *excepting* follows "always," "not," or "without" (*not excepting* the juniors; *always excepting* the athletes). Note that *except* is a preposition and calls for the objective case ("No one *except* me knows the answer," not "*except* I"). Do not confuse *except* and *but*. In "I should have been there *except* I was ill," make it "*but* I was ill," since a conjunction, not a preposition, is required.

excepting. See *dangling participles*; *except/excepting*.

exception. See *with the exception of*.

exceptional/exceptionable. The meanings of these words are completely unrelated. *Exceptional* means "unusual," "out of the ordinary." A very bright student may be said to be exceptional; the courage of a soldier in the face of great danger may be considered exceptional. *Exceptionable* means "objectionable," something to which exception may be taken ("His egotistical remarks were *exceptionable*"). This word is used far less commonly than *exceptional*.

excerpt. See *extract/excerpt*.

excessively. See *exceedingly/excessively*; *overly*.

exchange. Not "They *exchanged* hats with each other," but "They *exchanged* hats." The word *exchange* has built into it the sense of "with each other."

exclamation point. See *quotation marks*.

excusable. See *salable*.

excuse. See *pardon/excuse*.

exhaustive/exhausting. Occasionally confused. *Exhaustive* means "thorough," "complete," "comprehensive" (an *exhaustive* study). *Exhausting* means "tiring" or "draining strength" ("Weeding the lawn is *exhausting* work").

exhibit/exhibition. Reserve the word *exhibition* to refer to a large public show, usually a major event held in a community building, an art museum, or a large fair. An *exhibit* is also a display, but generally of items from a single collection, a part of a larger show. The World's Fair, an exhibition of international importance, contained exhibits from many countries.

exhilarate. Sometimes misspelled *exhilirate*. Be careful.

exist is a word that tends to induce verbiage. "An arrangement like that *which exists* at the school" is reducible to "An arrangement like *that* at the school."

existence/resistance. Often misspelled *existance* and *resistence*, a switch of the *a* and *e* after the *t*. Note that *existence* has three *e*'s and no *a*'s and that *resistance* has two *e*'s and one *a*.

exorbitant. Sometimes misspelled *exhorbitant*, as in "We think their interest rates are *exhorbitant*." The word has no *h*.

expatriate. A *patriot* is a person who loves and supports his country. An *expatriate* is an exile, one who was banished from his native land, or a person residing of his own free will more or less permanently in a foreign country. The trouble sometimes occasioned by this term is the tendency to write it *expatriot* instead of *expatriate*.

expect. See *anticipate*.

expectorate. See *spit/expectorate*.

expertise. There is nothing wrong with this word, and it may be used even in formal speech and writing as a synonym for *expertness*. But bear in mind that overuse has made the word trite.

expletive has two disparate and unrelated meanings. In general usage an *expletive* is an oath or a word or phrase not necessary to the sense of the sentence but used to emphasize ("Damn it." "Good grief"). The word came into prominence during the Watergate investigation when presidential tapes were made public. In a number of instances they were blanked with the notation "expletive deleted." Grammatical *expletives* are anticipatory subjects—*it* is, *there* is, *there* are (which see).

explicit. One who exclaims, "But I gave you *explicit* instructions," meaning "complete" or "full," is not being accurate. *Explicit* means "clearly expressed," "distinct," "unequivocal." But that which is plainly set forth may not necessarily contain all the information. Something might have been left out. Some authorities, however, insist that *explicit* always means "lucidly *and* completely expressed." The antonym of *explicit*, which is *implicit*, means "understood though not expressed," "implied" ("*implicit* faith in your mother's love").

expurgated. See *unabridged/expurgated*.

exquisite is preferably pronounced with the stress on the first syllable—*eks*-kwiz-it.

extant. See *extent/extant*.

extemporaneous/impromptu. In the minds of most people these words are virtually synonymous. True, they both indicate that a performance or a speech had little or no preparation. Strictly speaking, however, an *extemporaneous* speech is one the speaker has outlined in advance. This means that what he delivers is unmemorized but that he was set for it. An *impromptu* talk is completely improvised, spontaneous, ad-lib, so to speak, because the speaker had no previous notice ("At his surprise retirement party, Frank made a witty *impromptu* speech"). (See *ad-lib*.)

extent/extant. Distinguish carefully between these look-alikes. *Extant* refers to that which is still in existence ("His works after all these years are still *extant* and deserve to be read"). *Extent* has a sense of measurement. It means "range" (the *extent* of the farmland), but in some uses it means "comprehensiveness." (See *degree/extent*.)

exterior/external. These words bear the sense of "outer" and "outside." Their applications are different, however, and the words are not interchangeable. *Exterior* is generally a noun and its opposite number is *interior*. We speak of painting the exterior of a house, and certainly we live in its interior. Adjective *external* means "that which is outside and apart" (*external* influences, *external* appearances, *external* conditions). Its antonym is *internal*.

extol.　See *rebel/extol*.

extra- is usually prefixed with no hyphen (*extramarital, extramural*), but *extra-long*.

extra, as in "Today is *extra* warm for May," is colloquial. In better writing use "very" or "unusually."

extract/excerpt, when referring to quoted material, are synonymous but usually given different significations. An *extract* is a passage taken from a book or other publication. And so is an *excerpt* except that it was selected to be quoted. An *extract*, too, may be quoted, but it may have been taken out of the publication for other reasons, as material for a study group, for example. *Excerpts* usually are shorter than *extracts*.

extraneous.　See *intrinsic/extrinsic/extraneous*.

extrinsic.　See *intrinsic/extrinsic/extraneous*.

fabricate/manufacture. To express the notion of putting together, constructing, *fabricate* is the better word ("This intricate piece of machinery was *fabricated* in our laboratory"). *Manufacture* suggests the actual making of something, stressing the labor ("We *manufacture* millions of safety pins").

façade. Although unnecessary, the cedilla is used by some careful writers. And since a *façade* primarily is the front of a building, saying "front *façade*" is also unnecessary. Omit "front." (See *accent marks*.)

faces. "He was unmoved, but all the others' faces blanched." Since none of the others had more than one face, change to "but the face of each of the others blanched."

face up to is a phrase condemned for its wordiness, the argument being that *up to* is superfluous, since one "faces" a bad situation or the facts, not "faces up to." The controversy has simmered down, however. Most usage critics now approve of the longer phraseology because "up to" adds a sense of resolution. A person who faces up to a situation is determined to see it through.

fact. "He remembered *the fact* that he was to leave at six." Nothing is lost if *the fact* is deleted except two wasteful words. The same is true in "The doctor repeated *the fact* that smoking is injurious to health." In some constructions the locution may be necessary, but it should be used as sparingly as possible. And remember that a fact, to be one, must be true. Avoid the redundant "true facts"; there are no false ones. Instead of "owing *to the fact that*," make it *since* or *because*. Rather than "We call your attention to *the fact that*," say "Were you *aware that*." "In spite of *the fact*" is reducible to *though* or *although*. (See *due to the fact that*.)

factitious/fictitious. These sound- and look-alikes have a sense in common—falsity. *Factitious* means "artificial" or "not spontaneous." It is something manufactured to suit a purpose. Contrived applause by the producer of a play is factitious. That which is *fictitious* is not real; it is imaginary. Most often the word is applied to mental concepts: novels, plays, and stories. But it is equally applicable to any product that has an entirely imaginary basis.

factor. See *contributing factor*; *element/factor/feature/phrase.*

fail. Do not use *fail* to displace the idea of "not." Instead of "He *failed* to appreciate the new form of dance," make it "He *did not* appreciate. . . ." Rather than "He *failed* to enjoy . . ." or "He *failed* to hear . . .," say "He *did not* enjoy" or "He *did not* hear."

failing. See *fault/failing.*

fairly/quite/rather. A person who likes something *fairly* well likes it a little, but not very much. Saying "fairly well" is not a compliment. If he likes it *quite* well, he means more than "fairly well." He is willing to recommend it. If he likes it *rather* well, he really likes it, even more than usual or more than expected. (See *relatively*; *quite*.)

faker/fakir. The second is not a fancy spelling of the first. In fact, the words are not related. A *faker* is a trickster, a swindler, a fraud. A *fakir* is a Muslim or Hindu religious person, a beggar, known for his feats of magic.

fall. See *seasons, capitalization of.*

famous/notorious refer to persons who have received widespread notice. Except for that sense, the words have opposite meanings. And yet *notorious* is sometimes mistakenly used for *famous* (seldom is the reverse true). *Famous* connotes good repute; *notorious*, ill-fame. A banker who is favorably known (*famous*) for making liberal loans cannot properly be said to be *notorious* for his liberality.

fan. See *shortened words.*

fantastic should mean "fanciful," "bizarre," "extravagant," but colloquially it is a popular term to express enthusiasm. In that sense it is to be avoided in formal discourse.

fantasy/phantasy. These homonyms are sometimes mistakenly spelled, each for the other. The former is a product of imagination, a fanciful invention, a caprice. The latter is a visionary notion. Note that these words do not end in *cy* but in *sy*. Most dictionaries, despite the thinking of Fowler and Partridge, regard these words as variants. Prefer *fantasy*.

farther/further. Although more and more these words are being used interchangeably, even by good writers ("Let's look into it *farther*" or *further*), it is better to use *farther* to denote longitudinal distance—the comparative of *far* ("We have a little *farther* to travel")—and *further*, the abstract distance—an unmeasurable distance, the progress of thought or condition. Adjective *further* means "additional" ("We'll inform you of any *further* developments"); adverb *further* means "to a greater extent" ("Let's pursue the matter *further*").

fashion/mode are interchangeable terms when they refer to prevailing customs of dress. One's clothing is in *fashion*, or *fashionable*, if its style is accepted. The same may be said of one's *mode* of dress (*modish* is conforming to current fashion). In some uses, however, the words have different applications and different meanings. *Fashion* is used to distinguish the style of dress and the patterns of social behavior of a group or a period in history ("During the Revolutionary War period *fashion* decreed silk hose for diplomats." "The style of dancing much in *fashion* during the seventeenth century was the minuet").

Mode may also refer to a method of doing or acting, to how something is done ("The latest *mode* in auto repair is by computer." "The fastest *mode* of traveling is by airplane").

fatal/fateful. Although synonymous in some respects in that something *fateful* may prove to be *fatal*, that is, cause death, the primary meaning of *fateful* is "highly significant," "of momentous importance," and it need not be of deadly consequence. On the contrary, it may refer to an event of great pleasantness ("On this *fateful* day he received the Medal of Honor"). Note that *fatal* is not comparable. Nothing can be more fatal than *fatal*.

father/mother/aunt/uncle. In general, these words should not be capitalized ("I will ask my mother." "I saw your aunt yesterday"). Capitalize the term only when it precedes a proper name ("I saw Uncle Charles yesterday") or substitutes for a proper name ("I saw Mother this morning").

fathers-in-law. The plural form ("The *fathers-in-law* are arriving at the same time") is obtained, as in the example, by pluralizing *father*, not *law*—not *father-in-laws*.

fault. "I *fault* him not." The question is whether *fault* may serve as a verb. Judged by the opinions of current critics, the verbal use of *fault* has as many yea votes as nays. Use it if you find it useful, as many of us do. But remember that in some contexts "blame" or "criticize" may be more appropriate.

fault/failing both suggest a shortcoming. A *fault* is a defect or a flaw, which may be a part of someone's personality or character. It means that something is not as it should be. A *failing* is a relatively minor weakness. One may outgrow a failing but be less likely to change a fault. Reserve *fault* for serious shortcomings.

faux pas, "a blunder," is pronounced foh-*pah*, not *fox pass*. The plural of *faux pas* is *faux pas*.

favor in "She *favors* her mother" is colloquial. In formal English use *looks like* or, better still, *resembles*.

faze, meaning "to disturb," "to worry," or "to bother," is an informal term. Its frequent use in such expressions as "Nothing *fazes* my boss" certainly has become tiresome. Further, and this is even more annoying, the word is sometimes confused with *phase* as in "Birthdays no longer *phase* me." Note that *faze* is almost always used negatively.

feasible/possible. In some uses the meanings of these words overlap. *Feasible* means "capable of being done"; *possible* means "capable of happening." Although whatever is feasible is possible, the opposite is not always so. For example, it is possible that the home team will win today's game, and, considering the clouds overhead, it is possible that the game will be rained out. In neither case would *feasible* serve. *Feasible* is correctly used in "Everyone agreed that the chairman's plan was *feasible*." A sense of "suitability" is inherent in *feasible*. Although *possible* is often followed by *that*, *feasible* may never be. Say "It is *feasible* for him to . . .," not "It is *feasible* that. . . ."

feature. See *element/factor/feature/phase*.

February is the only month that causes a spelling problem. The first *r* is the troublemaker. It is often erroneously omitted by those who say *Febuary*. And so with those who write *goverment* instead of *government*. Most likely their misspelling, too, can be attributed to faulty pronunciation. Be careful not to drop the middle *n*.

feel. See *believe/feel/think*.

feel bad/feel badly. Both expressions are correct, but they mean different things. To *feel bad* is to be ill or worried (*bad* is an adjective; linking words like *feel* take adjectives). To *feel badly* is to have an impaired sense of touch (perhaps the fingers are numb or gloved); here *feel* is a dynamic verb modified by adverb *badly*, which describes the "how" of the action. (See *good/well*; *bad/badly*.)

feel like is colloquial for "want to." In "I *feel like* eating early," I *feel like* helping my neighbor," and "You must *feel like* resting," recast using a form of *want*." Note: "I *feel like* it's going to rain" is equally questionable wording. (See *like/as*.)

feet. See *foot/feet*.

fellowman/fellow employee. Note the differences in spelling. A *fellow employee* (two words) may be a *fellowman* (one word), "a kindred person." *Fellowman* has no gender; it may refer to a woman.

feminine forms. See *-ess*.

ferment/foment. In the minds of some writers the figurative sense of *ferment* and *foment* is confusing because the words sound somewhat alike and both may mean "to cause trouble" or "to agitate" ("The striking machinists *fomented* unrest among office employees"). In this usage *foment*, meaning "to incite" or "to arouse," is to be preferred.

fervent/fervid. Both imply a strong feeling, meaning "intense." The sense of *fervent* is "showing warmth of feeling, extreme earnestness" (a *fervent* plea). *Fervid*, which usually qualifies a concrete action—a plea, a writing—is said of someone who is very emotional, possible feverish (the coach's *fervid* speech).

fever/temperature. "I'm happy that today my son has no *temperature*." Of course, the mother meant "no fever." The colloquial use of "temperature" for *fever* is impermissible in serious writing. But its use in everyday speech is not to be criticized, for, after all, when your kid registers normal, who cares what you call it.

FIGURE • **97**

few, an adjective, means "not many." As a noun it means "a small number," in contradistinction to "many." If *few* men attended a play, scarcely any were there. If *a few* men were there, some attended, but perhaps not so many as was hoped for. If there were *quite a few*, many attended. This last expression, best reserved for informal usage, ignores the meaning of *few* ("not many") and, quite oppositely, conveys the idea of "a lot."

fewer/less. These words cause constant problems, and what agreement there is among current authorities concerning their use is far from unanimous. The general rule is that *fewer* is used with units that can be counted (*fewer* houses, *fewer* calories)— hence it is usually used with plural nouns—and *less* with inseparable quantity, an amount in bulk (*less* sand, *less* weight)— hence it is usually used with singular nouns. The guideline, then, is to determine whether the item mentioned consists of countable units. If so, use *fewer* (*fewer* rights); otherwise, *less* (*less* freedom). One caution. It is correct to write "He earns *less* than $950 a week," for the sum of money is thought of as a total sum, not 950 separate dollars. But do not settle for *less* if the word required is *fewer*.

fiancé/fiancée. It is not difficult for someone untutored in French to confuse these words, especially since they are pronounced alike. A woman's bethrothed is her *fiancé*, spelled with one *e*. The betrothed woman is the man's *fiancée*, spelled with two *e*'s. Both have an acute mark as shown. (See *accent marks*.)

fictitious. See *factitious/fictitious*.

field in the phrase *the field of* when referring to a subject is redundant and can almost always be omitted. ("He won a prize *in* [not *in the field of*] chemistry." "Martha plans a career *in* [not *in the field of*] accounting").

fight with, as in "He *used to fight with* the French in Morocco," is ambiguous. The question raised is, "Which side did he fight on?" Was he in the French army or did he fight against the French army? If the latter is true, clarify by using *against*. If the former is true, change by inserting *along* before *with*.

figuratively. See *literally/figuratively*.

figure meaning "to think or suppose," as in "I *figured* I ought to leave early," is informal.

figurehead. Remember that a *figurehead* is only a symbol. It has no power. Hence, do not call an esteemed elder statesman the figurehead of the United States Government. Such a remark is not complimentary; it is, in fact, deprecatory.

figure of speech. See *metaphor/simile.*

figures. If a *figure* is used to repeat an amount written in words, it should be enclosed in parentheses—for example, twenty-five hundred (2,500) dollars. Note that the figure is not preceded by a dollar sign and that the word *dollars* follows the figure. If *dollars* had preceded the figure, the dollar sign would be called for: twenty-five hundred dollars ($2,500). (See *numbers.*)

filet/fillet. Except when meaning "lace" or in *filet mignon*, use *fillet* (double *l*), "a slice of boneless meat or fish," in all instances.

Filipinos. See *Philippine Islands.*

final/finale. These words have a shared meaning in that both refer to something that comes at the end. *Final* is an adjective, as in "This is the *final* game of the day." *Finale* is a noun meaning "the closing number of a concert or musical entertainment" ("This aria signals the *finale* of the opera"). When *final* refers to the last of a series of games, it is used in the plural, *finals* ("The *finals* of the tennis championship are now being played"). The plural word there becomes a noun.

finalize. Although word-usage critics deplore this word, they have been unable to restrain its linguistic progress. True, it sounds pompous, and "complete," "conclude," or even "make final" would, in this regard, serve better; but the war is over. Dictionaries include it, and certain persons prefer it because of its snappy sound and its sense of finality. Nevertheless, many serious writers think it inept and express themselves in another way.

final outcome. Omit *final*. Since *outcome* is a final consequence, the phrase *final outcome* is redundant.

find. See *locate/find.*

finest of two. See *better/best.*

finished, in formal usage, is preferred to *through* in such a sentence as "The lecturer *has finished* (rather than *is through with*) his introductory remarks."

fire. In colloquial speech, an employee peremptorily dismissed from employment is said to have been "fired," an expression borrowed from the field of firearms. Just as a bullet is discharged from a gun, so an employee is discharged from employment. They both have been "fired."

first. See *before/first.*

firstly/lastly. Although *firstly* is an acceptable adverb, *first* is preferable, especially in enumerations: *first . . . second . . . third*, and so forth. But *lastly* as an adverb, although used by Shakespeare and other distinguished authors, today has little following.

firstly/secondly. Writers sometimes wonder whether an enumeration should say *firstly . . . secondly*, or *first . . . secondly*, or *first . . . second.* They may use whichever they prefer. Style is personal. The first terms, however, are considered old-fashioned. Good writers use either the second or the third, with the third—*first . . . second*—weighted more heavily.

first of all. Drop the useless *of all.*

first two/last two. This is the correct way to express these terms, not "the two first" and not "the two last."

fish. See *moose/fish.*

fission, "to split or divide," is preferably pronounced *fizh*-un rather than *fish*-un.

fix. Although everyone understands that in "My brother's in a terrible *fix*" the brother has a serious problem, in better writing choose a more suitable noun, such as *predicament.* Use *fix* as a verb only, in the sense "make fast" or "repair."

flaccid, meaning "flabby," is pronounced *flack*-sid.

flagrant. See *blatant/flagrant.*

flair/flare. Often mistakenly interchanged, as in "He has a natural *flare* for detecting fake paintings." A *flare* is an outburst of flame or light (figuratively quick tempers *flare*); a *flair* is an instinctive bent, a natural talent, an aptitude. One has a flair (a knack) for picking out the right place, spotting trouble, or learning foreign languages—or detecting fake paintings.

flaming inferno, as in "The house looked like a *flaming inferno*," is tautological. Both words denote "fire." Make it an *inferno.*

flammable. See *inflammable/flammable/inflammatory.*

flare. See *flair/flare.*

flat plateau. See *tautology.*

flaunt/flout. "What surprised everyone was that a senator could *flaunt* the law and get away with it" is a typical misuse of *flaunt* for *flout,* now so prevalent that some dictionaries treat the words as synonyms. But they shouldn't; the meanings of these words are distinctive and ought to be kept so. To *flaunt* is to exhibit ostentatiously or conspicuously, to show off. To *flout* is to mock or scorn or to treat with contempt. A person who defies the law flouts it.

flew/fled. It is incorrect to say a jailbird *flew* from the prison while the gates were open. *Flew* is the past tense of *fly; fled* is the past tense of *flee.*

fliers. See *flyers/fliers.*

flotsam and jetsam. *Flotsam* figuratively means "odds and ends" or "the outcasts of society." Originally it was the wreckage of a ship or its cargo found afloat after a ship had sunk. *Jetsam* is cargo cast off (or jettisoned) from a ship in distress to lighten the load. Now used only metaphorically, as in "Vagrants and drifters that sit in downtown doorways are the *flotsam and jetsam* of our community," the phrase has become a cliché.

flounder/founder. To *flounder* (a blend word from *founder* and *blunder*) is to struggle about clumsily like a fish out of water. To *founder* is to sink, and considering its ancestry, all the way to the bottom. Its Latin progenitor was *fundus,* which means "bottom."

flout. See *flaunt/flout.*

fluctuate. See *vacillate/fluctuate.*

flunk is colloquial for *fail* ("Adrian *failed* [not *flunked*] geometry."

flyers/fliers. Not to be confused. Handbills are *flyers* not *fliers. Fliers* are airmen.

focus. One can, metaphorically, *focus* attention on the subject at hand in the way one uses a magnifying glass to enlarge a single point. It is proper to say the *focus* of the investigation was the credibility of the informer. But when *focus* is used to cover a wide field, so that it no longer concentrates on a point, its sense becomes unintelligible. A teacher cannot logically focus on the careers of all his students. This is like switching from a rifle to a blunderbuss.

follows. The expression *as follows* is idiomatic in the sense "it follows," *it* being understood. Say "The items are *as follows*," not *as follow*.

foot/feet. No one has trouble with such a statement as "We have a *seventy-foot* lawn," but it is a mistake to continue and say, "and my brother is *six-foot tall*." He is six *feet* tall. In the first example noun *foot* qualifies noun *lawn*. When one noun qualifies another, the first usually is singular. In the second example *tall* is an adjective.

forbade, the past tense of *forbid*, is pronounced for-*bad*.

forbear/forebear. These words raise particular problems because *forbear* is not only a verb, meaning "to desist" or "to refrain from," but also a noun, a variant spelling of *forebear*, "an ancestor." The noun is usually found in the plural ("His *forebears* [or *forbears*] came from Holland"), and its stress is on the first syllable. The verb is stressed on the second. Preferably choose *forebear* (with two *e*'s) when an ancestor is meant.

forbid/prohibit. These synonyms take different constructions. *Forbid* is followed by *to* or a gerund, never by *from* (*forbid* someone *to* do something, not *from* doing it). *Prohibit* is in an opposite camp. Unless followed by an object noun ("The principal *prohibits* ball playing during school hours"), it takes *from*, not *to* ("South Koreans *are prohibited from* entering North Korea").

forceful/forcible. Occasionally *forcible* appears where *forceful* would be more suitable. *Forceful* means "powerful," "vigorous and effective"—full of force ("His presentation was *forceful*, and, we must add, his personality was *forceful*, too"). *Forcible* means "having force" or "that which is effected by force or violence" ("The fireman made a *forcible* entry into the building").

forego/forgo. Whether *forgo*, which means "to abstain or refrain from," "to do without something to which one is entitled," may properly be spelled *forego* depends on the authority consulted. Dictionaries treat it as a variant spelling. But it is wiser to omit the *e*. *Forego* (with an *e*) means "to go before," "to precede." Its most common form is the participle (the *foregoing* statement). For the curious-minded, the past tense of *forego* is *forewent*. One can live a lifetime without ever hearing it.

foregone conclusion is an inevitable conclusion, a decision formed in advance. It is a cliché.

forenames. See *given names*.

forensic. Be sure the context makes clear which of its two meanings is intended—related to judicial procedure or pertaining to public discussion.

foreseeable future is accepted idiom. Everyone knows, or should know, that fifty years from now is not what is meant. It is the expected immediate period that one may reasonably consider. The expression is not precise, of course, but it is understandable—and useful.

for ever/forever, meaning "for always," may be written as two words, as it was originally—*for ever and ever*—but the single word now predominates.

foreword/forward. Spelling these words is sometimes troublesome. Remember that *foreword*, which contains the word *word*, is an introductory statement. In all other uses, *forward* is correct.

for example/for instance. Have no concern about interchanging these phrases (meaning "as an example"), although *for example* is the commoner expression in texts. When the words are used by themselves—*example, instance*—their meanings are not entirely alike. An *example* is a sample, a part of something. It also is a thing to be imitated—a pattern, a model. An *instance* is something serving as an example by way of illustration. It is a type of example that proves a point ("Spending so much time with his neighbor's baby is an *instance* of his love of children"). (See *i.e./e.g.*)

for free, as in "At the movie we each got a pretzel *for free*," sounds like street language. Drop *for*; *free* is enough. Of course, if you paid nothing, you got it *for nothing*, which is a good English phrase.

forgo. See *forego/forgo*.

for instance. See *for example/for instance*.

formal English. See *English, levels of*.

former. See *ex-/former; latter/former; was a former*.

for nothing. See *for free*.

forte. When *forte* means "a strong point," it is pronounced with one syllable, *fort*. When it is used as a musical term, meaning "very loud," it has two syllables, *for*-tay.

for the purpose of is a wordy phrase. In "The course was given *for the purpose of* teaching tax reform," an economical recast would be "The course was given *to teach* tax reform."

fortuitous/fortunate. Although a fortuitous occurrence may be fortunate, the words are not synonymous. *Fortuitous* means "accidental" or "unexpected" ("Meeting my uncle in Chicago was *fortuitous*"). Since a fortuity is a happening by mere chance, it may turn out to be fortunate or unfortunate. *Fortunate* means "having good fortune" or "marked by good luck." Certainly it need not be *fortuitous*.

forward. See *foreword/forward*.

for you to should ordinarily not follow a verb ("We want *for you to* leave early"). Drop *for*. But the phrase is correctly used immediately after a noun ("Salvatore set up a *meeting for you to* be interviewed") or an adjective ("Angie would be *delighted for you to* visit her"). (See *like for; mean*.)

founder. See *flounder/founder*.

Fourth Estate is a well-known phrase referring to "the press." For those desiring to know what the other three estates were called, their names follow: Lords Spiritual, the Lords Temporal, the Commons.

fraction. A person learning that a friend has lost a fraction of his assets might wonder how much was lost. Almost all or almost none? A fraction may be ninety-nine one-hundredths; it need not be a small part. Clearly, a more informative term would have been helpful—a large part, a small part. When *fraction* is preceded by *only*, it connotes only smallness ("Fortunately he lost *only a fraction* of his assets").

fractions not hyphened. A hyphen is not used with a fraction that is not serving as an adjective. "Today he paid *one half* of the tax," not *one-half*.

Frankenstein, the physician in Mary Shelly's ghost story, built a live monster from bones he had collected. Ultimately the monster took its creator's life. Although Frankenstein did not name the monster, in general speech the monster has been given the name of its creator, *Frankenstein*. A person responsible for a self-destructing situation is said, figuratively, to have created a *Frankenstein*.

free. See *for free*.

free gift. Since by definition a gift is free, the expression *a free gift* is redundant, as redundant as *a free pass*.

frequent. See *recurring/frequent*.

frequently. See *commonly/generally/frequently/usually*.

friable is not to be confused with *fryable*. That which is *friable* is readily crumbled (dry soil). That which is *fryable* can be fried (eggs or potatoes). Note that most dictionaries do not list *fryable* as a word in the English language, but it is used as such and is easily understood.

friend. See *personal friend*.

frightened/scared should be used with *by*, not *of*. A person may be frightened or scared *by* thunder, not *of* thunder (*scared* is less formal than *frightened*). But *afraid*, a state of habitual fear, may properly be followed by *of*. Which means that a person, grammatically speaking, may be afraid *of* thunder. (See *afraid/ frightened*.)

frivolous. It may sound frivolous to say that *frivolous* sometimes comes out *frivilous*. It shouldn't.

frolic needs a *k* inserted before suffixes *-ed* and *-ing—frolicked, frolicking*. But note *frolicsome*, no *k*. And in *politics,* note that a *k* has been added in *politicking. Traffic* needs a *k* before suffixes *-ed* and *-ing—trafficked, trafficking*.

from. Often used elliptically in matters of death, as in "He died *from* a coronary attack," meaning that he died from the effects of a coronary attack. It is preferable to follow *die* with *of*, not *from*: "He died *of* pneumonia." (See *between/from*; *suffer*.)

from/from ... to. In "His research resources were *from* the local library," omit *from* and avoid a redundancy. Likewise, in "Jonathan earned *from* $12 *to* $14 dollars last week," *from* is unnecessary.

fryable. See *friable*.

-ful. Whether *-ful* or *full* is used with, say, cups or hands, depends on the sense being applied. The rule is that the plurals of nouns ending in *-ful* are formed by adding an *s*—"fuls." Hence, "Take two *spoonfuls* of medicine daily," but "On the table are six *cups full* of sugar." The first implies a measure; the second, separate cups.

fulfill. See *skillful*.

fulsome. The newspaper reported that the governor lavished fulsome praise on his devoted colleague. What the paper meant, of course, was that the praise was great, full and unstinting. *Fulsome* does not mean that at all. It means "excessive" or "disgusting." *Fulsome praise* is insincere and therefore offensive. If the devoted colleague had even a smattering of linguistic knowledge, he would feel insulted.

funeral obsequies. Omit *funeral*. An *obsequy* is a funeral rite or ceremony.

funny, colloquially, signifies many meanings, primarily "curious, odd, or strange" ("It's *funny* that he didn't call me back"). The word properly means "humorous" or "comical." Also incorrect is the use of *funny* to suggest a foolish impropriety ("He tried to get *funny* with me").

furnish. Everyone knows what *furnish* means, as in to furnish a house. But some critics deplore its use in the sense of "supply" ("We shall *furnish* you with the material you need"). Since the opinions of authorities differ on this point, the decision whether to use *furnish* to mean "supply" is up to the writer.

further. See *farther/further*.

fuse together. Omit *together* to avoid a redundancy. To be fused is to be united as if by melting together.

future. One who speaks of the *near future* or *the not-too-distant future* is not being precise. But he is understood and the expressions have become established in everyday speech. Of course, saying *soon* for the first and *eventually* for the second is more in keeping with better English, even though those terms do not pinpoint the time either. (See *foreseeable future*.)

future plans. See *past records*.

gainfully employed is a long and pretentious way to say "working."

galore, an adverb meaning "in plenteous amounts," is a jocular colloquialism.

gambit, an opening move in chess that sacrifices a pawn to gain an advantage, is, in general usage, an opportunity or tactic in an overall strategy that involves a concession or sacrifice. Since the move takes place at the beginning of a negotiation or business transaction, saying *opening gambit* is redundant. Drop *opening.* With non-chess players it may be the very reverse. They are more likely to drop *gambit* and use *opening.*

gamut refers to an entire range of anything—the colors of the spectrum, the A to Z of a discussion, or the whole series of notes on the musical scale. Pronounce *gam*-uht.

gantlet/gauntlet. These words may be synonymous in common usage. But certainly not by derivation. In fact, the original meanings of these words bear no relationship to each other. A *gantlet,* commonly pronounced *gawnt*-leht, was a military punishment in which offenders were made to run between two rows of soldiers who beat them with clubs as they ran by. A *gauntlet* (same pronunciation as *gantlet*) was a protective glove worn by fighting men. Challenges to a duel were made by disdainfully flinging down a *gauntlet,* since a glove was a traditional symbol of defiance.

garçon. See *accent marks.*

garish. See *gaudy/garish.*

gather together. See *join together/gather together; fuse together.*

gauge, a standard of measurement, is a commonly misspelled word. Note it is not *guage,* but *gauge,* with an *au,* but pronounce *gāge.*

gauntlet. See *gantlet/gauntlet.*

gay is so commonly equated with "homosexual" rather than "merry" that one must be careful to avoid ambiguity or, worse, the unintended meaning. It is chancy to say you had a *gay* time.

gender. "Being of the male *gender*, I feel that I must take a strong stand." *Gender* is not a proper synonym for sex. It is a grammatical term applicable only to words. Change the example to "Being a male, I . . ." or, better yet, "Being a man, I . . . ." And note that *gender* is always masculine or feminine, never male or female. (See *one*.)

genealogy. Often misspelled. Not *ology* but *alogy*.

generally. See *commonly/generally/frequently/usually.*

generally speaking. See *dangling participles*.

general rule, as a. Redundant, since *rule* implies "a usual or customary action or behavior."

genuine is properly pronounced *jehn*-yoo-ihn. The last syllable does not rhyme with *vine*.

gerund. See *-ing words*.

get. See *got/gotten*.

get up. See *rise/arise/get up*.

gibe/jibe. Those who wonder whether to use *gibe* or *jibe* to mean jeer or mock, taunt or deride, should know they're free to use either form. The words are interchangeable. But when employed in its informal sense, "to be in harmony with," "to agree," the only spelling acceptable is *jibe*. (*Jibe* is also a nautical term, but that is not being considered here.)

gift. "She *gifted* him with a yellow sombrero." Although some dictionaries recognize *gift* as a verb, meaning "to make a present of," others, as well as most usage critics, disapprove of it. Why not make it "She *gave* him a yellow sombrero." (See *author/ host*.)

gild/guild. To *gild* is to cover with a thin layer of gold. A *guild* is an organized trade group. Be sure to spell these words correctly. "Thomas belongs to the typesetters *guild*," not *gild*.

girlfriend/boyfriend. Writers not knowing whether to spell these informal terms as one word or two, or whether to spell one solid and the other as a phrase, are understandably in a quandary. The fact is that lexicographers do not agree among themselves; there is authority for each of the various spellings. Some dictionaries list *boyfriend* as a single word and *girl friend* as two words. Others do not list *girlfriend* at all. The choice recommended here is to spell these labels as one word. But if you choose to do otherwise, at least treat them consistently.

given name. Since the professed faith in the United States is chiefly Christian, it is understandable that someone might ask another "What is your Christian name?" But because the question is not applicable to those not of that faith, "given name" or "first name" is preferable, for then no objection can be raised on any account.

glamour is our only British-born *-our* word (*honour, favour,* etc.) that retains its *u.* But note that its adjective form is spelled *glamorous* and its verb form *glamorize* ("He *glamorizes* everything he does").

glance/glimpse. These synonymous words suggest a brief look at something. To *glance* at the President is to have a momentary sight of him. And so is to *glimpse* the President. But it is more natural to convert *glimpse* into a noun and say, "We caught a *glimpse* of the President." *Glance,* like *glimpse,* is both a noun (to take *a glance*) and an intransitive verb, *to glance* (always followed by *at*).

glean. In centuries past, after a harvest the field was gone over again to see what had escaped the reaper. This revisit by the gleaners was laborious and usually not particularly rewarding. Thus gleaning came to mean more than a gathering; it implied a collecting of bits slowly and tediously, a sense that may be conveyed metaphorically in speech today. This means that one cannot glean what happened the moment he walks into a room filled with people, nor glean a person's financial status by spotting luxury cars in his driveway. To glean is to work steadily, acquiring slowly, bit by bit—laboriously. (See *aftermath.*)

glimpse. See *glance/glimpse.*

gloaming is a poetic word. But if you use it, be sure to know what it means. It means "evening twilight."

gloomy. See *pessimistic/gloomy.*

glutton. See *gourmet/gourmand/glutton.*

go/going/gone. Do not use *to* after these words in an interrogative sentence beginning with *where* ("Where's he *going*" [not *going to.*] "Where has she gone" [not *gone to*]). (See *where.*)

gobbledygook is speech or writing that is filled with big words and involved phrases difficult to understand. Coined by the Honorable Maury Maverick to imitate the cries of a turkey, *gobbledygook* is a forceful but informal term.

good/well. *Good* is an adjective. When suitable, it may follow a copulative, or linking, verb (*feel, sound, smell, taste, touch,* and a few others such as *seem, appear, grow*). "It sounds *good.*" "It looks *good.*" The adverb form of *good* is *well* ("The car runs *well*"). However, *well,* meaning "healthy," serves as an adjective when used after a linking verb. Note that "He looks *good*" refers to appearance, attire, general demeanor and "He looks *well,*" to physical condition. A person who seems happy looks good; a person who seems healthy looks well. (See *feel bad/feel badly.*)

good and, as in "good and mad" or "good and hot," a colloquial intensifier, means "to a considerable extent" or "very." In formal English use "very." (See *nice and; try and.*)

goodly is a good word, even though not often seen or heard. It means "comely" (a *goodly* youth), but in its most common use it means "considerable, rather large, fairly great." One may speak of a "good annual dividend," meaning "substantial," or of a *goodly* return on his investment.

good will/goodwill have the same meaning and are interchangeable, despite their different spellings. Purists who insist that the denotation of *good will* (spelled as two words) is "friendly disposition" and that the denotation of *goodwill* (or *good-will*) is "a business asset," although the distinction may have some merit, are waging a losing battle.

got/gotten. The past tense of *get* is *got* and the past participle is *got* or *gotten.* As in similar situations where one has a choice of participles, the selection depends on euphony. To *get* is to come into possession, but *have got,* when referring to mere possession, is redundant. For example, "*I've got* a pen," although considered good idiomatic English, should, strictly speaking, be recast "I *have* a pen." A sentence such as "*We've got* to avoid getting our feet wet" needs only "We *have* to avoid" or "What we *must* (or *ought to*) avoid." "*Have* you *got* a moment?"

works well without *got* or, as reworded, "Do you *have* a moment?" But in spoken English *have got* is more common and certainly more emphatic—and more natural ("*I've got* what you want"). Some modern writers would hold that "I've got a cold" and "He's got a bright idea" are acceptable idiom on any level of English.

got married is better stated *were married* ("Agnes and Bill *were married* last week"). But "He got sick last week" or "He got rich because of a lucky find" is considered idiomatic English. The sense of *got* in these examples is "became."

gourmet/gourmand/glutton. Confusing these words may be a source of embarrassment. Although they all refer to a lover of food, a person called a *gourmet* is complimented; if called a *gourmand*, affronted; and if called a *glutton*, insulted. The tastes of a *gourmet*, an epicure and a connoisseur of food and wine, are well regarded. A *gourmand* enjoys life at the dining table so much that he overindulges; hence *gourmand* is a deprecatory term. A *glutton* has such an insatiable appetite that he will eat anything and as much of it as he can get, ignoring table manners while gobbling away. Of the three, only a *gourmet* is a restrained eater.

government. See *February*.

graduated. Use *from* after the verb to avoid the telescoped colloquialism "He *graduated* high school today."

graffiti/spaghetti. "He tossed a *spaghetti* at the *graffiti* that was on the wall." Grammatically this cannot be done. One noodle taken from a bowl of spaghetti is a *spaghetto*, an Italian singular noun. Writings scribbled on a wall are *graffiti*, a plural noun, which takes a plural verb (the *graffiti were*). One scrawling is a *graffito* (a *graffito was*).

grammatical errors. Insisting that the phrase "a grammatical error" is a contradiction in terms and therefore an impossibility ignores the most important definitions of *grammatical*, "that which relates to grammar" and "the systematic description of the ways of language." It is grammatically correct to speak of grammatical errors, and the expression is well established.

granddad/grandfather/grandmother/granddaughter/grandson. Spell all of these as given, with no hyphen, not "She is a grand-mother." And note the double *d* in *granddad* and *grand-daughter*—not *grandad*, not *grandaughter*.

gratuitous. Be sure that when you offer your services it is wanted, for *gratuitous* means both "freely given" and "unnecessarily intrusive." A book given as a gift is gratuitous. And so is unsolicited advice. The difference is that the book is welcome. The advice may not be.

gravamen. See *onus/gravamen*.

gray, the color, is spelled with *a*; *grey* in *greyhound*, a sleek-looking dog, is preferably spelled with *e*.

great. See *big/great*.

Great Britain/United Kingdom. Although often used interchangeably, these terms should be differentiated. *Great Britain* is an island comprising England, Wales, and Scotland. The *United Kingdom* consists of Great Britain plus Northern Ireland.

great majority. See *majority*.

greyhound. See *gray*.

grievous is sometimes misspelled *grievious*. Be careful.

grisly/grizzly. Sometimes confused—for example, "a *grizzly* sight" instead of "a *grisly* sight." *Grizzly* applies to grayish hair and is usually said of a gray beard or a gray bear. *Grisly* means horrifying or gruesome.

groom. See *bridegroom/groom*.

ground/grounds. Interchangeable in the sense "the basis for an opinion." A person who stands his ground may have good *ground* (or *grounds*) for his point of view.

grounds of. See *on the grounds of*.

group is treated as a singular noun when it refers to a single unit but plural when it refers to individual members of a collection ("That *group* of gymnasts *have* received the most medals at the meet." "That *group* of Japanese gymnasts *is* probably the best at the meet"). Other nouns treated the same way are *breed, brand, class, type, species, variety*.

grovel. See *enthuse*.

guarantee/guaranty. When used as a noun, referring to an assurance that something will perform satisfactorily, either spelling is proper ("The two-year *guarantee* [or *guaranty*] expires soon"). The verb is always *guarantee*.

guess. See *reckon/guess*.

guild. See *gild/guild*.

guilt. "He suffered from *guilt feelings*." Writers who wish to avoid criticism would do better to say *guilty feelings* or to recast the sentence, "He had *feelings of guilt*." In the opinion of most authorities, *guilt* is a noun only, and is therefore impermissibly used as an adjective. Dictionaries support this view.

gypsy/gipsey. Spell these words either way that pleases you. Both spellings are acceptable, but the one that predominates is *gypsy*.

habit/custom. Frequently interchanged, yet their senses are distinguishable. *Habit* is a spontaneous or natural act resulting from frequent repetitions of the same act ("Johnstone has a *habit* of pulling his necktie when he's nervous"). *Custom* evolves from the similar habits of many people that, with time, become the accepted practice of the group or community ("It is a *custom* here to attend church on Sunday." "In Bridgton the *custom*, after the garbage men have driven away, is for the neighbors to water the streets"). A *custom* is followed; a *habit* is acquired. Be careful not to refer to a "usual" or "customary" habit. Habits, by definition, are always usual and always customary.

habitable/inhabitable. Do not be confused by the first syllable of the second word. The *in-* does not mean "not." In fact, both words have the same meaning, "able to be lived in." The difference between them is that *habitable* refers to houses and *inhabitable* refers to large areas, like valleys, plains, or even countries. If the area is not inhabitable, it is *uninhabitable*.

habitual, when a preposition is needed, is followed by *with*.

habitual custom. Redundant, since *custom* is the result of habitual practice. Omit *habitual*.

had better. See *better had*.

had have/had of are ungrammatical constructions. Neither *have* nor *of* may follow *had* ("If I had [not *had have* or *had of*] gone, I would have been happy").

hadn't ought to is an impropriety for *shouldn't* ("Dana *shouldn't* [not *hadn't ought to*] leave so early").

had of. See *had have/had of*.

hail/hale. The sentence "The felon was *hailed* into court" needs correcting—*haled* for *hailed*. To *hale* is "to haul" or "to cart away" (as to prison). To *hail* is to greet, to salute, to cheer ("The astronaut was *hailed* throughout the city") or to call (as a cab). Although a robust person is *hale*, this adjective is wrongly used in "a hale fellow well met." It should be "hail fellow," a fellow who is genial upon being greeted.

hairbrained. See *harebrained*.

hale. See *hail/hale*.

half. Wondering about its proper usage? Just remember not to use two *a*'s or *a* and *an*. Not "*a* half *a* cup" or "*a* half *an* hour," but *a half* cup and *a half* hour (or less formally, *half a* cup and *half an* hour).

half/quarter. Use a singular verb if quantity in volume or bulk is denoted, but a plural if the reference is to separate persons or items. ("*Half of* the *gas is* processed through AT Co." "*Half of* the *oranges are* in wooden crates.")

halfhearted/halfheartedly. A spirited person may greet his friends heartily—that is, enthusiastically; but if he is dejected, he will not be greeting them half heartily. The adverb required is *halfheartedly*, a form of *halfhearted*.

half-mast/half-staff signify a flag flown midway up a pole as a symbol of mourning. Flags at *half-mast* are flown on ships and at naval installations; flags elsewhere are flown at *half-staff*. Only the terminology is different. Not everyone, however, agrees with this statement. Some usage critics hold that the common expression on land and sea is *half-mast*.

handfuls. See *-ful*.

handicap/hindrance. Confine the use of noun *handicap* to mean "a disadvantage" or "a disability" and *hindrance* to something that impedes progress. This means that a handicap may also be a hindrance. A person with a speech defect may find that his handicap is a hindrance when trying to become a radio commentator.

handle/manage. Those wondering which of these verbs to use may be assured that, when they mean "to control" or "to influence," they are interchangeable, although in some uses one or the other is to be preferred. Either verb, for example, may serve in "Miss Huggins *handles* (or *manages*) every situation well" and in "The coach *handles* (or *manages*) the players to the owner's satisfaction." But when a manual activity is implied, *handle* is more suitable ("Leo *handles* the levers deftly"), and when a nonphysical activity, *manage* is more appropriate ("Roberto is *managing* every detail since the boss fell ill").

hanged/hung. Using *hung* for *hanged* when death by hanging is meant is a gross error. A person is hanged; a picture is hung.

happen. See *occur/happen/take place.*

happen into, as in "I *happened into* my friend's store yesterday and saw my math teacher," is low colloquial. Avoid.

happen to. "I *happen to* know that our neighbors are planning a divorce." Delete *happen to.* It happens to serve no useful purpose.

harass, meaning "annoy" or "irritate," may be pronounced *har*-uhs or huh-*rass. Har*-uhs is more prevalent. The pronunciation huh-*rass* might lead to a misspelling, since it seems to rhyme with *embarrass.* Note that *harass* has only one *r.* (See *embarrass; tantalize/harass.*)

harbor. See *port/harbor.*

hardly/scarcely. "He had *hardly* reached home than it began to snow." "*Scarcely* had I undressed than the doorbell rang." Since these adverbs are not comparatives, they should not have been followed by *than* but by *when.* Another caution. *Hardly* and *scarcely* have negative connotations and should therefore not accompany another negative. In "*Without hardly* a spoken word from father, everyone knew what he meant," delete *hardly.* Or change to "With *hardly.*" (See *barely; can't hardly; double negatives.*)

harebrained, meaning "giddy" or "flighty," is spelled as given, and not *hairbrained.*

harmony/melody are sometimes loosely interchanged terms. But they ought not be. Although both refer to a combination of musical sounds from voices or musical instruments, their uses should be differentiated. *Harmony* is the sounding of two or more musical tones in a chord. *Melody* is the arrangement of sound organized in a sequence of tones that make up a tune.

has. See *do/did.*

has not yet/has not already. Correct combinations. Action that continues to the present takes *has* or *have,* and not *did.* Therefore, "Travis *did not receive* his report card *yet*" should be reworded "Travis *has not yet received* his report card."

hastily improvised. See *tautology.*

hate/dislike. Be careful not to intensify unreasonably the wording of your aversions. Seldom is the word *hate* justified.

You might hate war and Arab terrorists, but otherwise *dislike* is the more suitable term. To *dislike* is to regard with displeasure or distaste. This word is strong enough to apply to spinach.

have. Use *have* after *could, may, might, must, shall, should,* and *will,* not *of.* Not "We *could of* gone if we had more money," but "We *could have.*" (See *do/have.*)

have got to is a colloquial expression for "must," "should," or "ought to." "I *have got to* have my car repaired" in serious writing should be rendered "I *must* (or *should*) have my car repaired." And "I *have got to* prepare this report before tomorrow" should be amended to read "I *ought to. . . .*" (See *got/ gotten.*)

have reference to. See *with reference to.*

headquarters. "The company is *headquartered* in St. Paul." In careful writing *headquarters,* "a center of operations," is not a verb but a plural noun. Make it "The company has *its headquarters* in St. Paul."

health reasons. "He was rejected for *health reasons*" is objected to by many grammarians on the ground that the word *health* is not an adjective. Recast the example "for reasons of health."

healthy/healthful. Some usage authorities maintain that *healthy,* in addition to its normal senses, can represent those implied by *healthful,* thus obsoleting the word *healthful.* Other authorities take a different tack, recommending that established meanings of these words be preserved: *healthy,* "possessing health"; *healthful,* "conducive to health." Traditionally, persons and other living things in good health were said to be *healthy,* and salutary climate, wholesome food, and the like, *healthful.* But because *healthy* is now widely used to refer to temperate climate or to a place good for health, such use can no longer be rightly criticized—although it need not be adopted either. You may say, and correctly so, "*Healthful* climate will keep you *healthy.*" In brief, *healthy* is having good health; *healthful* is health-giving.

heartrending is the way to say it. *Heartrendering* is incorrect. Fat is rendered.

heat up. See *hold up.*

hectic originally meant "feverish." Its sense has broadened to mean "excited," "filled with activity" (a *hectic* day). *Hectic* is now standard English.

height. Sometimes misspelled *heighth*, with three *h*'s, and sometimes misspelled *hight*, without the *e* after the initial *h*. Watch it.

heinous, meaning "odious," is pronounced *hay*-nuhs, the first syllable rhyming with *may*.

he is a man who needs only *he is*. Rather than "*He is a man who* is musically talented," reword and save words: "He is musically talented."

help. See *cannot help but*.

hence/thence/whence. *Hence* is still a useful word, but *thence* and *whence* are old-fashioned. Built into each of these words is the sense of *from*. Therefore, do not say *from hence*, *from thence*, or *from whence*. For example, in "He went to Chicago *from whence* he left for the coast," omit *from*, despite Psalms CXX:1 in the Bible: "I will lift up mine eyes to the hills, from whence cometh my help."

herb, a seed plant used for medicines or cooking, has a silent *h*. It is pronounced *uhrb*. *Herbaceous*, which means "like an herb," sounds its *h*—huhr-*bae*-shuhs.

here. This simple adverb is sometimes misplaced in constructions beginning with the demonstrative *this*. Place it after the noun (*this* book *here*, not *this here* book). Similarly *that there* girl should be reworded *that* girl *there*. Still better is simply *this book* and *that girl*.

here is/here are are anticipatory constructions when used in a sentence with a delayed subject. In "*Here* is my plan" and in "*Here* are my suggestions," each verb agrees with its subject— *plan* and *suggestions*.

herewith. A bit of archaic legalese that is best replaced by modern phraseology, even if a few more words have to be expended. In "I'm sending you our catalog *herewith*," drop *herewith* for "with this letter."

heroes. See *-o*.

her's is as substandard as *his'n*. There are no such forms in English. Of course *hers*, with no apostrophe, is a correct possessive pronoun ("This book is *hers*"). But note that *she's* and *he's* are recognized contractions for *she is* and *he is*; they're not possessives.

heterodox. See *orthodox.*

heterosexual. See *homosexual.*

hiccup/hiccough. Don't let the spelling of these words bother you. Use the one you prefer. Both are standard and pronounced alike (*hihk*-uph). The former spelling is commoner.

hike, as in "to hike up the prices," meaning "to increase," is colloquial.

him/himself. See *-self/-selves.*

hinder is followed by a gerund introduced by *from* or *in* ("Stephen *hindered* his sister *from* leaving." "The manager *hindered* Saul *in* carrying out his plan").

hindrance is spelled as given, not *hinderance.* There is no *e* between the *d* and the *r.* (See *handicap/hindrance.*)

historic/historical. Although often confused, these words have distinctive senses. *Historical* is the general, all-purpose word meaning "of or related to, or based on, history." In simpler terms, it refers to anything that concerns or contributes to history (a *historical* novel, a *historical* document, a *historical* society). *Historic* means "historically important," of such significance as to be assured a place in history (a *historic* battle, a *historic* landmark, a *historic* occasion). Whether *a* or *an* should precede these words is a matter of preference. The trend favors *a.* (See *a/an.*)

historical present/literary present. When a statement is historically true, use the present tense in a dependent clause: "We learned that the earth *is* round." The literary present tense is employed when speaking of a significant past event or a statement made by an important historical or literary figure, or when making a reference to a narration of past events. "Thoreau *urges* us to do without luxuries." In *Hamlet,* the actor describes the fight between Pyrrhus and Priam: "Anon he *finds* him striking too short at Greeks; his antique sword . . . *lies* where it falls" (italics added). (See *was/is.*)

histrionic. Although a person whose name is enshrined in *history* may have engaged in *histrionics,* the italicized words are unrelated. The term *history* need not be defined. *Histrionic* refers either to acting or to overacting, a display of excessive emotion. The context must make clear which meaning is intended.

hit or miss is the proper idiom, not *hit and miss*.

hoard/horde. Sometimes misspelled, one for the other. A *hoard*, literally "a hidden treasure," consists of things stored or accumulated for future use—the squirrels' hoard of nuts. A *horde*, originally nomadic tribes of Mongols and Turks, is a crowd of people, sometimes ill-behaved ("*Hordes* of Christmas shoppers create chaos on December 24"), or any multitude— animals, insects, gangs, crowds.

Hobson's choice is an unpleasant one. It is a choice between what is offered and nothing. The phrase was named after Hobson, a liveryman in England, who told his customers which horse they could ride. Either they took it or walked.

hoi polloi. This Greek term consists of two words *hoi* (meaning "the") and *polloi* (meaning "many"). Its anglicized meaning is "the masses," "the ordinary people." Clearly, saying "the hoi polloi" is redundant, the equivalent of saying "the the people." When you do not need *the* with this expression, omit it. If you do use *the*, do not feel abashed. Many reputable writers refer to *the hoi polloi*. It is no more redundant than the *City of Minneapolis*, in which *-polis* is Greek for "city."

hold up, as in "to hold up the meeting," is an acceptable idiomatic expression, but not *heat up*, as in "to heat up the room." Amend to "heat the room."

home in formal usage should be preceded by *at* (*at home*) after verbs that do not imply motion. Therefore, not "Stay home," but "Stay *at* home." (See *house/home*.)

homely/comely. A girl may be homely or comely. *Homely* means "unattractive"; *comely* means "of pleasing appearance." These antonyms do not rhyme. The latter word is pronounced *kuhm*-lih.

homicide/manslaughter/murder. The troublesome word in this trio is *homicide* because some people equate it with *manslaughter* and *murder*. *Homicide* is the killing of a human being by another, and it may, of course, constitute a *manslaughter* or a *murder*. But those killings are unlawful, criminal, which cannot be said of all homicides. A *homicide* may be accidental, or committed in self-defense, or be an ordered legal execution.

homonym/homograph/homophone. In Greek, *homo* means "same." Each of the key words means that a word has a sameness with another word. A *homonym* has the same spelling and pronunciation as another word but is different in meaning—the *bark* of a dog, the *bark* of a tree; *boil* (a sore), *boil* (as water). A *homograph* is a word spelled identically to another but having a different meaning and pronunciation—*wound* (an injury), *wound* (a tightened spring). A *homophone* is a word that has the same pronunciation as another but an entirely different spelling and meaning—*air* and *heir*; *feat* and *feet*.

homosexual is a term not applicable exclusively to males. The first element, *homo-*, is Greek for "same," which makes clear that *homosexual* designates sexual attraction between members of the same sex, whichever it may be. This *homo-* is the same as that in *homogeneous*, "of the same kind." Latin *homo* means "man," and that word is the front end of *homo sapiens*, "man as a thinking creature." The antonym of *homosexual* is *heterosexual*. (See *gay*.)

Honorable. See *Reverend/Honorable*.

hope is sometimes incorrectly used in the plural after *no* ("Gladys had *no hope* of recovering her stolen pin," not *no hopes*).

hopeful. See *optimistic/hopeful*.

hopefully. Trying to convince people that *hopefully* is used incorrectly in "*Hopefully* the train will arrive according to schedule" is a difficult, if not a hopeless, task. The objection raised by usage critics to this loose construction is that hope is being attributed to something that cannot hope; the train will not be steaming in full of hope. What is meant by *hopefully* is "it is to be hoped that" or "I hope that" ("I hope that the train will arrive according to schedule"). To avoid a misusage of *hopefully* in this kind of construction, a few more words are required.

horde. See *hoard/horde*.

horribly. See *intensives*.

hospitable. Often pronounced with a *spit*, stressing the second syllable. The accent should be on the first syllable—*hahs*-piht-abl.

host/gift. True, nouns may be converted into verbs when there's a need for them. For years people have *painted* houses, and *oiled* bicycles. No one criticizes those verbs or avoids using them. But this is not to condone a similar use of *host* and *gift*. Those words, as transitive verbs, sound graceless. Furthermore, they are unnecessary, since the language can convey the ideas that these words connote with such expressions as "serve as host for" or "be host to" or "entertain" and "give a gift to" or "present (someone) with a gift." Certainly verbs *host* and *gift* do not belong in better writing. (See *author/host*.)

house/home. "The city manager's *home* was put up for sale last week." Wrong. A house was put up for sale. A structure built for residential purposes is a *house*. A *home* is where the heart is. A married couple buy a house and create a home. Clearly a *home* is not salable; a *house* is (even though no one will ever convince real estate agents—and some usage critics—of this truth).

how is sometimes mistakenly used for *by which* or *under which* in a sentence such as "The treasurer said he knew of no plan *how* it could be financed." Change *how* to *by which*. In "I told my son *how* I wouldn't stand for anymore of his nonsense," change *how* to *that*.

how come, meaning "why," may be a delightful expression coming from the mouth of a young child ("*How come*, Mom, we're not going to the movies?"), but it does not belong in educated writing.

however, how ever. When the idea to be expressed is general, meaning "in whatever manner" ("*However* we draft the document, it will be good enough") or the sense is "nevertheless" ("*However*, we can draft a better document"), spell it as one word. If *ever* is employed to emphasize ("*How ever* did you walk from the station in this pouring rain?"), use two words.

human. An issue sometimes raised is whether *human* may properly replace *human being*. Or must it always serve as an adjective? In formal and technical writing the answer is to use only *human being* as a noun, restricting *human* to its sense "pertaining to people." At least this is the opinion of many good writers. Others, a growing group, accept *human* as a noun synonymous with person.

human/humane. Should you describe a person known for his kindness and compassion as *human?* Preferably not. Use *humane* instead, a word that implies those qualities.

humble has two unrelated meanings. One is modest in spirit, not proud. The other is low in position or of low estate. A man of humble birth may not be *humble*—that is, he may have no feelings of humility. Those who pronounce *humble* as *umble*, thinking it is the correct or a more elegant pronunciation, are mistaken. The *h* should be sounded.

hung. See *hanged/hung.*

hurricane/typhoon. Easily confused by anyone with no meteorological background. Distinguish by calling this kind of disturbance a *hurricane* if it arises east of the International Date Line and a *typhoon* if it arises west of the Date Line.

hyper-/hypo-. Spell compounds as one word. The first means "over" (*hyperacidity, hypercritical*) and the second, "under" (*hypochondriac, hypodermic*).

hyphen. A compound modifier used before a noun, consisting of an adjective and noun or participle, is hyphened (*long-term loan, much-wanted criminal*), even if the adjective ends in -*ly* (*a scholarly-minded publisher*). But no hyphen follows a -*ly* adverb (*widely known lawyer, simply dressed waitress*). Misplacing a hyphen can materially change meaning. Be careful. Consider a slow moving-van and a slow-moving van, two gallon-buckets and two-gallon buckets.

hyphens (suspended). Although constructions in which the parts of a compound are separated by a conjunction are unusual, they do surface once in a while. Combine the parts with hyphens ("It is a *two-* or *three-year* project." "My miserly uncle is more likely *to under-* than *to overspend"*).

hypocrisy, meaning "insincerity," is spelled as given, not hypocrasy.

hypothecate/hypothetical. These are unrelated terms. To *hypothecate* is to mortgage or pledge to a creditor as security for a loan or debt. A borrower may hypothecate stock to justify a loan application. *Hypothetical* refers to something assumed or supposed, like a *hypothetical* example.

I

-ible/-able. These sound-alike suffixes are a constant source of perplexity to everyone concerned with correct spelling, especially since there is no reliable rule to follow (*hospitable, incredible; indefatigable, indefensible*). The only safe course to take is to look the words up in a dictionary. And for whatever good this information may do, more words end in *-able* than in *-ible*. But note that some words are spelled identically except for this ending. The difference makes a considerable difference in the meaning, as shown by *impassable* (that cannot be passed) and *impassible* (having no feelings).

-ics. The number applied to nouns ending in *-ics* may be troublesome. The rule is to treat the noun as singular when used to denote a subject of study or a science ("Mathematics *is* my favorite course." "Acoustics *is* the science of sound"), but plural when it denotes activities or practical matters ("The acoustics *are* defective." "The athletics at this school *are* varied"). (See *acoustics; economic/economical.*)

idea is so vague a term that it is often preferably replaced by a specific noun: *understanding, surmise, intention, scheme, theory, object.*

identical takes the preposition *with* or *to*. "This house is *identical with* or *to* that one." Most authorities favor *with*.

idiom. See *dialect/idiom/jargon/vernacular.*

idiosyncrasy, "a personal peculiarity," is spelled as given, with a *crasy*, not a *cracy*, and certainly not a *crazy*.

idiot/imbecile/moron. Although a person who does something foolish is sometimes called by any of these terms, psychologists distinguish between them as being applicable to different levels of mental deficiency. An *idiot* has so little understanding that he cannot take care of himself. An *imbecile* has a higher level of intelligence (equivalent to a mental age of about seven) and can perform simple tasks. A *moron* has a low intelligence quotient, but one high enough to manage daily personal needs and even to be gainfully employed on a job that primarily involves physical work.

i.e./e.g. The abbreviation *i.e.*, which stands for Latin *id est*, meaning "that is," introduces a definition ("It is a way of life, *i.e.*, a way of life in this community"). *E.g.*, an abbreviation for *exempli gratia*, "for example," introduces an example ("He was all mixed up, *e.g.*, he didn't know where he was to go or when"). In formal texts use *that is* and *for example*. Avoid the abbreviated forms except in footnotes. After an example introduced by *e.g.*, do not add *etc.* Not "He enjoys many types of music, *e.g.*, sonatas, fugues, etc." *Etc.* suggests other unlisted examples.

if. A noun clause that begins a sentence is preferably not introduced by *if*; use *whether* ("*Whether* it will snow is uncertain"). *If* takes a subjunctive if the notion that follows is not true (contrary to fact) ("*If* I *were* a ballplayer"—but I'm not) and an indicative if the thought is true or probably true ("*If* I *was* absent from the meeting, I must have been out of town"). (See *provided/providing*; *whether/if/that*.)

if and when. Seldom necessary. Choose one. Dropping *if* or *when* causes no loss in meaning. (See *when, as, and if*.)

if worst comes to worst is an illogical expression. To indicate a worsening condition or situation, the correct form is "if worse comes to worst." But the expression as Cervantes said it—"Let the worst come to the worst"—is well established and here to stay. In fact, it has been around since 1594.

ignorant, meaning "uninformed," is followed by *in* ("Randall is *ignorant in* matters pertaining to law"); when used in the sense of "unawares," by *of* ("Sadie is *ignorant of* her daughter's longing to study ballet"). (See *illiterate/ignorant*.)

ignorant/stupid. Sometimes confused. To be *ignorant* is simply not to know something. A person who has little education is ignorant about many things. A *stupid* person is mentally unable to learn. Of course, stupidity may be the cause of ignorance.

ilk is a word best avoided unless its meaning is made clear by the context. As a Scots term, *ilk* means "of the same place or name," but most people use it pejoratively in the sense of "kind," "sort," or "class" ("If the boss hires more people of that *ilk*, I'm gonna quit").

illegible/unreadable. "Her scribbled letter is altogether *unreadable*." It would be better if that last word were *illegible*, since its only meaning is that the quality of handwriting or printing is so poor that it can't be read. *Unreadable* too has the sense of undecipherable, but it may also refer to the contents of the text, implying it is too technical or simply boring—or offensive.

illicit. See *elicit/ illicit.*

illiterate/ignorant. To say that a person who doesn't know is *illiterate*, instead of *ignorant*, is itself a sign of ignorance. *Illiterate* means "unable to read or write," which does not mean unknowledgeable. Although *illiterate* is equated with "ignorant" in common language, it may be wise in better English to substitute for either of those words a more precise term—for example, *untaught, uneducated, uninformed, unaware.*

illusion. See *delusion/illusion*; *allusion/illusion.*

illusive. See *elusive/illusive.*

imbecile. See *idiot/imbecile/moron.*

immature/premature share the sense "not being ready," but each in a different way. The first means "not developed" (a child is *immature*); the second, "too soon" (a *premature* announcement). That which is *immature* is not completed. That which is *premature* has occurred before the expected time.

immerge. See *emerge/immerge.*

immigrant. See *emigrant/immigrant.*

imminent. See *eminent/imminent.*

immoral. See *amoral/immoral/unmoral.*

immunity/impunity. Distinguish carefully between these words, for they are sometimes confused. *Immunity* means "exemption" (*immunity* from smallpox). *Impunity* also means "exemption" but from punishment. A person who does as he pleases, knowing he will suffer no consequences, feels he may act with impunity.

immured/inured. Watch their spellings. *Immured* means "shut in," "imprisoned," or "enclosed" ("Rudolph Hess was *immured* for many years in a prison in England"). *Inured* means "accustomed," "hardened by exercise" ("Long-distance swimmers become *inured* to ice-cold water").

impact. Before yielding to the flourish of this vogue word, give some thought to a more suitable replacement. This means that except when *impact* is used in its ordinary denotation, "a striking of one thing against another," "a collision," it is best avoided, as the following indicate: a law that has an *impact* on drug use (*reduces*); the *impact* of the chairman on the panel (*influence*); comprehending the *impact* of his proposal (*significance*).

impassable/impassible need a moment of pause to ensure correct spelling. *Impassable* refers to something that cannot be traveled on ("The muddy road is *impassable*"). *Impassible* connotes lack of emotion, implying that a person is unfeeling or incapable of feeling pain ("The whippers on slave boats must have been *impassible*"). (See *solid/stolid.*)

impeach. Many of us mistakenly believe that *impeach* means "to find guilty." It does not. It means "to bring charges against or to indict a person for the purpose of removing him from office *if found guilty.*" It therefore is the equivalent of "to accuse," not "to remove."

impediment. See *obstacle/impediment.*

impel/induce are not exact synonyms, even though in common usage they are frequently interchanged, as in "I don't know what *impelled* (or *induced*) Joan to change her mind." *Impel* means "to drive or force," "to cause to move"; *induce*, "to lead on," "influence," "persuade." The distinction between these verbs, observed by some writers, is that *impel* suggests that some force or outside influence is present; *induce*, a belief strong enough to convince one to take action. But it is not always possible to tell whether a person was motivated by outside compulsions or inner convictions.

imperative/imperious. Distinguish between these terms carefully; they are not synonymous. *Imperative* refers to that which is commanding or authoritative ("The notice said it was *imperative* that the job be completed by week's end"). *Imperious* refers to that which is domineering, overbearing, dictatorial ("The duke's manner is *imperious*").

implicit. See *explicit.*

imply/infer. To *imply* is to suggest without saying so directly—that is, to make no explicit statement. To *infer* is to surmise or deduce, to derive by reasoning. A speaker implies; his audience infers. Be careful to avoid such a sentence as "Do you mean to *infer* that the nurse was negligent?" Use *imply*.

imply/insinuate. To *imply* is to suggest, to hint. It is a neutral word containing no deprecatory overtones. To *insinuate* is to hint slyly, to convey an idea by trickery. It connotes deviousness, as evidenced by its definition, "to enter or introduce by devious ways."

important essentials. Since *essentials* are indispensable or basic, they are, by definition, important. Prefacing *essentials* with *important* is redundant.

importantly. "The production manager successfully turned the business around; more *importantly*, he saved its life." Although *importantly* is frequently so used, preferably it shouldn't be. *Important* says it more logically—and better—for the elliptical construction is "what is more important," the sense of the sentence being that the life of the business is more important than its turn around. Nevertheless, some writers prefer *importantly*, and its use is far from uncommon.

impossible is not comparable. Do not say "It's the *most impossible* idea I've ever heard." (See *absolutes*.)

impracticable/impractical. More often *impractical* is misused for *impracticable* than the other way around. That which is *impracticable* is not feasible. It cannot possibly be carried out or accomplished ("His idea of making water run up hill is *impracticable*"). That which is *impractical* serves no useful purpose or costs too much. It could be done, but with too great an expenditure of time, energy—or money.

impresario is sometimes misspelled as though it began with *impress*. Be sure to use only one *s*.

impromptu. See *extemporaneous/impromptu*.

impulsive. See *compulsive/impulsive*.

impunity. See *immunity/impunity*.

in-. Solid as a prefix (*inadmissible, intangible, inaccessible*).

inability/disability. These words imply a lack of ability, but their applications are distinctive. *Inability*, in addition to lack of ability, means "lack of capacity, power, or means," being unable (*inability* to pay one's debts, to play a tuba, to water-ski). *Disability* is something disabling (deafness is a *disability* for a singer; lameness, for a soldier). It is said that a person's inabilities are congenital. And although some disabilities may also be, others may be attributable to injuries or illness.

in addition to. A parenthetical phrase beginning with *in addition to, besides,* or *with* following the subject of a sentence does not create a grammatical plural. The number of the subject and verb is not affected by those intervening words. ("*Madame Butterfly,* in addition to three other operas, *is* part of the current repertoire"). (See *as well as; together with/along with.*)

in advance of. See *before/prior to.*

in all probability is a wordy way of saying "probably."

in any way, shape, or form is a trite colloquial redundancy. If a person is in good form, he is in a good way, and in good shape. Why say the same thing thrice?

inapt. See *unapt/inapt/inept.*

inasmuch as should be written as shown, not *in as much as.* The objection to this clumsy expression, even in its correct form, is that it is excessive for *because, since,* or *for* ("We left early *inasmuch as* it was starting to rain"—*because*). Use a single word.

in a state of mind is an expression that contributes nothing to a sentence except wordiness. In "My employer was *in a* receptive *state of mind* to my proposal," the italicized words, if deleted, would shorten the sentence without changing its sense.

in back of. See *back of.*

in behalf of. See *behalf.*

incapable. See *unable/incapable.*

in case. See *case.*

incidence/incidents/instance. The meaning of *incidence* is "the way something (such as a tax or disease) falls upon or distributes itself"; *incidents,* "happenings or events"; *instance,* "illustration," "example." "The *incidence* of the disease known as AIDS seems to be increasing." "This harrowing *incident* I hope never to experience again." "Lincoln is an *instance* of a poor boy who became President." (See *for example/for instance.*)

incidentally/accidentally. One who writes "*Incidently,* I met him *accidently*" should rewrite the key words—*incidentally, accidentally,* each spelled with five syllables.

incisive. See *decisive/incisive.*

inclined to believe, a wordy expression ("I am *inclined to believe* you're right"), is best avoided when *believe* alone will serve ("I *believe* you're right"). (See *is of the opinion that.*)

inclose. See *enclose/inclose.*

includable, not *includible,* is the correct spelling. Note the *able.* But *collectible,* not *collectable,* is preferred. Note the *ible.*

include/including. "The plan *includes* these four items" is wrongly put if the plan is made up of only four items. To indicate that fact, use *comprise.* If the plan consists of more than four, of course *include,* which indicates that at least one member is un-named, is correct. (See *comprise.*) *Including* is governed by the same conventions as those for *include.*

incomparable. See *uncomparable/incomparable.*

incomprehensible. See *indescribable.*

inconceivable. See *indescribable.*

in connection with/in this connection. *In connection with* is a wordy way of saying *about* or *concerning.* Prefer a single word. ("We recently heard a lecture *in connection with* economic con-ditions in South America"—*about* economic conditions). The phrase *in this connection* can usually be omitted with no loss in sense; it is never considered good usage.

in consequence of is merely a wordy way of saying *because of* or *due to.*

incredible/incredulous. Discriminate carefully between these words. *Incredible* usually applies to a statement that cannot be believed. It is, in a word, "unbelievable." *Incredulous* means "skeptical." A story beyond belief is incredible; the person hearing the story (and disbelieving) is *incredulous.*

inculcate/indoctrinate. Bear in mind that although *inculcate* (from its Latin progenitor, *inculcare*) means "to ground in," and so "to impress," and *indoctrinate* (from *docere*) "to instruct," the result is the same regardless of the terminology used. A person whose religious principles have been inculcated into her has become indoctrinated with the principles of that religion. The verbs take different prepositions—*inculcate, in* or *into*; *indoctri-nate, with.* Remember, you don't *inculcate* a person; you *inculcate* the idea or belief. But note that some authorities say you may inculcate something *in* someone or someone *with* something.

incumbent means "the present officeholder," which makes the expression *present incumbent* redundant. Omit *present*. (See *present incumbent*.)

indentation/indention refer to a notch or recess in a border. They may be freely interchanged when the reference is to the blank space at the beginning of a paragraph.

indescribable/inexplicable/incomprehensible/inexpressible/inconceivable/unthinkable. Although the meanings of these words overlap, their senses can be differentiated. That is *indescribable* which cannot be pictured in words. *Inexplicable* refers to something that cannot be explained or interpreted; *incomprehensible*, to that which cannot be intelligently understood; and *inexpressible*, to that which cannot be satisfactorily put in words. *Inconceivable* suggests that something is incapable of being conceived; it cannot be visualized and is therefore incredible, as unbelievable as the story of the test pilot who forgot his parachute. What is *unthinkable* cannot be thought of, perhaps because it is so degrading, so horrible, or so difficult to imagine, like nuclear war.

index. The plural form is "indexes" except in science, where it is spelled "indices."

indict/indite. Easily confused because they are pronounced alike. To *indict* is to charge with an offense ("The grand jury, we are sure, will *indict* him"). To *indite* is to compose or put into writing ("The chief mate will *indite* the letter of dismissal"). *Indite* sounds bookish. Avoid it.

indirect discourse. See *may/might*.

indirect object. When the indirect object precedes the direct object, the preposition *to* is understood. Particularly with verbs *give, pay, send,* and *write,* use an indirect object and avoid a "to" construction: "I *gave him* the book," rather than "I gave the book to him." And so "I *paid* the *bank* what I owed on my loan"; "The teacher *sent* the sick *pupil* a book"; "She *wrote me* a letter last week."

indiscriminate/indiscriminating may change their prefix to *un-* and retain the same meaning, "not discriminating." In fact, *undiscriminating* is the more usual and the preferred form. However, the adjective *indiscriminate,* meaning "having no sense of discrimination," "mixed up," is the only correct word; *undiscriminate* is not acceptable.

indispensable. See *absolutes.*

indisposed/undisposed. *Indisposed* means "slightly ill," "unwell." *Undisposed* (often used with *of*) means "unresolved," "not disposed of," as is a motion that has been tabled.

individual. Properly used as a noun when human beings are contrasted with a group ("The rights of both *individuals* and society must be given equal consideration"). But avoid as an all-purpose substitute for *person.*

indoctrinate. See *inculcate/indoctrinate.*

indubitably. See *undoubtedly/doubtlessly.*

induce. See *impel/induce.*

induction. See *deduction/induction.*

inductive/deductive have a sense in common in that both pertain to reasoning processes, but they are often confused. *Deduction* is drawing a conclusion from a general principle. It is, to put it in reverse, reasoning from the general to the specific. *Induction,* quite oppositely, is reasoning from particulars to generalizations. By deduction one concludes that since all petunias are flowers, and this is a petunia, it must be a flower. By induction one reasons that since every pine tree we have examined has cones, we can therefore expect all pine trees to have cones.

inedible. See *uneatable/inedible.*

in effect/in fact. *In effect* is not usually set off by commas ("He is *in effect* the manager"), but *in fact* generally is ("It was not, *in fact,* the clothing we had selected") except when the absence of commas will improve cadence ("He *in fact* was present").

ineffective/ineffectual. Use *ineffective* of something that does not produce the desired result. That which is ineffective is useless. This adjective may be used of persons or things ("My diet pills turned out to be *ineffective*"). *Ineffectual* is applied only to persons and means "powerless" or "incompetent" ("He was sexually *ineffectual*"). A distinction between these words observed by some writers is to apply *ineffective* to a certain characteristic of a person and *ineffectual* when the incompetence is general.

ineluctably is a fancy word for *inevitably*. Avoid it.

inept. See *unapt/inapt/inept*.

in excess of. Wordy for *more than* or *over* (*more than* is more formal). But either may properly replace *in excess of* in "*In excess of* four hundred high school students attended."

inexplicable. See *indescribable*.

inexpressible. See *indescribable*.

in fact. See *in effect/in fact*.

infectious/contagious. The use of these words troubles some people, possibly because both refer to communicable diseases that are contracted through the spread of germs. But, whereas an *infectious* disease is transmitted by germs that may be in the air or in water, as from colds or influenza, or microorganisms communicated through any other means, a *contagious* disease is spread only by actual bodily contact with the diseased person or by touching something previously handled by him.

infer. See *imply/infer*.

inferior to/superior to. The writer has ignored idiomatic usage in "You'll get service *superior than* that which you have ever had." The accepted expression is *superior to* ("a service *superior to* that which"). Its opposite number, *inferior*, also takes *to*, not *than*.

infinitive. "Anthony was fool enough *to have risked* his fortune" needs only "fool enough *to risk*." The present tense of an infinitive expresses action contemporaneous with that of the main verb. (See *split infinitive*; *to infinitive*.)

infinitive, subject of the. The answer to the question whether "I" in "The police took him and *I* to be robbers" is used correctly is—it is not. Although a subject usually is in the nominative case, the subject of an infinitive does not follow the normal rule. Its subject is in the objective case. Hence the example should read, since *me* is the objective case-form of *I*, "him and me."

inflammable/flammable/inflammatory. In the minds of some people, *inflammable* means "not flammable" (*in*, "not," plus *flammable*, "burnable"), especially since *in-* in many English words means "not" (as in *inactive* and *inaccurate*). Because a misunderstanding of the word *inflammable* might be disastrous, *flammable* was coined to warn that a fluid was combustible. Today *flammable* and *inflammable* have the same meaning and are interchangeable. Bear in mind that *incombustible* refers to an object that won't burn but *inflammable* to one that will. *Inflammatory* is a figurative term meaning "tending to inflame," "kindling passion or anger."

influence, with the accent on the first syllable, meaning "the power of persons or things to act on others," is properly used in a sentence such as "He used his *influence* to persuade his colleagues to vote his way." But do not say, "He's got *influence*." Make it "He is *influential*."

informal English. See *English, levels of.*

informer/informant refer to someone who furnishes information. The chief difference between them, in current usage, is that an *informer* provides an investigating organization with incriminating information against another. An *informant* merely informs or provides information to another, which, incidentally, may be about himself.

infra dig is unrelated to any archeological project. It means "beneath one's dignity," and is an abbreviation of Latin *infra dignitatem*. The term sounds pretentious in most cases.

infrequent. See *unfrequent/infrequent.*

ingenious/ingenuous. These words are easily confused. *Ingenious* (pronounced in-*jeen*-yus) means "inventive," "clever," "original," "resourceful." An ingenious person adapts wisely to situations and handles them skillfully ("Councilman Thomas submitted an *ingenious* plan to improve the flow of traffic"). *Ingenuous* (pronounced in-*jen*-yoo-us) means "artless," "free from deceit," "unsophisticated." Such a person is frank and open, with undisguised feelings ("Her *ingenuous* manner made the guests feel welcome").

-ing words. "The track coach liked his running." "The teacher saw him running." Which sentence is correct? They both are. In the first sentence the object of the verb *liked* is "running," a verbal noun called a *gerund*. In the second sentence the object of the verb *saw* is "him," which is modified by "running," a verbal adjective called a *participle*. The difference between the two sentences is that the former emphasizes the action (*run-*

ning); the latter emphasizes the one doing the action (*him*). Note the pronoun introducing a gerund is in the possessive case.

inhabitable. See *habitable/inhabitable.*

inhuman. See *unhuman/inhuman.*

in-law. Frequently misspelled in the plural. Make it *sons-in-law,* not *son-in-laws; daughters-in-law,* not *daughter-in-laws,* and so forth.

in lieu of. Preferably replaced by *in place of* or *instead of.* Either expression would serve better in "*In lieu of* tails and white tie, we wore tuxedos."

innocuous/inoculate. Two words bound to eliminate some spelling-bee contestants. Note that the first has a double *n,* but not the second.

innumerable means "countless." Note the redundancy in "An *innumerable number* of supporters waved at the candidate." Make it "*Innumerable* supporters . . ." or replace *innumerable* with "A *large* (or *countless* or *incalculable*) number." And do not confuse it with *numerous.* That word means "of great number," although not so great a number as that suggested by *innumerable.* We may say that *innumerable* implies "a very great number," so large as to be uncountable.

inoculate. See *innocuous/inoculate; vaccinate/inoculate.*

in order to (that). *To* is the usual sign of the infinitive. Sometimes the wordier *in order to* is substituted for the sake of rhythm, occasionally to accentuate meaning. But generally this substitution is not recommended. It is excessive in "He went home *in order to* get his wallet." Omit *in order. In order that* is longer but no more effective than *so that* or *that* in many instances. However, it is necessary in such a construction as "*In order that* he might finish early. . . ."

in re. See *re/in re.*

in reference to. See *with reference to.*

in regard to. See *regard/regards.*

in routine fashion says in three words what *routinely* says in one.

inside of. See *outside of/inside of.*

insignia. In "He has a large *insignia* on his garage door," *insignia* is technically incorrect, since it is a plural noun. Strictly speaking, there cannot be "*a* large *insignia*." The singular form of *insignia* is *insigne*. However, because few people know that word, *insignia* has taken its place and is now accepted as both a singular and a plural ("The insignia *is* . . ." "The insignia *are* . . ."). *Insignia* has developed a plural of its own, *insignias*, now interchangeable with *insignia*. (See *agenda*.)

insinuate. See *imply/insinuate*.

insofar (used with *as*) means "to such extent." Although once written as three words (*in so far*), the words have coalesced and are now written as one. Avoid *insofar* if you can, for it tends to lead to wordiness. Try replacing it with *although, except that*, or *so far*.

in spite of. See *despite/in spite of*.

in spite of the fact that. See *fact*.

instance. See *for example/for instance*.

instincts. See *natural instincts*.

insurance/assurance. A company in the business of insuring is an *insurance company*. What confuses some people is that some such companies in Canada and Britain are called *assurance companies*. Those companies, however, sell life, not casualty, insurance. The reasoning behind the distinction is that a holder of a life insurance policy is assured that at some indefinite future time (at the assured's death) benefits will be paid on its account. This assurance cannot be given by casualty companies because their responsibility is contingent on the happening of a loss that may never occur.

insure. See *ensure/insure*.

intensive pronouns. See *-self/-selves*.

intensives, words employed to add emphasis, are usually best omitted. If used at all, they should be carefully selected. In formal discourse do not use *too, such*, or *so* as intensives, as in "Adeline is just *too* pretty"; "This class is *such a* bore"; "Clarence is *so* funny." And be careful of needlessly adding such modifiers as *awfully, horribly, terribly*, or *simply*. They are deadwood and should be lopped off in such sentences as "Our teacher is *terribly* funny" or "Mose is *simply* wild about pickled herring." (See *awful; simply; so/that; such/this; terribly*.)

inter-/intra-. These prefixes are written solid (*international, intermarriage; intrastate, intramural*). *Inter-* means "between," "among," "together"; *intra-*, "within," "inside." *Interscholastic* sports involve different schools; *intrascholastic* sports are engaged in within one school.

in the back of. See *back of.*

in the course of is a wordy way of saying *in, during,* or *while.* "We spoke about it *in the course of* our general conversation" (*during*).

in the event that goes a long way to say *if.* "*In the event that* it rains, we'll postpone the trip." Simplify. "*If* it rains."

in the first instance. It is better just to say *first.*

in the immediate vicinity of says no more than "near." *In the vicinity of* (without *immediate*) is often used to mean "about" ("He paid *in the vicinity of* $20,000 for that car"). *About* would save three words and be more precise, too. (See *in the neighborhood of.*)

in the light of is the correct wording. Do not omit the *the.* Do not say *in light of.*

in the line of is an unnecessary colloquialism. It should be excised in "What does the library have *in the line of* home decorating books?" Why not just say, "What home decorating books does the library have?" But note that "in the line of duty" is correct phraseology.

in the near future can economically be reduced to *soon.*

in the neighborhood of. If appropriate, prefer *nearly* to this wordy expression ("He spent *nearly*—rather than *in the neighborhood of*—$5,000"). (See *in the immediate vicinity of.*)

in the . . . part of adds nothing but prolixity. Rather than "My uncle lives *in the* southern *part of* Georgia," say "My uncle lives *in southern* Georgia."

in the process of. Usually an unnecessary phrase that, if deleted, makes a sentence tighter and more forceful. "A patient *in the process of* convalescing requires fresh air daily" needs only "A convalescing patient requires fresh air daily."

in this connection. See *in connection with/in this connection.*

in to/into. When written as two words, *in* is an adverb and *to* a preposition ("We were told to go *in to* see the manager"). As a preposition expressing motion from one place to the inside of another, *into* is written as one word ("The doctor walked *into* the operating room").

intra-. See *inter-/intra-*.

intrinsic/extrinsic/extraneous. *Intrinsic* means "belonging to a thing by its very nature," "essential." The *intrinsic* value of a coin is the cost of its material and manufacture, but its worth as a collector's item is much more. *Intrinsic* has two near-antonyms—*extrinsic*, meaning "not essential or inherent," "caused by external circumstances" ("Its *extrinsic* worth far exceeds its face value"), and *extraneous*, "coming from the outside," "not pertinent," "foreign" ("This paragraph does not belong; it contains *extraneous* material").

intrusive/obtrusive have a sense in common of saying or doing something that has not been solicited. *Intrusive* suggests that something was unasked and unwanted; it is an uncalled-for thrusting in or upon a person. *Obtrusive*, a thrusting out, is a pushing ahead, a forcing of others to pay attention. Figuratively such a person is said to be forward.

inured. See *immured/inured*.

invaluable. Difficult as it is to believe, *invaluable* is sometimes wrongly used to mean "not valuable," possibly on the assumption that the *in-* in *invaluable* means "not." It does not; the *in-* is an intensifier. Something invaluable is priceless; it is beyond value. The antonym of *invaluable* is *valueless*.

inveigh/inveigle look somewhat alike but have different meanings. They should be distinguished. *Inveigh* means "to speak strongly against" and *inveigle*, "to entice or cajole."

invent. See *discover/invent*.

in view of the fact that. Note that *because, since,* or *considering that* means the same but says it more briefly.

irreducible minimum. See *tautology*.

irregardless is not a word in the English language. Use *regardless*. (See *disregardless*.)

irrelevant. Sometimes misspelled *irrevelant*. Be careful not to transpose the *l* and the *v*.

irreparable. See *repairable/irreparable*.

irresponsible. See *unresponsible/irresponsible*.

irreversible. See *irrevocable/irreversible.*

irrevocable/irreversible. That which is *irrevocable* cannot be called or brought back. That which is *irreversible* is unalterable, unable to be changed. The distinction between these words is narrow. In general application, however, *irrevocable* is usually applied to orders or decrees and to single acts ("His decision to seek other employment is *irrevocable.*" "Yesterday belongs to the *irrevocable* past"). *Irreversible* connotes a longstanding activity or characteristic that can no longer be changed ("His addiction to drugs is such as to make it *irreversible*").

irritate. See *aggravate.*

irruption. See *eruption/irruption.*

is of the opinion that. A person who has such an opinion believes in what he says, and *believes* is the better way to express it ("He *is of the opinion that* war is imminent"—*believes that*). (See *inclined to believe.*)

is when/is where. Although a *when* or *where* clause leads easily into a definition, its use is not recommended. "Ignorance *is when* a man doesn't know" should be recast "Ignorance is the *absence* of knowledge," and "Drunkenness *is when* you've drunk too much" should be reworded "Drunkenness is the *condition* of a person who has drunk too much." *When* and *where* are generally adverbs. A noun (*ignorance, drunkenness*) requires as its predicate complement another noun or noun phrase or clause, not an adverbial clause.

it. See *there/it.*

italics. Numbers, letters, and words used as words rather than for their meaning are underlined, which means italicized in print ("The sentence had three *s*'s, two *g*'s and *u*'s, and the word *verbose* twice"). Note that the pluralizing *s* is not italicized.

it goes without saying. See *needless to say.*

it is/it was. In sentences such as "*It is* a long way to Tipperary," and in "*It was* Willie's touchdown that won the game," the expletive *it* anticipates the real subject, which follows the singular verb ("*It is* the man who pays." "*It is* the men who pay"). (See *there is/there are.*)

it is I. In formal discourse the pronoun following *it is* should be in the nominative case; hence *it is I* or *he* or *she* or *they*. In informal usage the objective case sounds more natural (it's *me*, it's *him*, it's *them*). However, many educated people, although accepting and using "It is *me*" in everyday speech, would not say "It is *them*," but "It is *they*."

it . . . it. It is confusing if expletive *it* and pronoun *it* appear in the same sentence. Avoid. "*It* is wise to check the air in your spare tire regularly so that *it* will be usable when needed" can be better stated "A wise motorist checks the air in his spare tire regularly so that *it* will be usable when needed."

it's/its. "The car got it's hood painted today." Every educated person knows that *it's* should have been *its*, that *it's* is a contraction of *it is*, and that *its* is a possessive pronoun. Why does this error appear so frequently? Pure carelessness? Possibly. But the apostrophe might have deceived the writer into believing that *it's* is a possessive form. It looks like one. Be careful.

Japanese, it should be noted, is spelled with only one *e* before the *s.*

jargon. See *dialect/idiom/jargon/vernacular.*

jealousy. See *envy/jealousy.*

jetsam. See *flotsam and jetsam.*

jewelry has three syllables—*joo*-ehl-rih (not *jool*-rih)—and so does its most exciting gemstone, *die*-uh-muhnd (not *die*-muhnd).

Jewish synagogue. Is there another kind? Is there such a thing as a Moslem or a Christian synagogue? The question, of course, is rhetorical.

jibe. See *gibe/jibe.*

jittery, meaning "nervous or uneasy," is a good word; but it is best replaced in formal writing with one more suitable to the text.

job/position. A *job* is a piece of work or an undertaking for a fixed price. A *position* is employment above manual labor. No matter, a person who has a position has a job to do.

join together/gather together. Almost always tautological, as in "Let's *gather together* to see what's best to do." If *together* is used for the sake of emphasis as in "What therefore God has joined together, let no man put asunder," the writer must feel strongly about it. Never justifiable, however, is the combination *link together* or *meet together.*

Jr., Sr. Whether to use a comma before *Jr.* or *Sr.,* as in "Mr. J. L. Whitman, Sr. will serve as chairman," is a matter of choice; there are no rights or wrongs. It has been customary to use the comma, but a trend away from it is picking up momentum. Of course, the practice of the owner of the name, if it is known, is the one to follow. In journalistic style the comma is omitted.

judge/adjudge are synonymous in the sense "to consider," "to estimate," "to decide." *Judge* is a common verb; *adjudge*, a formal

140

verb, sometimes seen as a substitute for "order" or "decree." In fact, *adjudge* is so formal, and sounds so awkward, that it is best left to the judges.

judge/jurist. Frequently confused, even by journalists. A jurist is a person skilled in the law. He may be a practicing lawyer or a law professor. He need not be a judge, although all judges are expected to be jurists.

judging. See *dangling participles.*

judgment. Do not spell this word *judgement.* Omit the "e" after the "g." (See *abridgment; acknowledgment.*)

judicial/judicious. Sometimes confused because of their similarity in appearance. *Judicial* pertains to courts and judges. *Judicious* means "wise or sensible," as is a person who shows good judgment.

juggernaut, sometimes capitalized, is a force that no one can withstand. The term is used properly if the force is ruthlessly crushing. It must destroy or, if the word is used metaphorically, at least cause serious damage.

junction/juncture. When one begins a sentence "At this particular *junction*," the probabilities are great that he means *juncture.* A *junction* is a coming together or a place of meeting, say, for railway lines or electric wires in a junction box. Or it might be the point where two rivers join. *Juncture* is the preferred term when the reference is to time or to a serious state of affairs, a crisis ("We must reconsider at this *juncture* because the state of our affairs is critical").

junta, "a group of military officers holding state power in a country after a *coup d'état*" or "a council or committee, especially for legislation," is usually given the pronunciation *huhn*-tah.

jurist. See *judge/jurist.*

jury. See *collective nouns.*

just. "It is *just exactly* three o'clock" is tautological. One meaning of *just* is "exactly." Choose either *just* or *exactly.* Saying "It is *just about* right" is contradictory. It says it both precisely and approximately, which doesn't make sense. Place *just* close to the word it modifies, generally before it: "With only ten minutes to spare, he *just* showered" (but didn't shave). "On our visit we saw *just* her mother" (and no one else).

just/justly. Adjective *just* and adverb *justly* both refer to that which is prompted by fairness and reason. One may say the minister was a *just* person and his sense of decency was *justly* recognized. Adverb *justly* always precedes the verb it qualifies. (See *only*; *wrong/wrongly*.)

just as means "in the same way," which means that *just the same as* is redundant. Make it "He studied at Stanford, *just as* (not *just the same as*) his brothers did." (See *the way/just as*.)

just deserts. See *desert/dessert*.

just recently. One meaning of *just* is "recently" ("He *just* got here"), and one meaning of *recently* is "just" ("He *recently* arrived"). Saying "He *just recently* arrived" is therefore redundant. Use one word or the other. (See *just*; *just yet*.)

just yet. Often used colloquially instead of *now* or *still*. In "The concrete is too wet to walk on *just yet*," recast using one of the suggested replacements—for example, "The concrete is *still* too wet to walk on."

juvenile is often mispronounced by adults (which see), especially when they speak of a person behaving childishly—"He's acting like a *juvenile*" (stressing the last syllable and rhyming it with "mile"). *Juvenile* is correctly pronounced *joo*-vehn-ihl.

karat. See *carat/karat/caret*.

keep continuing. See *continue on*.

keep from, meaning "refrain from," is a colloquialism. In formal English use "refrain from" or "help" in a sentence such as "Anthony could not *keep from* hollering back."

ketchup/catsup. When asking for this tomato-based, spicy sauce be not concerned whether you call it *ketchup* or *catsup*. Some cookbooks spell it one way and some the other. The entries of dictionaries simply mirror these references. Consider your own taste.

kidnap is a not a noun. *Kidnapping* is. Not "Leon was indicted for *kidnap* and murder." Make it *kidnapping* and murder. (See *diagram/program/kidnap*.)

kilt. "We laughed when we saw him wearing kilts." The kilt-wearer laughed back at our ignorance. The correct expression is *wearing a kilt*. The pleated skirt is singular.

kind. Two of the most common errors made with *kind* are exemplified in the following sentences: "Walter is the *kind of a* man everyone likes." "*These kind of* apples are delicious." In the first, *a* is superfluous; neither *a* nor *an* belongs after *kind*, since *kind* indicates a class. (A counterargument is that the *a* or *an* serves a purpose in some constructions—"What kind of painter is he?" asks whether he is a house painter, a portrait painter, and so on. "What kind of a painter is he?" inquires about his capability as a painter.) The second example should be amended to read "This *kind of* apple" or "These *kinds of* apples." Mixing singulars with plurals in this kind of expression is to be avoided. What has been said about *kind* applies to *sort* except that *kind* is preferred to *sort* for a more explicit reference: "We recommend this kind of therapy." (See *manner of*; *sort of*; *these kind/ those sort*; *type*.)

kindergarten ends in *garten*, not *garden*, even though in German *Garten* means "garden."

kindly, as in "*Kindly* send me your catalog," is disapproved by most word-usage critics. *Kindly* means "in a kind manner," which is not what was meant. Prefer "would you be good enough to . . ." or simply "please. . . ."

kind of, when used to mean "rather" or "somewhat" ("She's *kind of* cute"), is colloquial.

kind of/rather/somewhat.   In better speech and in writing do not use *kind of* to mean "rather" or "somewhat." Instead of "It is *kind of* humid" and "Nathan was *kind of* surprised," say *rather humid* and *somewhat surprised.*

kiosk, an outdoor newsstand, is pronounced with a *kee* (not a *ki* with a long *i*), *kee*-ahsk.

kith and kin.   Although everyone knows that *kin* means relatives (not *a* relative, however—there's no such thing as *a* kin), probably more tourists visit Tibet annually than there are users of this phrase who know what *kith* means. It means "friends and acquaintances." But no one calls them "my kith." The phrase *kith and kin* has become fossilized in the language because of its frequent, though meaningless, use.

knot.   In "We sailed along at ten *knots* an hour," *an hour* is redundant. A *knot* is a unit of speed of one nautical mile an hour. It is not a measure of distance.

know/realize.   Precisians discriminate in the use of these words, although they agree that their meanings overlap. To *know* is to understand. To *realize* is to understand clearly and fully. What distinguishes these words from each other is the degree of understanding. If a person apprehends, he *knows*. If he apprehends thoroughly, grasping possible consequences, he is said to *realize*. *Realize* emphasizes the idea of completeness.

knowledge.   See *a little knowledge*; *to my knowledge/to the best of my knowledge*.

known to be.   Try *is* as a substitute.

kudos.   A pompous word, best confined to crossword puzzles. In "Elgart was entitled to all the *kudos* he received," *all* indicates more than one. However, *kudos*, which means "praise" or "renown," is singular. Delete *all*.

L

La/Le are capitalized in proper names (Fiorello La Guardia, Eva Le Gallienne).

labor. See *belabor.*

lack for is colloquial for *lack.* In "Nebraska does not *lack for* arable land," drop *for.*

lady. See *woman/lady.*

laid/lain. The past tense and participles of *lay* and *lie* are often confused. Bear in mind that *lay* (its principal parts are *lay, laid, laid*), a transitive verb, takes a direct object. Therefore, "I *laid* the *pen* on the desk" and "He has *laid* those *rumors* to rest." Intransitive *lie* (its principal parts are *lie, lay, lain*) never takes a direct object ("The patient *lay* in bed for ten days." "The newspaper *has lain* on our neighbor's front walk for a week"). (See *laying/lying.*)

lama/llama. The more familiar word is *llama,* a South American animal. Be sure to use a double *l.* Spelled with one *l, lama,* it means a Tibetan Buddist monk or priest. Generally both words are pronounced alike.

lamentable. Dictionaries offer a choice of two pronunciations for this word meaning "deplorable," a stress either on the first syllable—*lam*—or on the second—*en.* Stressing the first syllable is to be preferred.

lapse. See *elapse/lapse*; *period of time.*

large. See *loom/bulk.*

large portion of/large number of. Nothing is achieved by using either of these phrases except the expenditure of ink. It is better to economize and say *much of* or *most of* or *many,* depending on the context. Instead of *"A large portion of* his wealth was inherited," make it *much of.* Instead of *"A large number of* fans welcomed our hero," make it *many.*

last/latest. *Late* has two superlative forms—*last* and *latest.* Although both mean "coming after all others," they have different applications. *Last,* in the sense of "final," may refer either to position (the *last* boy in the row) or to time (the *last* show of the night). *Latest* implies not so much finality as "the current" or "the most recent" ("I know that my sister's *latest* boyfriend will not be her *last*").

last but not least is not a troublesome but a tiresome phrase. Avoid this cliché.

lastly. See *firstly/lastly.*

last-named. See *latter/former.*

last two. See *first two/last two.*

later on. Omit *on.* Say "We will go later," not *later on.*

latter/former. This sentence needs correcting: "Representatives of the miners, transport, and electrical unions conferred; a member of the latter union presided." *Latter* and *former* may be used of only *two* persons or objects; *former* designates the first of two and *latter* the second. Thus the previous sentence should be amended to read, "A member of the *last-named* union presided." The use of these terms, even if correct, is often criticized because they make a reader go over old ground to see which is which. But since they are word-savers, and sometimes avoid a monotonous repetition of nouns, almost every writer occasionally finds them useful.

laudable/laudatory. The sentence "The governor's remarks at the inauguration were *laudable*" probably needs correcting. *Laudable* means "deserving of praise," "commendable" (a *laudable* plan). *Laudatory* means "expressing or bestowing praise" (a *laudatory* book review). The governor's remarks, in all probability, were *laudatory*, not *laudable.*

lawful/legal. *Lawful* has a broader connotation than *legal.* That which is lawful is allowed by or is not contrary to law. The law may pertain to the laws of the state or a church, or to moral law or ethical doctrines. *Legal* refers only to the law of the land— law enacted by human beings. One refers to "a legal document" or "the legal profession." On the other hand, we speak of "a lawful undertaking," "lawful claims," "lawful business practices." A man who has wedded will find that both words apply to him. He has a lawful wife and a legal marriage.

lawyer. A general term for a member of the legal profession—often called *attorney*. But although an attorney at law is empowered to act for another person, so may a layman if he is made an *attorney in fact*. The word *attorney*, therefore, does not apply solely to members of the legal profession. British lawyers are called either *barristers* (those who plead in court) or *solicitors* (those who represent clients before the lower courts and prepare cases for barristers to plead in higher courts).

lay. See *lie/lay*.

laying/lying. Even some well-educated people persistently say, "I can't disturb my father now because he's *laying* down." "My dog likes *laying* down every afternoon in the sun." These "down" words are forms of "to lie," meaning "to recline"— "I *lie* down" or "I *am lying* down"; "We *will lie* down" or "I *will be lying* down." The confusion involved in all the *lie/lay* forms has been attributed to the identicalness of the past tense of *lie*, which is *lay*, and the present tense of *lay*, which also is *lay*. The present participles of these verbs, respectively *laying* and *lying*, should be carefully distinguished. If what immediately follows *lying* is not a noun or a pronoun, as in "lying down" or "lying in bed," use *lying*. If a noun follows—"The chicken is *laying* eggs"; "The gardener is *laying* sod"—then use *laying*. (See *laid/lain*.)

Le. See *La/Le*.

lead/led. *Led* is the past tense and participle of the verb *lead*, which means "to conduct or escort." Occasionally *led* (rhymes with *fled*) is misspelled *lead* (rhymes with *plead*), perhaps because it and the metal *lead* are spelled alike. (See *mislead/misled*.)

leading question. The belief that a leading question is either embarrassing or unfair ("Have you stopped kicking your dog?") is incorrect. A leading question is simply one that suggests the answer desired ("You went to Des Moines last week, didn't you?").

least/lest. These words are unrelated and should not be confused with each other. *Least*, the superlative form of *little* (its comparative degree is *less*), is used of amount (the *least* amount of salt) and of importance (the *least* value). *Lest* is a conjunction meaning "for fear that" ("Be careful *lest* you slip on the ice") and "that," after words of fear or danger ("I was afraid *lest* he should ignore our plea"). *Lest* always takes a verb in the subjunctive mood, with or without *should*.

leastways/leastwise. Do not use these dialectal terms either in speech or in writing. They mean "at least," "at any rate," and their definitions are a better way of expressing them. (See *-wise*.)

leave/let. Some authorities say *"Leave me alone"* means "Get out of my sight," whereas *"Let me alone"* means "Don't bother me." Others say that the expressions are interchangeable and that they mean "Get away." Most word specialists prefer *let* in formal discourse. In other analogous uses, *leave* is unacceptable. *Let* alone carries the sense "to allow," "to permit"; *leave* means "to depart." In "My mother berates me for *leaving* my homework go," make it *letting*. Change *leave* in "Children, *leave* us all go now" and in *"Leave* it remain the way it is" to *let*. (See *let alone*.) But note that many *let* and *leave* idioms are established and are correct English. "The bus driver *let* me off at the corner." "My uncle is sure to *leave* a legacy."

lectern. See *dais/podium/lectern*.

led. See *lead/led*.

legal. See *lawful/legal*.

legendary/mythical have a sense in common. They both mean "fabulous"—that is, beyond belief. *Legendary* is opposed to historical ("Robin Hood is a *legendary* person"); *mythical* is opposed to actual ("Venus was the *mythical* goddess of love"). That which is *legendary* is traditional (a *legendary* tale). A *mythical* place, like Serendip, exists only in myths; it is not based on reality. A *mythical* person in nonexistent. No matter how firmly people believe he is alive, the belief is unprovable; hence made up. This latter definition has given rise to another meaning for *mythical*—a deliberate artifice.

legible. See *readable/legible*.

lend. See *loan/lend*.

***l* endings.** Those writers who double a final *l* before a suffix (*travelled, travelling; cancelled, cancelling*) follow the British style. The preference in America is not to double (*traveled, traveling; canceled, canceling*). A word that is both noun and verb, *marshal*, is often seen with an unnecessary *l* (*marshall*, noun; *marshalled*, verb). Make it *marshal, marshaled*.

less. See *fewer/less.*

less/well. Hyphen *less* and *well* compounds before a noun (*a less-motivated student, a well-read book,* but not following a noun ("His name is *less known* in the city." "He is a physicist *well liked* in his profession").

lest. See *least/lest.*

let. "Let you and I leave promptly" needs grammatical surgery. Change *I* to the objective case *me.* "Let you and *me* leave promptly." (See *leave/let.*)

let alone is an informal expression in the sense "much less." In formal style "We cannot afford a Chevrolet, *let alone* a Porsche" needs amending to *much less* a Porsche. (See *leave/let.*)

let's, a contraction of *let us,* is standard English but best confined to speech and informal writing. *Let's us* is an illiteracy. Clearly either *'s* or *us* should be omitted. *Let's* already says *let us.*

liable/likely/apt Although their meanings have come to overlap somewhat, especially in the sense of "probability," the words are often interchanged, even though one or the other would be more suitable. Careful users still treat them distinctively. *Apt* means "naturally inclined, appropriate, suitable" (*apt* to dance when he hears music, an *apt* choice of words). *Likely* suggests a likelihood, that which is expected or probable ("The heavens say it is *likely* to snow today"). *Liable* means both "obligated" ("A father is *liable* for the debts of his minor children") and "exposure to something regrettable, unpleasant consequence" ("If you don't study, you're *liable* to fail"). The most common misuse of these words is *liable* for *likely,* as in "You are *liable* to see him playing tennis any Sunday." This usage is so widespread that perhaps it has achieved legitimacy. Nevertheless, if nothing disadvantageous or burdensome is involved, use *likely,* not *liable.*

liaison, "a connecting link," is a tricky word to spell. Note the *iai.* Stress the last syllable—lee-ae-*zawn.*

libel/slander. These words mean "defamation," which is an injury to a person's reputation. The same defamatory statement may be a libel or a slander. Which it is depends on how the statement was made. If written and published, it would be libelous; if spoken, it would be slanderous. Popular usage ignores these distinctions; careful users of English observe them.

light. See *in the light of.*

lighted/lit. Since either form is correct (both are past tenses and participles of *light*), your ear must select one or the other. The governing factors are rhythm and euphony, tenuous guidelines indeed. In some instances, however, *light* has developed an idiomatic sense. For example, you are more likely to use *lighted* as the adjective form ("Allan is dangling his *lighted* cigarette") and *lit* when a verb is called for ("Allan *lit* his cigarette").

lightening/lightning. Occasionally misspelled. More often *lightening* appears where *lightning* is intended. *Lightening* is the lessening of weight; *lightning* is an electrical discharge.

light-year. "Considering how much time the project has taken, we must be *light-years* away from our goal." This sentence is wrongly put. A light-year is a measure of distance, not of time. For the technically minded, a light-year is the distance that light travels in one year in a vacuum, or 5,878,000,000,000 miles.

likable. See *salable*.

like/as. The grammatical world was thrown into a tailspin by a cigarette company which insisted that "Winston tastes good *like* a cigarette should." Since then, reams have been written to explain the differences between *like* and *as* and their distinctive uses. And yet questions concerning correct usage are easily answered. *Like*, which means "similar to" or "such as," is a preposition that compares nouns and pronouns. *As*, the equivalent of "in the way that," is a subordinate conjunction that compares adverbs, adverbial phrases, or adverbial clauses. *Like* is used when a comparison is made of two persons or things, ("Jerry looks *like* his father." "This house is *like* my mother's"); *as*, when a verb follows the questioned word ("Do it *as* I told you"). Note the verb *should* in the "Winston" sentence. This means that in formal English we can't "Tell it *like* it is." (See *as/like*.)

like compounds are spelled solid (*catlike, ladylike*) unless preceded by a noun ending in a double *l* (*bell-like*). Whether to hyphen if only one *l* precedes or if a combination seems awkward is a writer's decision to make. For example, although *boylike* is spelled as given, *girl-like* is often seen with a hyphen—and so is *molasses-like*.

like for. Not infrequently one hears this kind of sentence, "My teacher said she would *like for* us to finish promptly." The verb *like* in that construction takes a direct object, which may not be introduced by a preposition. Delete *for*. (See *for you to*; *mean*.)

like for instance, a not uncommon conglomeration of words, is nonstandard. In "I hate certain kinds of movies, *like for instance* war pictures or pictures of violence," delete *like* and insert a comma after *instance*.

likely. "It is *likely* to snow tomorrow" is good grammar, but not "It will *likely* snow tomorrow." In the first sentence *likely* is an adjective; in the second, an adverb. Convention is firm that *likely*, when used adverbially with a verb in the future tense, must be accompanied by a qualifier such as *most*, *quite*, or *very*, as in "It will *most likely* snow tomorrow." Illogically, adverbs *probably* and *possibly* need not be qualified. "It will *probably* snow tomorrow" is unobjectionable. Caveat: A few authorities accept *likely* to mean "probably."

likes of in the sense "of a kind" is nonstandard. Do not say "He was such a poor actor the *likes of* which I'd never seen." Make it "such a poor actor as I'd . . ." or simplify, "I've never seen such a poor actor."

likewise. It is more gracious, and it is grammatically accurate, too, when acknowledging the introduction "I'm glad to meet you" to reply "I'm glad to meet you, too" rather than "Likewise." One meaning of *likewise* is "similarly," but it is not applicable here.

limited/delimited. "The debaters' introductory remarks are being *limited* [not *delimited*] to five minutes." *Delimited* means "marked off; fixed lines that separate boundaries" ("A six-foot fence *delimits* my neighbor's property from mine"). *Limited* means "confined within limits," that is, restricted, kept within bounds. It is often mistakenly used as a synonym for "slight" or "little." Instead of "Elaine has a *limited* time to spend," say "a little or a short time." And rather than use *limited* in the sense *few* or *small*, select a more precise word: *inadequate* capital, *scant* income, *meager* background.

limp/limpid. "After Carol's long run she fell *limpid* in my arms" confuses weakness with clarity. *Limpid* means "clear or transparent" (*limpid* pools), not "lifeless." To fall *limp* is to lack firmness or energy. Perhaps these words are confused because *limpid* is sometimes falsely influenced by *limp*.

linage/lineage are easily confused because each is a variant spelling of the other. The first, *linage*, is the number of lines of written or printed matter ("Printers charge according to *linage*"). The second, *lineage*, means "lineal descent from a common ancestor" ("Ambrose is proud of his *lineage*"). Note that each word has its own pronunciation—*linage* has two syllables; *lineage*, three.

line. See *in the line of*.

lineament/liniment. A *lineament* is an outline or contour of the body, especially of the face; a *liniment* is a soothing liquid rubbed on the skin, an ointment. Do not forget the *a* after the first *e* in *lineament*.

linguist is a word with two unrelated meanings. A *linguist* is a person who speaks several languages fluently. Or he may be a person specializing in linguistics, the science of language, and yet speak only one language.

linguistics is the science of language. Note that, although the word *linguistics* looks like a plural, it is singular and governs a singular verb.

liniment. See *lineament/liniment*.

linking verbs. See *copulative verbs*; *feel bad/feel badly*; *good/well*; *look*.

link together. See *join together/gather together*.

liquefy/rarefy. *Liquefy*, meaning "to make into a liquid," is spelled, unlike *liquid*, with only one *i*. Note the *e*. *Rarefy* is also spelled with an *e*, even though *rarity* has none.

listen, rather than hear, implies hearing with close attention: *listen* to the lecturer, *listen* to the President; but *hear* the rain, *hear* the waterfall.

literally/figuratively. Unfortunately, some writers occasionally misuse *literally* by attaching it to an expression that is clearly metaphorical. "Thompson *literally* hit the ceiling." "Agnes laughed so hard she *literally* split her sides open." "The President's speech *literally* brought the house down." None of these examples should be taken literally. *Literally* means "actually" or "in a manner true to the exact meaning of the words it accompanies." In each instance *literally* should be omitted. And not replaced by *figuratively*. All metaphors are figurative. *Literally* is properly used in a sentence that says what it means; a sentence that ordinarily seems metaphorical, but in this case is intended to be taken at its face value ("I *literally* threw the book at him, but, unfortunately it bounced off his left foot").

literary present. See *historical present/literary present*.

little knowledge. See *a little knowledge*.

lived. See *long-lived*.

livid/lurid. Perhaps the wisest thing to do with these words, when referring to color, is not to use them. Their original meanings are little understood or else completely ignored. *Livid* meant "of a bluish leaden color." But few persons today would believe that it means anything other than "red," a bright red at that. When a person is enraged ("furious" is a popular meaning of *livid*) and his face becomes *livid*, it should be ashen, but more likely it will be red. Hence to satisfy both the populist and the etymologist, name the color and avoid the word *livid* entirely. *Lurid* is another troublesome word. It means ghastly yellow (flame with smoke), the color of a sick person whose face is wan or pallid. Today *lurid* is most often used figuratively in the sense "sensational." A carnival with flashing lights and kaleidoscopic figures is "lurid," the very opposite of pallid.

llama. See *lama/llama*.

loan/lend. The better practice is to use *loan* as the noun and *lend* as the verb. Not "He *loaned* me his book" but "He *lent* me his book." The past tense of *lend* is *lent*, not "lended" or "loaned."

loath/loathe. Not to be confused. The first, which rhymes with *both*, is an adjective meaning "reluctant," "disinclined," or "unwilling" ("Masterson was *loath* to see his uncle"). The second, which rhymes with *clothe*, is a verb meaning "to detest" or "to abhor" ("Morris *loathes* pork sausages"). To distinguish the spellings of these words, remember that *loathe* and synonym *hate* both end in *e*.

locate in the sense of "settle" is impermissible in formal language.

locate/find should not be used synonymously. To *locate* is to find by search—that is, by hunting for something in a particular area. To *find* is "to meet with or to come upon by chance," without considering a particular place.

long-lived. Speakers troubled by the pronunciation of this word should think of "life" because it was the progenitor of this adjective. Both *life* and *lived* (in "long-lived") have a long "i"—and this applies also to *short-lived*. The past tense of the verb *live* (*lived*) is of course pronounced with a short "i."

longshoreman/stevedore. The basic distinction between these words is one of employment. A *longshoreman* (originally called an *alongshoreman*) works along the shore, loading and unloading vessels. A *stevedore* employs longshoremen. Although often used interchangeably in general speech, the words have these distinguishable meanings.

long way/long ways. "The school is a long ways from home." The school should teach that the accepted expression is "a long way."

long words. Note that although *long-suffering, long-range,* and *long-term* are spelled as given, with hyphens, *longstanding* and *longtime* are written solid.

look. When *look* means "to seem" or "to appear," it is followed by an adjective ("He *looks* rich"), as is true of *feel* (which see) and other *copulative verbs* (which see). When *look* is used as an intransitive verb meaning "to see with the eyes," its modifier is an adverb (*look* lovingly, *look* longingly).

look/looks. Those who like the sense and look of a sentence like "By the *looks* of things, we're headed for a recession" should use *look* rather than *looks* ("by the *look* of things").

looking. Change "We saw *as ugly a looking* animal today as we have ever seen" to "We saw *as ugly-looking* an animal. . . ."

loom/bulk. Idiom prescribes that these verbs be modified by *large* and not *largely* ("The ship *loomed large* in the moonlight").

loosen/unloosen mean "to unfasten or undo." You may decide whether to loosen or to unloosen your belt. The result will be the same. In this case the *un-* does not mean "not." (See *ravel/unravel.*)

lots of/a lot of. Expressions in which *lot* or *lots* mean "much," "a great deal of," or "a great many" (*a lot of* money, *lots of* vegetables), although occasionally seen in the works of respected writers, generally are avoided by formalists. But if used in this sense as the subject of a sentence, its verb should agree in number, not with *a lot* or *lots*, the grammatical subject, but with the noun or pronoun that follows *of* ("*Lots of* food *is* here." "*Lots of* books *are* on the shelf." "*A lot of* time *has* been wasted." "*A lot of* employees *have* reported in sick"). And note that *a lot* is spelled as given, with two words. Not *alot*.

loud. "He certainly spoke *loud*." Certainly this is the way most people say it, but formal writing prefers *loudly*, even though *loud* it just as good an adverb.

lovable. See *salable*.

love. Do not use this word loosely. If you *like* minestrone, say it that way, not "I *love* minestrone." Use *like* wherever it will do.

lunch/luncheon. Use the word *lunch* for an afternoon meal that is informal or customary. But if you invite a group to a structured occasion, your invitation should call it a *luncheon*. A more formal affair calls for a more formal word.

lurid. See *livid/lurid*.

lusty/lustful. Although both terms were derived from the same ancestor, their current meanings are far apart. *Lusty* has a favorable connotation—full of healthy vigor, robust ("Athletes are a *lusty* lot"). Its sense of healthfulness and strength has been extended to areas other than personal health (a *lusty* attitude toward his profession, a *lusty* swing of the bat). *Lustful* has acquired a pejorative sense—excessive sexual desires, lecherousness ("Women shunned him because of his *lustful* nature").

luxuriant/luxurious. "With so much wealth, it's no wonder he lived *luxuriantly*." The word required was *luxuriously*. *Luxuriant* means "thick," "growing profusely"; *luxurious* means "characterized by luxury or sumptuousness." The words are most frequently confused when used as adverbs: *luxuriantly, luxuriously*.

lying. See *laying/lying*.

_M_

machinate, meaning "to contrive," "to plot or to devise a plot," is pronounced _mak_-ih-naet. Its noun form, _machinations_, is a commoner word.

mad is colloquial in the sense of "angry." In formal English use _annoyed_ or _angry_. When _mad_ is combined with _about_ ("I'm _mad about_ chopped liver"), it is on a low rung of informal speech.

madam. This polite form of address to a woman is a variant import of French _madame_, and the American equivalent of _Mrs._ The plural form of both _madam_ and _madame_ is _mesdames. Mrs._ is an abbreviation for old English _mistress_, but only the abbreviated form is placed in front of a married woman's name. _Mrs._ has no plural, although some respected word-users recommend _Mmes._

Madison, Dolley. Those who have occasion to write the name of the wife of the fourth United States President should, to spell it properly, know that it is _Dolley Madison_, not _Dolly_. Incidentally, her given name was Dorothea.

maître d' is a term that has made some people wonder why it ends with _d'? Maître d'_ is an abbreviation for French _maître d'hôtel_, which means "master of the house." But as generally applied today, it refers to the headwaiter of a fancy restaurant. Pronounce it _meh_-truh-doh-_tehl_.

major is a comparative adjective meaning "greater in importance, size, amount, extent," and so on. A reference to "_the_ major orchestra of the year" is therefore incorrect. It might be "_a_ major orchestra" because a comparison is then being made with other orchestras that performed during the year. Some writers, rather than _major_, wisely choose a term such as _chief, great, principal, main,_ or _important_, which, although not synonymous with _major_, may be more suitable to the context.

majority. A majority is the larger number of a group divided into two unequal figures. If there are two candidates for an

156

office, the one receiving more votes than the other has a majority. But be careful not to use this term of things that are not countable. Do not say the majority of the sand was dumped on the left side of the yard, or the majority of the time we loaf. Say *most of*. Even when persons or items are countable, *majority* sounds pretentious where *most of* is what is meant. Rather than "*The majority* of the cousins dislike picnics," say "Most of." When the *majority* is much more than half, it may be termed *a great majority*, but not *the greater majority*. *Majority* takes a singular verb when the reference is to a precise number ("The *majority was* 496"), but a plural when the reference is to members of a group considered individually ("The *majority* of the boy scouts in our troop *were* good cooks").

malapropism is using the wrong word that sounds like the right one ("an *allegory* on the banks of the Nile"). Do not confuse *malapropism* with *spoonerism*, the accidental transposition of initial sounds in adjacent words ("The Lord is a *shoving leopard*").

manage. See *handle/manage*; *run/manage/operate*.

manageable. See *spelling*.

man-hater. See *teeth*.

mania. See *phobia/mania*.

maniacal, "affected with madness," "insane," is pronounced ma-*nye*-uh-kul, its second syllable sounding like a long *i*.

manifold/multiple. Distinguish these words. *Manifold* means "of many kinds" (*manifold* responsibilities). *Multiple* means "having many parts" (*multiple* interests).

manila envelope. See *roman letters/russian dressing*.

manner is a noun bound to cause wordiness. One often hears a sentence like "He did it *in a gracious manner*" rather than the more economical "He did it graciously." Or *in a stupid manner*, which means "stupidly." Replace *in a . . . manner* with an adverb.

manner born. See *to the manner born*.

manner of is a classifying phrase and therefore may not be followed by *a* or *an* ("What *manner of* man is he?" not "What *manner of a* man is he?"). (See *kind*; *type*.)

manslaughter. See *homicide/manslaughter/murder*.

manufacture. See *fabricate/manufacture*.

manuscript/typescript. The word *manuscript* literally refers to anything (a letter, a document) written by hand (Latin *scriptus,* "written," and *manus,* "hand"). *Typescript* is defined as "a typewritten manuscript," a contradiction in terms. Actually *typescript* refers to a typewritten copy of material keyed into a typewriter. Nowadays a *manuscript* need not be handwritten; it may be typewritten or produced by a word-processor.

many a. In "*Many a* dog and *many a* cat have been protected by my daughter," change *have* to *has* (*has* been protected), since the *and* here does not create a plural subject. *Many a* governs the number of the verb and requires a singular verb. Of course, without *a, many* takes a plural verb (*many* dogs and *many* cats *have* been).

marginal does not mean "small." It means "barely within a standard or limit of quality." That which is marginal is on the edge of approval or disapproval. A test score that is marginal, if it passed, has only barely passed. If it failed, it almost passed. Do not equate *marginal* with "small."

marital/martial. The first pertains to marriage; the second, to war. The first may be the breeding ground for the second.

marriage. See *wedding/marriage.*

marshal. See *l endings.*

martial. See *marital/martial.*

masterful/masterly. Although some dictionaries ascribe the meaning "expert" or "skillful" to both these words, in precise usage they should be distinguished. A *masterful* person is not necessarily expert or skillful; he is imperious, domineering, strong-willed. He behaves like a master. *Masterly* alone means "adroit," "expert," "skillful." A person's work or performance is masterly if executed proficiently.

materialize. Two things to remember. First, *materialize* is not a fancy synonym for "happen, develop, or come into existence." Second, that which materializes becomes physically perceptible ("The money we expected never *materialized*"). The following sentence borders on the absurd: "We are delighted that the predicted loss of our city's population did not *materialize.*"

mathematics. See *-ics.*

matinée. From the French *matin,* which means "morning," comes the English word *matinée,* which means "afternoon performance." Logic plays no part in the evolution of some English words.

matricide. See *patricide/matricide/parricide*.

matter. Too often an expression with *matter* (*as a matter of fact, for that matter, as a matter of course, a matter of life and death*, and so on) is unnecessary, and trite. Avoid it where you can. In "Picking a winner is *a matter of* sheer luck" and in "Selecting the stock leader for next year is *a matter of* guesswork," *a matter of* should be dropped. Sometimes a verb substituted for *a matter of* makes a more forceful sentence, and certainly a less hackneyed one ("Writing *is a matter of* skill and perseverance" reads better, "Writing *requires* (or *involves*) skill and perseverance").

may/might. "I'm thinking that I *may* take a course in psychology." "I'm thinking I *might* take a course in psychology." Both sentences are correct, and between *may* and *might* you may take your choice. However, in the opinion of some grammarians, *may* expresses a greater degree of probability than *might*. "I *may* go to the movies" implies that I have given serious thought to going and the likelihood is great. *Might* also connotes a possibility but one more remote. In ordinary speech the distinction between these words is little understood and even less observed.

Bear in mind that if the ambassador says "I *may* visit the White House tomorrow," in indirect discourse *may* becomes *might* (all verbs are put in the past tense): "The ambassador *said* he *might* visit the White House tomorrow." (See *can/may*.)

maybe/may be. *Maybe* is an adverb meaning "possibly," "perhaps" ("*Maybe* we'll leave soon"), and implying considerable uncertainty. *May be* is a two-word verbal phrase that expresses a corresponding meaning, "possibility" ("It *may be* that we'll leave soon"). Some writers prefer *perhaps* to *maybe*, perhaps because it sounds more formal.

maybes. See *dos, don'ts, and maybes*.

me/myself. See *-self/-selves*.

meager/meagre. See *theater/theatre*.

mean, in strict formal English, when used to express intention, is followed by a noun clause headed by *that*: "The adviser did not *mean* that they should suspend their research." In daily conversation *that* is acceptably omitted. But what is not acceptable is "The adviser did not *mean* for them. . . ." In the sense "disagreeable" or "ill-tempered," *mean* is informal. (See *for you to*; *like for*.)

meaningful is a meaningless word in many contexts. It should be used carefully, and sparingly, especially since everything said or written has meaning. But avoid such expressions as "a meaningful relationship."

meantime/meanwhile. Preferably use *meantime* as a noun to describe the interval between one event and another ("In the *meantime* I arranged for a vacation") and *meanwhile* as an adverb referring to the intervening time ("My wife was late; *meanwhile* I prepared dinner").

measure up, as in "to measure up to the requirements," is a colloquial expression that some authorities admit into formal English.

mediate. See *arbitrate/mediate*.

medium/media. "The television *media* is prepared to cover the election." Make it *medium*—there's only one. "The radio and television *media* are carrying the story live." Now there are two. (See *criterion*; *phenomenon*.)

meet/meet with. Although both mean "to encounter," they are not to be interchanged, since their usages are different. ("I usually *meet* my uncle strolling along a shopping street." "Helen *meets with* her bridge club every Wednesday"). In its ordinary sense *meet* means "to make the acquaintance of"; *meet with*, "to join company." You meet your neighbor when he moves into his house; you meet with your neighbor when you wish to discuss a common problem. *Meet with* has other idiomatic meanings ("to undergo," "to experience"), as in "Bruce *met with* a serious accident last week."

meet together. See *join together/gather together*.

meet up with. See *put up with*.

mêlée, "a confusing fracas," is pronounced with no accent—*may-lay*.

melody. See *harmony/melody*.

memento/momento. *Momento* is a mispronunciation, and an incorrect spelling, of *memento*. Souvenir hawkers peddle "mementos." And Webster's Third lists *momento* as a variant spelling. Despite all that, use only *memento* to mean "souvenir."

memorandum. For its plural, use either the Latin form *memoranda* or the English form *memorandums*. *Memorandas* has not been accepted into the English language.

menstruate has three syllables, not *mehn-strate* but *mehn*-struh-aet.

mental attitude is redundant, since almost all attitudes are mental. Drop *mental* unless a contrast is being made with an emotional or spiritual attitude.

meritorious/meretricious. The first word means "possessing merit," "deserving of honor." The second means "possessing the traits of a prostitute," from Latin *meretrix*, "a prostitute." The connotation of *meretricious* is that someone was lured to a bad or evil end by deceitful attractions. The purpose of a meretricious staging is to conceal evil-doing.

metal/mettle. Be careful to spell these words correctly. *Metal* is a class of substance (gold, tin, lead). *Mettle* is a basic quality of character, like fortitude or courage.

metaphor/simile, figures of speech, are terms that share a sense in common in that they point to a resemblance or make a comparison. A *metaphor*, an implied comparison, is applied directly—that is, with no introductory words. It is never literally true ("She is a doll." "He is a tower of strength"). Of course she is not really a doll, nor is he a tower. A *simile* expresses a comparison between two unlike objects by using *as* or *like* ("She is *like* a doll"). Be sure that a reference to one of these figures of speech is called by its right name. Do not confuse.

meter/metre. See *theater/theatre*.

meteorology is a science that deals with the weather. Note that it begins with *meteor*. Do not spell it or pronounce it *meterology*.

method/methodology are not interchangeable terms. A *method* is a way of doing something. *Methodology* is the system of methods or procedures. Those who, instead of *method*, use the latter term thinking it sounds more impressive, are wrong on two counts.

meticulous/scrupulous. Interchanging these words is not uncommon, but it ought not be done. *Meticulous* means "finicky," "fussy." *Scrupulous* means "conscientious." Note that *meticulous* does not mean merely "careful" or "thorough"; it implies painstaking concern about small details, as is a person who is overcareful. But it should also be noted that in today's prevalent use, *meticulous* has a favorable connotation, that of being exact or precise. For the sake of clarity the context should make clear whether *meticulous* means "careful," a commendable sense, or "overcareful," a questionable one.

mid-. Spell compounds as one word (*midair, midday*) unless the second element is capitalized (*mid-Pacific*).

midnight. See *noon/midnight.*

midriff is the section between the chest and the waist. Regarding garments, *midriff* has two opposite meanings—a garment which reveals this section and a garment which covers it.

might. See *may/might.*

might of is an impropriety for *might have* ("He *might have* [not *might of*] gone if he had been invited"). (See *should of; would of.*)

might perhaps. "We spoke to him at length. Now he thinks he *might perhaps* do it." Both *might* and *perhaps* suggest a possibility. To avoid a redundancy, use one or the other.

mighty. It is mighty informal to use *mighty* this way—as an adverb meaning "very" or "exceedingly." Use it as an adjective signifying power or great size (*"Mighty* Mouse").

mileage. See *usage/mileage.*

milieu, "surroundings," "environment," is pronounced me-*lyuh.*

militate/mitigate. "His lack of education *militated* against his advancement." The key to the correct use of *militated* in the example is the preposition *against,* since *against* always follows *militate* but not *mitigate.* The combination *mitigate against* does not exist. *Militate* means "to have an adverse effect or influence on"; *mitigate,* "to lessen, moderate, or make less severe" ("The defendant's plea was so moving that the judge *mitigated* the sentence"). Note that *mitigate* always takes a direct object.

million/millions. When troubled by whether to use the singular or plural form, remember that *million* is used with specific numbers—two million people attended—and *millions* in other cases—millions of insects in the swamp. Incidentally, *million,* although a singular form, may serve as either a singular or a plural. It normally is treated as a plural—two million books *were* sold—but as a singular when money is involved—two million dollars *was* spent.

mimic/panic. These words add a *k* in all their other forms (*mimicked, panicking, mimicker, panicky*).

mineralogy has an *a* in the middle. Not *minerology*, but *mineralogy*. (See *genealogy*.)

minus. Everyone knows that *minus*, as in "Herman came *minus* his toupee," means "without" or "lacking." And so *minus* in this sense has come to be generally accepted. But in formal writing, prefer a replacement. Rather than "Florence is *minus* two teeth," make it "Florence lost two teeth" or "has two teeth missing."

minuscule is a word bound to pick up a few losers in a spelling contest. Although referring to something small, it does not begin with *mini*, as in *miniskirt* or *minibike*, but with *minus*.

minutia/momentum. You may use either plural form, the anglicized *minutias* and *momentums* or the Latin *minutiae* and *momenta*.

mischievous has three syllables only and is pronounced *mihs-chihv-uhs*. Note the middle syllable. It is not *cheehv*.

mishap/accident. An accident need not be an unfortunate occurrence. The primary meaning of *accident* is "something that happens by chance, without design." You might meet your college roommate by accident. The primary meaning of *accident* has shifted, however, so that it now suggests not only the unexpected but the unfortunate, like an automobile accident. A *mishap* is a relatively minor accident; injuries, if any, are superficial. A collision resulting in a fatality is an accident.

mislead/misled. Be particularly careful to use the latter form for the past tense of *mislead*. "The public was *mislead* by the ad" needs *misled*.

misplaced modifiers. "Do you *ever* think there'll be a substantial reduction in the federal budget?" is better stated "Do you think there'll *ever* be." Note the shift of *ever*. (See *only*.)

misquotations. Quotations are effective devices to spark up one's writing. But be certain not to misquote. For example, "To gild refined gold, to paint the lily" is correct, not *to gild the lily*; "pride goeth before destruction, and an haughty spirit before a fall," not *pride goeth before a fall*; "All that glisters is not gold," not *glistens*; "For whom the Bell Tolls," not *bells*; "I am escaped with the skin of my teeth," not *by*. And note that music hath charms to soothe the savage breast, not *beast*, and that money is not *the root of all evil*, but the root is the love of money. (See *more honored in the breach*; *nor any drop to drink*; *not all*.)

misspell. A particularly embarrassing word to "mispell" is *misspell*, as in this sentence. Note the two *s*'s.

mistakened is not an English word. Use *mistaken* ("He's *mistaken* [not *mistakened*] about the nature of the transaction").

mister. See *Mr.*

mistrust/distrust. Whether you *mistrust* or *distrust* someone, the point is you do not trust him. Although the key words have slightly different connotations, they're synonymous and interchanging them should cause no problem. *Mistrust* is the weaker of the two. It suggests a loss of confidence in a person or a suspicion as to his motives. *Distrust* connotes a settled belief that there can be no faith in the person concerning the matter at hand. A person who mistrusts someone, we might say, can be bent in another direction. A person who distrusts is rigid in his opinion.

mob. See *shortened words*.

mobile/movable. These words pertain to something movable; that is, not fixed in one place or position. The distinction between them lies in the ease with which the object can be moved. If it can be moved but only with great difficulty, like a large printing press, the object, although *movable*, cannot be said to be *mobile*. A vacuum cleaner is *mobile*.

mode. See *fashion/mode*.

modern/modernistic as applied to decorations, furnishings, and structures are synonymous, although different connotations have attached to each word. *Modern* is used correctly when referring to contemporary works and designs. And so is *modernistic*—except that its sense is often "exaggerated modern," that which is too experimental, too avant-garde, to merit acceptance as a satisfying aesthetic product. Be careful with this word. *Modernistic* may sound deprecatory.

modest/shy are not synonymous terms. A *modest* person is not necessarily *shy*. *Modest* means humble, free from vanity. A *shy* person is not assertive; he is timid, easily frightened. He dislikes being conspicuous. *Shy of* meaning "lacking" is colloquial. Rather than "We are *shy of* two dictionaries," make it "*short of.*"

modifiers should be so placed as to modify the proper word. Change "All the books were *not* lost" to "*Not* all the books were lost." And their position should not alter the meaning: "*Even* Ralph cannot see that far"; "Ralph *even* cannot see that far"; "Ralph cannot see *even* that far." Be particularly careful with the placement of *only, also, almost,* and *still.* (See *also; even; not all; only.*)

momentarily/temporarily. Although both these words refer to a limited time, they take different constructions. *Momentarily* is used when the main verb is in the future tense ("The doctor *will* return *momentarily*"); *temporarily,* when the verb is in the present tense ("The community *is temporarily* without electricity").

momento. See *memento.*

momentum. See *minutia/momentum.*

money. Its preferred plural form is *moneys* rather than *monies.* (See *dollar sign.*)

mongoose. You may not often have need to use the plural form of this word, but if you do, remember it is *mongooses,* not *mongeese.*

monologue is entertainment by a single speaker. If the speaker is entertaining only himself, and there is no audience, change *monologue* to *soliloquy* (Latin *solus,* "alone," and *loqui,* "to speak"). The spelling *monologue* is preferred to *monolog.* (See *catalog.*)

moose/fish. *Fish* enjoys two plural forms, *fish* and the less often used *fishes.* But *moose* has no alternative plural forms; it is always *moose* whether a singular or a plural.

moot. A problem word because it is used in two ways, each almost opposite to the other. Its primary sense is "arguable." Something debatable is *moot.* But *moot* has also come to mean "academic," "hypothetical," because the matter raised has already been decided, leaving no arguable point to settle.

more. See *better.*

more/rather. In "It was *more* sensible to sell the car in Oklahoma *rather than* to drive it to New York and sell it there," delete *rather. More* and *rather,* expressing the same sense, do not belong in the same sentence. You might say "Algernon worries *more* about you *than* he does about himself" or "Algernon worries about you *rather than* himself" (but not "worries *more* about you *rather* than himself").

more and more should not be followed by *than*. In "The Supreme Court has granted *more and more* powers to the Government than were originally intended," drop *and more*.

more honored in the breach, a quotation from *Hamlet*, means that it is more honorable to breach, or break, this custom than to observe it—that is, the custom is best not observed. The expression is often misinterpreted to mean that the custom—and in general usage some desirable activity—is more frequently broken or ignored and not enough observed. Either use it right or avoid it. (See *misquotations*.)

more importantly. See *importantly*.

more than. See *better than*.

more than/over. The problem here is whether good usage prefers one or the other when countables are involved. The predominant choice is *more than* ("The school now employs *more than* five substitute teachers"). But it should be borne in mind that although *over* has an informal ring, its use would not be wrong. Certainly where collective quantity is concerned, *over* is well established and enjoys some authoritative support ("Our royalties for six months came to *over* $20,000." "The fighter weighed *over* 180 pounds"). (See *in excess of; under*.)

more than one idiomatically takes a singular verb when followed by a singular noun as subject. Not logically, mind you, since it expresses a plural idea, but idiomatically ("*More than one* plan *has* been suggested"). Yet, when the phrase is divided—"Today *more* cars *than one were* stolen from the parking lot"—a plural verb (*were*) is required because plural *cars* governs the number of the verb. *All but one* also is notionally plural, but when the phrase is followed by a noun ("He swallowed *all but one* pea") or in the passive ("*All but one* pea *was* swallowed"), it is singular. When the phrase is separated from a following noun, the form of verb required is plural ("*All but one* of the peas *were* swallowed").

morning. See *time*.

moron. See *idiot/imbecile/moron*.

Moslem/Muslim. The words are interchangeable. Both refer to an adherent of Islam. Most believers in the faith, established by Mohammed, prefer *Muslim* because it is closer to the Arabic pronunciation.

most. "*Most* everybody is bound to make a grammatical blunder now and then," like the one in this sentence. The first word should have been *almost*, which means "nearly"—as almost everyone knows.

mostly all, as in "*Mostly all* the students left," should be rephrased "almost all" or "nearly all." Adverb *mostly*, which means "almost entirely," "for the most part," is used correctly in "Stella's interests are *mostly* in classical literature." "The members consisted *mostly* of old men."

most well-known. In "At the time of his death, Chagall was the *most well-known* painter in France," change to *best known*.

mother-in-law. When the mothers by the law attend a family reunion, they are *mothers-in-law*, not *mother-in-laws*. (See *possessive case forms.*)

motto. See *slogan/motto*.

movable. See *mobile/movable*.

Mr. is an abbreviation of *mister*, a title of respect addressed to men. Unless spelled as a word, *mister* is written only in its abbreviated form. Its plural form is not *Messers.* but *Messrs.*—one *e*.

Mrs. See *Madam*.

Mt. Fuji. See *Rio Grande/Sahara/Mt. Fuji*.

much. Often used to modify participles ("His plan has been *much* admired" or "*very much* admired"). *Very* may modify *much*, the adverb modifier of the participle, but *very* may not modify a participle directly unless the participle has lost its verbal function and is now considered an adjective ("We are *very* pleased," "*very* interested," "*very* worried"). Note that *much* is hyphened when part of a compound modifier (*much*-respected mayor, *much*-disliked controller) but not when used in a predicate position ("The controller is *much* disliked"). If *much* itself is qualified (a very *much* agitated producer), no hyphen is required. (See *very*.)

much less. This phrase remains tricky, considering how often it is used. It belongs only in negative, and never in affirmative, contexts ("My roommate is so sloppy that I wouldn't lend her my black gloves, *much less* my white ones").

multiple. See *manifold/multiple.*

mumps is one of many nouns that are singular, although plural in form. "*Mumps is* contagious," not "*Mumps are.*"

murder. See *homicide/manslaughter/murder.*

Muslim. See *Moslem/Muslim.*

must. See *got/gotten.*

must of is substandard for *must have.* (See *should of.*)

mutual. See *common/mutual.*

mutual cooperation is a trite and redundant way of providing emphasis. Equally redundant is *mutual teamwork.* In neither expression does *mutual* serve any purpose. The phrase *mutual advantage of both* needs *of both* excised, since implicit in mutual is that which is experienced by each of two or more persons.

myself. See *-self/-selves.*

mythical. See *legendary/mythical.*

nadir. See *zenith/nadir.*

naiveté. See *accent marks.*

naked/nude. These words are troublesome to some people—those who can't mouth them; those who can't write them; and those who can't bear even to read them—especially the word *naked*. The sense of both words is to be without clothing, bare, unclad. But in the minds of some, *naked* seems barer than *nude*. Between the two, *nude* is preferred in "polite" society, which has the benefit of great artists to support this preference. Goya, for example, didn't paint *naked* women; he painted *nudes.*

named for is preferable to *named after*. "Johnnie was *named for* his grandfather" rather than "*named after* his grandfather." And prefer *named* to *by the name of*. "A senator *named* Johnson" is better than "A senator *by the name of* Johnson."

namely. See *viz.*

nary (usually followed by *a* or *an*), as in "We'll give him *nary* a cent," means "not one." It is dialectal and should be so confined.

nation. See *countries/nations.*

natural instincts are two words that should not be mated because *natural* means "produced by nature" and an *instinct* is a natural feeling or an inborn tendency.

nature. Sentences employing *nature* in phrases such as "a remark of an adverse nature," instead of *an adverse remark*, or "a combination of a questionable nature," instead of *a questionable combination*, use *nature* superfluously. Eliminate it and see the improvement.

naught/aught. Those concerned with selecting a synonym for *zero*, or *cipher*, may choose either lead word. Some authorities prefer *naught*; others, *aught*. Although unattested, it is believed that *naught* came from a fusion of the *n* in *an* (of *an aught*) with *aught*; hence *naught*. *Naught* predominates.

nauseous, correctly used, means "arousing nausea." If you are *nauseous*, you make people sick, as gas fumes do. When you're feeling queasy, you are *nauseated*—that is, sick in the stomach. Remember that one feels *nauseated* not *nauseous*.

naval/navel. Be certain, when referring to the mark on the abdomen where the umbilical cord was attached, to write *navel*, and not *naval*. That latter word is used only of matters pertaining to the navy.

near disaster. "He spun his steering wheel sharply left and avoided a *near disaster*." Not a *near disaster*, but a *disaster*. What he had was a near disaster. But with *escape* or *accident*, make it a *narrow escape* or *what was almost an accident* rather than *near escape* or *near accident*.

near future is uneconomical wordage for *soon*.

nearly. See *close to*; *only*.

necessity/need. "There is no *necessity* to leave early." "There is no *need* to leave early." Although the words *need* and *necessity* are synonymous, idiomatically they are treated differently. *Necessity* may be followed by "of" or "for," but not by an infinitive, as in the first sentence. Make it "There is no *necessity for* his leaving early." *Need* is properly used with an infinitive, as in the second sentence. But sometimes the infinitive is not expressed with *to* ("You *need* not [*to*] leave").

née. "Mrs. Joan Smithfield, *née Joan McKellen*." She was born into a family that had a family name, but she was not born with a given name. She got that later. Make it "Mrs. Joan Smithfield, *née McKellen*. You may spell *née* with or without the French accent.

need. One may correctly say, "All the dog trainer *needs to do* is whistle" or "All he *need do* is whistle." Only when serving as an auxiliary verb before an expressed infinitive is *needs* (the third-person singular) necessary. (See *necessity/need*.)

needless to say is as unnecessary a formulation as *it goes without saying*, yet both serve to call particular attention to a thought about to be propounded. The expressions are useful transitional devices, especially when there is a shifting of thoughts. But be aware that some critics do not agree. They argue that what is needless to say should not be said. But that goes without saying.

negative misuses. A positive pronoun should not have as its antecedent a negative-noun compound. In "*No* athletes were permitted to leave the grounds during the day, and *they* were not allowed to sleep off the campus either," make it "Athletes *were not* permitted. . . ."

neglect/negligence. The distinction in the meanings of these words should be carefully noted. Both mean "a failure to attend to." *Neglect* refers to a failure to perform a specific act ("John's failure to pay his income tax by the due date was gross *neglect*"). *Negligence* may be a trait of character; it connotes habitual neglect ("His *negligence* at work cost him his job").

neighborhood. See *in the neighborhood of*.

neither, when not accompanied by *nor*, is singular and accordingly takes a singular verb. Meaning "not either," it may function as a pronoun or an adjective. "*Neither is* acceptable" (a pronoun). "*Neither* box *is* any good" (adjective).

neither . . . nor, meaning "not one or the other," is the proper combination; *neither . . . or* is always wrong. In "In politics I have favored *neither* the right *or* the left, but remained in the center," change *or* to *nor*. The sentence "*Neither* husband *nor* wife were present at the ceremony" violates another rule, that in this construction the verb agrees with the nearer noun. Therefore, "*Neither* husband *nor* wife *was*. . . ." As with all correlative conjunctions, the construction should be grammatically parallel. Change "*Neither* the captain was present *nor* the players at the annual dinner" to "*Neither* the captain *nor* the players *were* . . ." so that the alternatives are in structural balance.

nemesis. In Greek mythology the goddess of retributive justice was Nemesis. From her name (with a small *n*) evolved a word meaning "avenger." In popular usage, however, *nemesis* has come to mean "a longstanding and formidable opponent," an enemy. Sports reporters frequently equate *nemesis* with "traditional conqueror." If team A loses regularly to team B, B, it is said, is A's nemesis. This usage is not accepted in better writing.

nephew. Pronounced *nehf*-yoo in the United States except by persons of British descent, who say *nehv*-yoo.

nerve-racking is sometimes erroneously spelled *nerve-wracking*. *Wrack* was derived from an archaic word meaning "wreck" or "ruin." A *rack* was an instrument of torture on which a person was stretched. If your experience were nerve-wracking, it would wreck your nerves. More likely it was nerve-racking, meaning your nerves were stretched so much that you were beside yourself. If you *rack* (not *wrack*) your brains, you strain them to recollect something. If you wrack them, they might go to "wrack and ruin," which implies "destruction." But if you must use this feeble cliché, make it *rack and ruin*. Caveat: some dictionaries list *nerve-wracking* as a variant of *nerve-racking*, and some admit only *wrack and ruin*.

never is not the equivalent of *not*. Rather than "He *never* mentioned the subject during the two hours we spent together," say "He did *not* mention."

nevertheless. Usually followed by a comma when it stands at the beginning of a sentence ("*Nevertheless*, everyone thinks it should be done"). But euphony and rhythm determine whether to punctuate when its placement is internal ("Everyone, *nevertheless*, thinks it should be done" or "Everyone *nevertheless* thinks . . ."). (See *nevertheless/nonetheless*.)

nevertheless/nonetheless mean "however" or "in spite of." Two questions that sometimes arise are whether shorter words (*still, but, yet*) would be as effective and whether *nonetheless* should be written as one word. The answer in both instances is yes. *Nonetheless* originally was written as three words—*none the less*—but no longer.

newfangled, meaning "excessively novel," sounds like slang. But it isn't. And it is not a newfangled word either. It is an old one, long established.

new innovation is just as redundant as *old antique*.

newly. When *newly* is attached to an element which together form a noun, the compound is spelled as one word—*newlywed* ("He is a *newlywed*"). When a verb follows *newly*, two words are required ("He is *newly* wed").

news. In "The *news* are all good today," *news* is treated as a plural, probably because of its plural form. But it should not be; it's a singular word, and takes a singular verb. A story has it that Horace Greeley was telegraphed the question "Are there any news?" to which he replied, no doubt with tongue in cheek, "Not *a new*."

nexus, which is both singular and plural (another plural form is *nexuses*), is a link or connection and is not a synonym for *focus*. *Focus*, outside the field of optics, means "a central point of attention or activity." (See *focus*.)

nice has become a favorite in colloquial speech, perhaps because it is an omnibus word generally regarded as a synonym for *kind, agreeable, refined, good-tempered, pleasing, accurate, respectable,* and others too many to mention. Discriminating speakers and writers reject this blanket term for one more precise. In fact, in formal composition, the only meanings accepted for *nice* are "discriminating" and "precise": a *nice* distinction; a *nice* eye for color.

nice and is used colloquially as an intensive ("The room is *nice and* large." "The soup is *nice and* hot"). In more precise speech and writing, replace *nice* with "very" or some other appropriate word. (See *try and*.)

nickel. Its variant spelling is *nickle*. In educated writing *nickel* predominates.

niece. Sometimes misspelled *neice*. Check it before using.

nincompoop. See *dumbbell/numskull/nincompoop*.

nine. Remember that although all words that represent this number begin, in one form or another, with *nine*—*ninety, ninefold, nineteen, ninety-one, ninetieth*—the exception is *ninth*. Somewhere or other it lost its *e*.

no is often heard, and acceptably so, in a statement such as "My uncle is *no* better today." But in strict formal usage *no* would be changed to *not any*. And so with "Your dress is *no* different from my sister's" except that it would be recast *not at all*. (See *yes/no*.)

no ... and no, as in "*No* man *and no* woman belonging to the opposite party *is* allowed to enter," idiomatically takes a singular verb, even though the subject, conjoined by *and*, is apparently a plural. (See *every ... and every*.)

nobody. See *no one*.

nod. Some people misunderstand the meaning of a *nod*. A person who nods his head, that is, moves it up and down, means "yes," as is often done by bidders at an auction to indicate approval of a bid. Those who write "The chairman *nodded* his head no" have misconstrued the meaning of that movement.

no good, as in "That watch is *no good*," meaning "useless or worthless," is colloquial.

nohow. Avoid this common colloquial expression meaning "not in any way," "not at all," "by no means." Instead of "I do not agree with them *nohow*," make it "I do not agree with them *at all*."

noisome should not be confused with "noisy." The word in no way refers to *noise*. *Noisome* means "foul-smelling."

nom de guerre. See *pseudonym*.

nom de plume. See *pseudonym*.

non-. Spell *non-* compounds as one word (*nonreligious, nonbelligerent, noncooperative*) unless the second element is capitalized (*non-American*). (See *nonesuch*.)

none. If *none* can be logically made singular, it should be ("*None* of the six persons *is* missing." "*None* of the books *was* worth reading"). But the belief that *none* always connotes a singular sense is not supported by the weight of authority. Many of the most particular writers use either a singular or a plural verb with *none*, depending on the tenor of the sentence. Possibly the best rule to follow is to use a singular if the idea of *none* is "no one" or "not one" ("*None was* there." "*None* of them *is* to be selected") but a plural if the meaning suggested is "not any" ("No auto parts were delivered today, and *none are* expected"). Not everyone will agree with all your decisions anyway. If the case is questionable, as was said in the first sentence, prefer the singular.

nonesuch is not a compound introduced by *non-* but by *none*. Do not omit the central *e*.

nonetheless. See *nevertheless/nonetheless*.

noon/midnight. *Noon* is correctly designated 12M. The M stands for Latin *meridies*. *Midnight* is designated 12 P.M., the P meaning "post" or past the noon hour (*meridiem*).

no one, as the subject of a sentence, is spelled as two words without a hyphen. It is always singular; hence the verb it governs and all its referents are likewise singular ("*No one is* allowed to go without *his* passport"). These guidelines also apply to *nobody* except that it is spelled as one word.

noplace/someplace/anyplace/everyplace. Many authorities accept these "place" words as adverbs meaning *nowhere, somewhere, anywhere,* and *everywhere* ("I saw it *noplace*") and write them as one word. But it is safer, and more in keeping with formal style, to use *nowhere,* etc., instead of *noplace,* etc. Note that when *place* is used as a noun—"*Every place* was inspected"—two words are required, and its usage is accepted by everyone on all levels of writing. (See *nowhere.*)

nor. See *or/nor.*

nor any drop to drink is the way Coleridge put it in *The Rime of the Ancient Mariner,* not "Water, water everywhere, and *not* a drop to drink." During Coleridge's days *rhyme* was spelled *rime.* Today *rime* is hoarfrost, though some authorities accept it as a variant of *rhyme* (which see). (See *misquotations.*)

north. See *compass directions.*

no sooner. Follow by *than,* not *when* ("*No sooner* had the dance begun *than* (not *when*) the electricity was turned off").

nostalgia. The original meaning of this word—severe homesickness—should be preserved. But today's popular meaning is "longing for something in the past," and it is in that sense that *nostalgia* is most frequently used, even by careful writers.

not. See *never.*

notable/noted/notorious. Although *notable* and *noted* suggest the remarkable or the distinguished, and may be used either of persons or of things, *notable,* with its sense of worthy of notice or attention, is preferably applied to things or events, whereas *noted,* since it refers to the celebrated or famous, is more appropriately applied to persons. *Notorious* implies ill-repute, referring to a person whose character is unsavory. It is always used in an unfavorable sense ("He's a *notorious* card cheat"). (See *famous/notorious.*)

not about to, implying determination, as in "My uncle is *not about to* retire," is informal. Delete *not,* and the phrase as a positive becomes standard English. "He is *about to* retire" is acceptable on all levels.

not all. "All that glitters is not gold," although repeated ad nauseam, in strict formal English should be reworded, "*Not all* that glitters is gold" because gold is among those things that glitter. To be logical, you should place *not* before the word or phrase it qualifies. Note the difference in sense between "*Not all* the graduates are being accepted by colleges" and "*All* the graduates *are not* being accepted by colleges." (See *adverbs*.) Incidentally, and returning to the first example, Shakespeare wrote "All that *glisters* is not gold," not *glitters*. (See *misquotations*; *modifiers*; *not everything*.)

not . . . because. One may rightly wonder what was meant by "He did not win because he pulled a leg muscle." That sentence could mean either that, because of his lameness he did not win, or that he won, but not because of the condition of his leg, which is absurd. If you place a comma after *win*—"He did not win, because he pulled a leg muscle"—the first meaning becomes clear.

not by any manner or means is not only wordy but incorrect. Make it "manner *of* means."

noted. See *notable/noted/notorious*.

not everything is the preferred wording rather than *everything is not*. (See *not all*.)

nothing but often leads to a false agreement when followed by a plural noun, as in "*Nothing but* hills *were* seen from our window." *Nothing* is the actual subject, and it always requires a singular verb (*was*).

nothing like in "*Nothing like* this has been seen before" is used correctly, but it is not in "Sally is *nothing like* so athletic as her sister." Make it "Sally is *not nearly*. . . ." *Nothing like* is not to be used adverbially for *not nearly*. (See *nowhere near*.)

not only . . . but also. The rule is that correlative conjunctions should be set out in parallel forms to achieve a grammatical balance. Thus "He *not only* is short *but also* fat" should be rearranged "He is *not only*." When only one principal verb is used, *not only* immediately precedes the element it modifies ("He was *not only* lost but scared"). If the sentence contains two principal verbs, *not only* is placed before the first verb and *but also* in front of the second. ("They *not only* went bankrupt *but also* absconded with the remaining assets").

notorious. See *notable/noted/notorious*.

not that is a colloquialism for *not very*. In "He is not *that* tall," change *that* to *very* in essay prose.

nouns as verbs. See *author/host*; *headquarters*; *host/gift*.

no use, as in "It was *no use* to argue with the principal," should be rendered in careful English *of no use*.

now. See *at present*; *at this point in time*.

nowhere. If you saw it *nowheres*, you didn't. If you saw it *noplace*, you also didn't—at least not in formal English. The only acceptable form is *nowhere*; *nowheres* is substandard, as is *no place* according to some, but not all, authorities. (See *noplace/someplace/anyplace/everyplace*; *nowhere near*.)

nowhere near, meaning "not nearly" ("It is *nowhere near* ten o'clock"), is an everyday informal phrase that does not belong in educated speech or writing. Use *not nearly*. (See *nothing like*; *nowhere*.

now pending is a common expression heard in speech and seen in newspapers. Yet it is an obvious redundancy. If the matter is pending, it is not settled or concluded. *Now* is superfluous.

nth degree. From the mathematical symbol n—an unspecified or indefinite number—has evolved this popular term. Its current meanings are "extreme" (to live up to the *nth degree*) and "utmost" (to apply oneself to the *nth degree*), even though these senses are foreign to the expression.

nude. See *naked/nude*.

number. See *amount/number*; *quantity*.

number, the (a). "A large *number* of houseboats was seen sailing down the river" needs *were seen*. The word *number* takes a singular or plural verb depending on whether the elements involved are regarded as individual units or as a whole. To accord with the rule, simply make it "*The number is . . .*" and "*A number are . . .*" ("*The number* of errors *is* small." "*A number* of improvements *are* to be made"). (See *total*.)

numbers. If styling numbers is troublesome (and you are unsure whether to spell them out or use figures), a good rule to follow is to spell out numbers less than one hundred and to express in figures those above a hundred ("My uncle is *forty-seven* years old." "The lease runs for *ninety-nine* years." "There are *104* oranges in the crate.") A number that begins a sentence

(*"Fifteen* men on the Dead Man's Chest"—Robert Louis Stevenson) should always be spelled out.

numbers, plural. See *spelling of plural numbers.*

numerous. See *innumerable.*

numskull. See *dumbbell/numskull/nincompoop.*

-o. The problem, when pluralizing a noun that ends in *o*, is whether to add an *e* before the final *s*. Some grammars suggest rules to follow, but they're shot through with exceptions. To be safe, look the word up in a dictionary. This sentence could make one jump—"One's *heroes* may ride *burros* in *rodeos* and eat *potatoes* while wearing *sombreros*."

obdurate. See *obstinate/obdurate*.

obiter dictum (Latin for "said in passing") is an incidental statement, a passing remark, or an opinion uttered as an aside. The phrase is often used to refer to a judge's opinion that is not binding.

obligated/obliged. Occasionally troublesome because they both imply a commitment. *Obligated* is used of legal obligations ("We are *obligated* to repay the loan we made last week"). *Oblige* has a more general sense and is often used with reference to social favors ("We feel *obliged* to invite them to our home"). Where these words are interchangeable, prefer the less formal *obliged*.

oblivious. Those who use *oblivious* according to its original meaning, "forgetful of something known in the past," should follow it with the preposition *of*. Those who adopt its extended meaning of "unaware" or "unconscious of," may follow it with either *of* or *to*.

obscure/abstruse are sometimes mistakenly interchanged, possibly because they both imply that something is hard to understand. *Obscure* means "not clear." A statement or a document that is obscure needs explaining because it is not expressed clearly. *Abstruse* means "difficult to understand." An abstruse statement or document is as difficult to understand as one that is obscure, not because it is not clearly expressed, but because it is too complicated for the listener or reader to comprehend. Synonyms of *abstruse* are *recondite, esoteric, arcane*.

observance/observation. Do not misuse *observance* for *observation*. The first is "the act or practice of complying with a law, custom, command, or other prescribed duty" ("The library is closed for *observance* [not *observation*] of Labor Day"). *Observation* is paying attention or noticing. Caveat: Not all dictionaries make these distinctions, but most do.

obsolete/obsolescent. *Obsolete* usually serves as an adjective, meaning "no longer in general use." Its employment as a verb, meaning "to discard as being out of date" ("The book published today *obsoletes* all those written on the same subject"), is controversial in that some authorities do not accept its verbal use, whereas others, equally distinguished, do. Note that *obsolescent*, a sister word, means "becoming outdated."

obstacle/impediment. Often confused, since both suggest a source of interference or a stumbling block to progress or further action. An *obstacle* literally ("The overturned cart on the roadway was an *obstacle* to homebound traffic") or figuratively ("His partner's narrow outlook was an *obstacle* to further expansion") is something that stands in the way of progress. An *impediment* does not so much obstruct as delay, hinder, or retard. Its original sense, "to tangle the feet," in Latin came to mean "baggage," and hence a burden. An impediment is still a burden in some ways. Lameness, speech defects, or other physical disorders are an impediment to performing certain tasks or jobs.

obstinate/obdurate are not comparable words and are therefore not interchangeable, even though both have the sense of "stubborn." The first means "not yielding," often stubbornly so, like a child refusing to obey. The second, *obdurate*, means "hardened." A person who cannot be convinced, no matter how pressing or logical the argument, is obdurate. His is a firm or hard stand, not subject to influence ("The boss remained *obdurate* to his employees' requests").

obtrusive. See *intrusive/obtrusive*.

obverse/reverse. The side of a coin with the principal design—the side with a head on it—is the *obverse*. The opposite side is the *reverse*.

obviate is wrongly used in "His problem was *obviated* when his uncle paid the bill." *Obviate* does not mean "remove" but "make unnecessary" ("His payment *obviated* legal action").

obviously evident. See *tautology.*

occasion. Sometimes seen misspelled with two *s*'s and one *c*. Watch it.

occur/happen/take place. These terms are not exactly synonymous. Occurrences and happenings are not prearranged. They happen by chance. *Occur*, a more formal word than *happen*, lends itself to a more specific event ("The accident *occurred* on the first of last month"). *Take place* suggests an arrangement of an event as to both time and place ("The inauguration will *take place* in St. Louis at two o'clock"). And something that takes place is usually of a longer duration than something that happens or occurs. (See *transpire.*)

occurrence/allotment. Two commonly misspelled words. Note that *occurrence* has a double *c* and a double *r. Allotment* is spelled with a double *l* but a single central *t.* If a suffix beginning with a vowel is attached to *allot*, the *t* is then doubled—*allotted, allotting.*

oculist/ophthalmologist/optometrist/optician. These are labels for professional people concerned with the health of eyes. A physician who specializes in eye care, after training in the treatment of eye defects and diseases, is called either an *oculist* or an *ophthalmologist*, depending on the physician's preference. The medical profession, generally, prefers the latter term. An *optometrist* is a doctor of optometry. He has been trained to measure the range of vision and prescribe corrective lenses, but not to prescribe medicine. An *optician* is a person trained in the making of eyeglasses and other optical goods. He may also sell these products.

-odd. Use with round figures (30-*odd* books), never with a precise figure (not 31-*odd* books). Hyphen *odd* when part of a compound (*odd-looking, odd-designed*) to avoid ambiguity (not "We have ten *odd* floor plans"). But note that *odd lot* ("He's selling an *odd lot* of shirts") is not a compound. No hyphen.

odd. See *queer/quaint/odd.*

odd lot. See *-odd.*

oddly enough. See *curiously enough/peculiarly enough/oddly enough.*

odds always takes a plural verb ("The odds *are* that we'll lose"). Although "*What's* the *odds?*" in which *odds* is treated as a singular is sometimes seen, grammarians would prefer "What *are* the *odds?*"

odious/odorous are not to be confused. *Odious* is hateful; *odorous* is having, yielding, or diffusing an odor, especially a fragrant or pleasant one.

odor. See *smell/stench/scent.*

of. Commonly one sees a sentence like "Bill Gussman of Yeadon will address tonight's meeting." Technically speaking, *of Yeadon* needs surrounding commas because it is a nonrestrictive modifier ("Bill Gussman, of Yeadon,"). Only if another Bill Gussman were being distinguished from the Bill Gussman of Yeadon would commas be unnecessary. (See *double possessive*; *from*; *off of/alongside of/out of.*)

of any/of anyone. "Frederick turned out to be the largest benefactor *of any.*" "His father is the busiest man *of anyone* in our town." These sentences need correcting. Make the first "the largest benefactor *of all.*" In the second drop *of anyone.*

of course. Whether to use commas with *of course* is a question of euphony. One might say "Of course, I think you should go" or "Of course I think you should go." In the second example the omission of a comma after *course* causes that word to be stressed. (See *comma.*)

officious/domineering. Although the sense of both is "bossy," they are not interchangeable. An *officious* person is meddlesome, persistently offering unwanted advice or services. A *domineering* person is more than meddlesome; he is arrogant, overbearing.

off of/alongside of/out of. Preposition *of* does not belong after preposition *off* ("He jumped *off of* the truck." "Take your feet *off of* the chair") or *alongside* ("His horse was hitched *alongside of* the post office"). But *of*, not *from*, properly follows *out* in "We saw him the moment he came *out of* the courtroom." *From* would be incorrect.

offspring, meaning "progeny," originally was a plural word, but it has come to be commonly used in the singular ("The boy is his *offspring*").

of phrase. Troublesome because a singular or a plural verb may follow an *of* phrase involving such nouns as *abundance, half,* and *part.* ("*Half is* all one could ask for." "*Half* of the delegates *are* from Missouri." "A *part* of the pie *is* for Ellen." "A *part* of the profits *are* for Tillie").

often has a *t* that is as silent as the *p* in *pneumonia* (noo-*mohn*-yuh), the *l* in *solder* (*sah*-duhr), or the *t* in *rapport* (rap-*pawr*).

oftener. A question sometimes raised is, Which is preferable, *more often* or *oftener?* Writers may take their pick, for both are acceptable. Select the one that affords the proper rhythm for the sentence.

oftentimes. Do not use this archaic term; use *often*.

of which/whose. Traditionally *of which* was applied in reference to inanimate objects, things ("The book *of which* the cover was torn is being repaired"). Its companion (*whose*) related to objects that possessed life—people, animals, plants, and so on ("a man *whose* life is," "a Persian cat *whose* habit was," "a Sycamore tree *whose* bark is"). Because of the awkwardness of the *of which* phrase, however, the trend has been to employ *whose* regardless of the nature of the object involved ("His was a thesis *whose* principles [rather than the principles *of which*] have become generally accepted"). Probably most of today's writers use *whose* unfettered by prescriptive decrees. (See *who's/whose*.)

ok is sometimes spelled *okay*, but this form is not generally approved. Use no periods with *ok* but add an apostrophe, as indicated, with the following endings: *ok'd, ok's, ok'ing*. If the plural of *okay* is used, write it *okays,* without an apostrophe.

-old. Note the two hyphens in such a sentence as "She is a 31-year-old woman." Although "He is an old fogey" takes no hyphen, "He is old-fashioned" does.

old adage/old cliché. An *adage* by definition is old, and a *cliché* would not be a cliché if concocted yesterday. Delete *old* and avoid a redundancy.

old antique. Redundant. See *new innovation*.

older. See *elder*.

old-fashioned. See *-old*.

omnium gatherum has come to be recognized as a useful dog Latin term for a mixture of many things. *Omnium* is the genitive plural of *omnis*, "all," and *gatherum* is from *gather* plus the Latin ending *um*. The term does not belong in formal texts.

on/onto. Often interchangeable, but *onto* suggests motion toward the object specified; *on* denotes "rest" or "a position atop something" ("The children sitting *on* the grass got up and jumped *onto* the bench").

on/upon. The choice between these words is yours to make (depends *on* you, depends *upon* the weather). Favor *on* in all instances except when overruled by idiom ("He was put *upon*").

on account of is verbose for *because*. "We left early *on account of* the rain" is reducible to *because of the rain*. Be sure not to include both *cause* and *account of* in the same sentence. In "The *cause* of his dismissal was *on account of* his frequent absences," say, simply, "His dismissal was *on account of*" or "The *cause* of his dismissal *was*."

on an average of, as in "We take in *on an average of* $2,000 a day," functions as well without *on* ("We take in *an average of* $2,000 a day").

on behalf of. See *behalf*.

one. When the pronoun *one*, meaning "anyone," has to be repeated in a sentence, it is correct to do so, and ordinarily it should be done. If you object to a *one* . . . *one* construction, because it sounds stiff or awkward, use either *he* or *he or she*. Most writers would choose the masculine pronoun. Or change the subject *one* to "teacher," "pupil," "employee," or whatever is appropriate and then go with *he* and *his*. "When *one* (a pupil) needs help, *one* (he) should consult *one's* (his) teacher."

Do not use *one* unnecessarily. Rather than "My last sale was an easy *one*," make it "My last sale was easy."

one another. See *each other/one another*.

one of many/only one. Although *one* is clearly singular, a plural verb may be used after an expression bearing the sense of "one of many" ("*One* of every five politicians in this area *are* Republicans"). But *only one* takes a singular—always ("*Only one* of every five politicians in this area *is* a Republican").

one of the . . . if not the. "It was *one of the* first, *if not the* first, time he had ever played the game." The problem here is that *time* as a singular can logically follow *first*, but what happens with *one of the first times*, which needs a plural? If plural *times* is substituted, the problem is the same except it shifts. "One of the first *times*" is correct, but *times* will not accommodate "if not the first." The best solution is to place "if not the first" at the end of the sentence: "It was *one of the* first times he had ever played the game, *if not the first.*"

one of the last sometimes leads to an ungrammatical construction. For example, "Michael is *one of the last* persons, if not the last, I would consult" should be amended to read: *one of the last, if not the last person.*

one of those . . . who. It is hard to see why writers disagree about the number of the verb that follows this expression. Take the sentence "Russell is *one of those teachers who were* nominated as most helpful in after-classroom study." Those who would use the singular—"Russell is one of those teachers who *was* nominated . . ." do so on the belief that *one*, a singular pronoun, is the antecedent of *who*; hence the singular verb *was*. The error in their thinking is that *one* is not the antecedent of *who*; *teachers* is, which makes *were* in the example correct. Inverting the sentence proves the point. "Of those teachers who *were* nominated . . ., Russell *was* one." The rule is that *one of those . . . who* is followed by a plural noun and a plural verb because the antecedent of a relative pronoun (*those*, in this case) governs the number of the succeeding verb.

ones. See *spelling of plural numbers.*

oneself/one's self. Either of these spellings is permissible, but *oneself* is to be preferred. *One's self* sounds clumsy.

onetime/one-time. If you mean "former," use *onetime*, one word ("He was a *onetime* mayor of St. Louis"). If you mean "a single occasion," hyphenate the words—*one-time* ("It was a *one-time* chance in a lifetime").

ongoing at one time was severely criticized by some authorities as a needless, vogue word for "continuing." Some die-hards have changed their thinking, however, probably worn down by the persistent use of *ongoing* on all levels of writing ("The *ongoing* schedules have produced remarkable results"). Nevertheless, *ongoing* sounds like gobbledegook and is usually superfluous.

only. Although you should enjoy a latitude in the positioning of *only*, bear in mind two things. First, generally this adverb is best placed immediately before the word it limits ("He ate *only* one egg" rather than "He *only* ate one egg"). Second, the placement of *only* could affect the intended sense of the sentence ("Nick is painting *only* what is necessary." "*Only* Nick is painting what is necessary"). As a postscript, remember that one's idiomatic ear must sometimes act as a guide. Certainly "I *only* go there once a week" sounds more natural than "I go there *only* once a week." This placement of *only* before the verb, although technically inaccurate, is common, especially in speech, and is considered reputable English idiom. Other limiting adverbs— *even, ever, exactly, just, nearly*—are governed by the same conventions. "He does not *eat even* one potato" is the formula approved by prescriptive grammarians. But "He does not *even eat* one potato" is the way most people, including many of the educated, would say it. (See *modifiers*.)

only one. See *one of many/only one*.

on purpose. In formal English prefer *intentionally* ("He did it intentionally") to *on purpose*.

on the average is trite and tautological for *about* or *almost*.

on the basis of. A wordy expression generally replaceable by *on, by, after,* or *because of*.

on the grounds of can often be economically replaced by *because of*. "His dismissal was *on the grounds of* (better *because of*) poor attendance."

on the occasion of. Those who desire to tighten their speech and writing by cutting out unnecessary words (and this should be everyone) may see whether *when* serves just as well as the key expression. If so, use it.

on the other hand. This useful phrase, that reconciles a thought with one that preceded, may stand alone. The fact that "other" is mentioned does not mean that there had to have been another hand ("Surprisingly, although it is five o'clock, it is now dark. *On the other hand*, tomorrow, if the clouds are gone, it could be light at this hour").

on the part of is unnecessary wordage for "by" or "among." Change "The applause *on the part of* the fans was prolonged" to a more economical and effective "The applause *by*." And amend "There has been a better understanding of community relations *on the part of* Asian-Americans" to *among* Asian-Americans.

on to/onto. *On to* is written as two words when *on*, as an adverb, has an independent meaning and is part of the verb or modifies the verb ("Harold went *on to* Washington." "The chairman moved *on to* other matters." "We decided to hold *on to* what we had"). In all other instances, *onto*, meaning "to a position on," is a preposition written as one word ("The acrobat jumped *onto* the mat"). (See *on/onto*.)

onus/gravamen. The words are not synonyms. An *onus* is a moral burden, a responsibility ("After Mother's death, Dad assumed the *onus* of bringing up the five children"). A *gravamen* is the essential part of a complaint ("The *gravamen* of the charge was, not that he robbed the man, but that he beat him up").

onward/onwards. These are acceptable adverbs, as in to go *onward* or *onwards*, but most writers prefer *onward*.

opaque is used both literally (impervious to light) and figuratively (obtuse). Something *opaque*, since no light can penetrate it, is the very opposite of *transparent*, a quality that allows the passage of light. An *opaque* lampshade doesn't allow light to pass through. A person described as *opaque* is dull, certainly not bright. A person whose actions are *transparent* is said to be frank and open. (See *translucent/transparent*.)

operate. See *run/manage/operate*.

ophthalmologist. See *oculist/ophthalmologist/optometrist/optician*.

opinion. Since an expressed opinion reflects one's thinking, properly one should say "My opinion is . . ." and not *my personal opinion* or, even worse, *in my opinion, I think*. The latter expression should be reduced to *I think*.

opposite, used as an adjective, takes *to* or *from* ("His was an *opposite* position *to* [or *from*] his father's." "Ronnie's house is *opposite to* mine"). As a noun it takes *of* ("Black is the *opposite of* white just as night is the *opposite of* day"). But note that *opposite* is an adverb in "to stand *opposite*."

optician. See *oculist/ophthalmologist/optometrist/optician.*

optimistic/hopeful. Although used synonymously by many people, *optimistic* should be restricted to describe a frame of mind, one with a hopeful outlook. *Optimism* is an attitude that believes everything is bound to turn out right. *Hopeful* should be applied to specific situations—"Tony is *hopeful* that his application to Rutgers will be accepted."

optimistic/pessimistic take *about*, not *that*.

optometrist. See *oculist/ophthalmologist/optometrist/optician.*

or as the second element in an *either . . . or* construction needs no company. Not "either this *or else* that." Omit *else*.

or/and. The misuse of *and* for *or* can lead to ludicrous mistakes. In "This year we intend to promote a new color such as magenta *and* aquamarine" and in "Raymond prefers a citrus fruit such as an orange *and* a grapefruit," *or* should replace *and*, for a color cannot be both magenta and aquamarine nor a citrus fruit both an orange and a grapefruit.

or/nor. One way to avoid the problem of deciding whether to follow a *no* phrase with *or* or *nor* is to determine whether the negative sense of the *no* phrase carries through to the next phrase. If it does not, if the sense of the first phrase ends with it, *nor* is required to negative that second phrase, as in "No one is allowed to enter the back room, *nor* may any books be removed from the front room." If that sentence is recast—"No one is allowed to enter the back room *or* to remove books from the front room"—*or* has properly replaced *nor* because the negative effect now applies to both parts. But consider "His uncle has no money, *nor* has he interest in earning any." Here *nor* is the correct choice. Note: when a negative ("not") governs two or more verbs, use *or*, not *nor*, as the conjunction. "I could not have seen him *or* (not *nor*) given him any information."

oral/verbal. *Oral* means "spoken." *Verbal* means "expressed in words," either spoken or written. An agreement made during a conversation is *oral*; if reduced to writing, it then becomes a written agreement. Nevertheless, to some people—to many people—*oral* and *verbal* are synonymous terms. In fact, unless the context indicates otherwise, the chances are that a person speaking of something *verbal* means "oral." Despite that loose and widespread usage, a recommendation is that in precise discourse the distinction between these words be observed.

orate. See *enthuse.*

ordinance/ordnance. The meanings of these words are unrelated. An *ordinance* is a rule, law, decree, or regulation, usually of a city. *Ordnance* is military equipment.

orientate. See *preventative/orientate.*

orthodox, from Greek *ortho,* a combining form meaning "straight" or "right," denotes an "opinion" that is right (ours); any other (theirs) is *heterodox,* the wrong one.

other. Do not omit *other* when a general comparison is made. "Howard is a better athlete than the boys in his class" should be recast "better athlete than the *other* boys in his class." (See *the other.*)

other than. "He made no *other* drawing *but* that one." Make it "*than* that one." After comparatives, and *else, other,* and *otherwise,* use *than* (not *but* or *except*).

otherwise/other. "Those decorators, interior or otherwise, hired by the architect will meet at noon." "My father's income, earned or otherwise, is just enough to see him through." Make it "interior or other" and "earned or other." *Other* is an adjective meaning "different"; *otherwise* is an adverb and means "differently." Although no consensus among discriminating writers establishes *otherwise* as only an adverb, many regard it that way. They use *otherwise* when an adverbial form is called for ("He would not speak *otherwise* than in praise"). But note that *otherwise* as an adjective is widely accepted and considered idiomatic by some dictionaries.

ought/should. Their meanings overlap. One may correctly say, "If you *ought* to do something, you *should* do it." Or "If you *should* do something, you *ought* to do it." However, *ought* implies a higher degree of moral obligation or responsibility than *should* and is more imperative. You *should* be polite, but you *ought* to visit your sick mother regularly.

ought to. "He *ought* do it." "He *ought not* do it." In the first sentence *to* should follow *ought* ("He *ought to* do it") but not in the second, because idiom has decreed that in negative statements involving *ought, to* is unnecessary.

outline. See *brief outline/little sip.*

out loud is an expression that does not belong in formal usage. Use *aloud*. But in daily conversation the expectable phrase is "out loud." *Aloud* sounds so stuffy that only a pedant would say "for crying aloud."

out of. See *off of/alongside of/out of*.

outside of/inside of. The *of* is unnecessary when *inside* or *outside* is used as a preposition. "We went *outside* the house," not *outside of*. "The bucket is *inside* the barn," not *inside of*. In informal usage, *outside of* means "besides" or "except for," as in "*Outside of* my mother and my father there were three passengers in the van." Even informally *besides* or *except for* would do better. When *inside* (*outside*) is used as a noun, *of* of course must follow ("We're painting the *outside of* [or *inside of*] the house").

oval in shape does not need *in shape*. Omit. This dictum applies to any geometric description—round *in shape*, rectangular *in shape*, and so on.

over. See *in excess of*; *more than/over*; *under*.

over-/overly. Spell *over-* compounds as one word (*overabundance, overactive, overanxious, overexpand, overturn*). *Over-* means "above," "beyond," "inverted." *Overly*, meaning "excessively," has some acceptance, but *over-* in many cases properly expresses this sense, and more economically—for example, compare *overly cautious* and *overcautious*. *Overly* has few uses, primarily those associated with virtues (*overly frank, overly concerned, overly deliberate*).

overall has legitimate uses—a coverall garment worn by workmen and as the measurements between the extremities of, say, the back lawn. But as a vogue word it is overworked and exhausted. Good writers avoid it. Consider in its place *total, complete, general, supreme,* or any other suitable substitute. Sometimes *overall* is superfluous and should be excised, as it should in "The teller declared the treasurer elected by an *overall* majority of 22" and in "The swimmer's *overall* time was seven minutes."

overflow. "The Mississippi has overflown its banks again." Wrong. The past participle of *overflow* is *overflowed*. *Overflown* is said of an airplane that failed to make the runway.

overlook. This word has two contradictory meanings. To *overlook* means "to supervise." It also means "to ignore deliberately or to fail to notice." A question may arise, if a person was told to overlook a program, was he supposed to supervise it or ignore it? If the former, a better choice of words would be *oversee*. If *overlook* is used, to avoid ambiguity the context had better make clear the sense intended.

overly. See *over-/overly*.

oversight can be an ambiguous word in some contexts, for it has two distinct and unrelated meanings. Ordinarily *oversight*, as in "Not mailing that letter was an *oversight*," is an act of omission caused by one's negligence. But in "Sheldon had general *oversight* of the new construction," it means "supervision." One who has oversight—that is, oversees—is an overseer. (See *overlook*.)

overwhelming is not a synonym for "vast." In "There was an *overwhelming* difference of opinion," *vast* would be more appropriate. *Overwhelming* means "overpowering in effect or strength."

over with. To be avoided in the sense of "completed." In "When the meeting is *over with*, we will go to my house," *with* is unnecessary.

owing to is an idiomatically correct phrase meaning "attributable to" or "because of" ("*Owing to* the shortness of time, we hurried the job along"). Prefer *owing to* to *due to* in this kind of construction. But avoid *owing to the fact that*, which says no more than *because* or *since* and uses more words. (See *dangling participles*; *due to*.)

owing to the fact that. See *fact*.

oxymoron is a seemingly self-contradictory locution: cruel kindness, an honorable thief, make haste slowly, a sophomore (a wise fool).

pachyderm. An elephant is rightly called a *pachyderm*, but the elephant is not the exclusive possessor of this term. A *pachyderm* is any thick-skinned animal (Greek *pachys*, "thick," and *derma*, "skin") such as the rhinoceros or the hippopotamus—or, figuratively, any insensitive person.

pact/compact. When used to mean "an agreement" or "treaty," the words are interchangeable. One may talk of the recent pact made with Belgium or the recent compact. *Pact* has the advantage of being a shorter word; *compact* sounds formal.

pains may be construed as singular or plural ("Great *pains is* taken by our principal." "All possible *pains are* taken by this faculty").

pair. Use *pairs* as the plural form before a number higher than one. At one time usage preferred *pair* ("He has *two pair* of blue socks"), but no longer. Now we say "He has *two pairs* of blue socks." (See *twins*.)

pair of. "A *pair of* scissors *is* on the table." "This *pair of* tongs *needs* repair." These instruments have a sense of oneness; they take singular verbs. But note that *pair of* takes a plural verb when the meaning of the sentence is clearly plural ("A *pair of* robins *are* on our lawn").

pan, when used as a combining form meaning "every" or "all," does not take a hyphen (*panacea, pandemonium*) unless the second element is capitalized (*pan-Hellenic*).

panacea, "all-healing," a cure for all ills—from halitosis to bunions. It is therefore incorrect to offer a medicine for, say, indigestion as a panacea for that kind of ailment. A *panacea* is not a cure for a particular complaint.

panache, "a tuft of feathers worn ornamentally, especially on a helmet," is pronounced pae-*nasche*. In a figurative sense, it means "dash, swagger, verve."

panic. See *mimic/panic*.

pants. See *pair of*.

papier mâché. See *accent marks,* and note spelling *papier,* correctly pronounced pah-pee-*eh,* but in English generally sounded like *paper.*

paradox is something that seems false. Therefore, in "His comment is a seeming *paradox,*" *seeming* should be excised and the sentence recast, "His comment was *paradoxical*" or "is a *paradox.*"

parallel structure. A series of phrases or clauses should have the same grammatical or syntactical form—for example, "He explained painting, drawing, and how to sell pictures" should have *selling* for parallel structure.

parameter is a vogue word that strikes some writers as elegant and learned. But in general English it is neither. It is a pretentious expression used to mean boundary, perimeter, or limit, even though it means none of those things. In mathematics *parameter* is a term denoting "a quantity that varies with the conditions under which it occurs." The best advice is to confine *parameter* to a shelf marked "little understood expressions."

paramount. In the sentence "Cutting our deficit is our *paramount* concern," *paramount* is being used to mean "first" and in "Our *paramount* obligation is to pay off the stockholders," to mean either "first" or "important." These uses of *paramount* are loose and unacceptable extensions of its traditional meaning, "chief in rank," "supreme," "preeminent." And since *paramount* means "supreme," it is an absolute term that cannot be qualified. It is incorrect to say "more paramount" or "most paramount."

paraphernalia may take a singular or a plural verb. But be careful not to misspell it *paraphrenalia.*

pardon/excuse. Either word may be used as an apology for a breach of etiquette. But the latter term, as in *excuse me,* is commoner and more in keeping with today's style of speaking. *Pardon me* sounds affected to some people. Certainly small slips are excused; more serious faults—and crimes—are pardoned.

parenthetical phrases. When a parenthetical phrase such as *we thought* or *we believe* comes between a relative pronoun (*who, whom*) and its verb, the phrase stands on its own and leaves the sentence unaffected. It does not alter the case of the pronoun. For example, "The neighbor *who* (not *whom*) *I thought* was retired

194 • PARENTHETICAL PHRASES

went back to work." *Who* is the subject of the verb *was retired*. Commas are not required to surround a parenthetical expression where their absence creates no confusion.

parricide. See *patricide/matricide/parricide*.

part/portion/share. A *part* is less than the whole. Gaul, as all Latin students know, was divided into three parts. A *portion* is a specific part. It is that part allotted or given to someone for a purpose ("I will give each child a *portion* of my wealth"). A *share* and a *portion* are the same, but a share is a portion viewed by the receiver ("My *share* is 10 percent").

partake is not a troublesome word—if one would only remember not to use it. *Partake* is so stilted and old-fashioned that it is bound to dull any sentence. Instead of *to partake of*, as in "*partake of* a meal," say *have* or *eat*. *Partake of*, properly, means "have a share in," "participate in."

part and parcel is an unnecessarily wordy expression in which *and parcel* contributes nothing to its meaning. If what is meant is an essential part of something, then express it that way.

partially. See *partly/partially*.

participle. See *-ing words*; *much*; *very*.

particular. One wonders what purpose *particular* serves in such phrases as "no particular purpose."

partly/partially. If these words are interchanged, but clearly so in their contexts, no harm is done. It is wise, however, to remember that *partially* in addition to its sense of "in part," "not wholly" (which is also the meaning of *partly*), means "with partiality or bias." Therefore, a report, *partially* written, may be either incomplete or biased. It is best to refrain from using *partially* when *partly* will do.

part of. See *on the part of*.

part-time. See *pastime/part-time*.

party. Often inappropriately used for "person." Except in a legal context, *party* implies a group of persons, not *a* person. Of course, telephone operators need not listen in on all this, for their "Your *party* is on the line" is so firmly set as an expression in telephone lingo that we might be taken aback to hear anything else.

passable/passible. Do not confuse. Changing the second *a* in *passable* to *i* changes the meaning. *Passable* means "able to be traversed" or "good enough." *Passible* means "able to feel" or "emotionally sensitive." (See *-ible/-able*.)

passed/past. Be careful not to interchange; the words are completely unrelated. When the word required is a verb, meaning "to go by," use *passed*; otherwise, use *past* either as an adjective meaning "former" or "previous" or as a noun meaning "a former time." "Having *passed* all his examinations, Harvey thought he could conquer the world." "The defendant conceded his *past* association with the underworld." "The *past* is gone forever."

passive voice. See *active voice/passive voice*.

past. See *passed/past*.

pastime/part-time. A *pastime* is a diversion to help pass the time pleasantly. But observe that, although a combination of *pass* and *time*, it is spelled as given, with one *s*. *Part-time*, a period less than full time, is spelled with two *t*'s, and preferably hyphened. But it may be spelled solid (*parttime*).

past records is as redundant as the "future plans" of those who engage in "advance planning." (See *plan ahead/advance planning*.)

past tense/present perfect tense. Differentiate. "I have seen three rabbits this morning" should be reworded "I saw," since the past tense denotes past time. The present perfect tense refers to action begun in the past and completed near or within the present—for example, "We *have credited* your account as instructed."

patricide/matricide/parricide. Each of these terms refers to a killer or the act of killing. Although uncommon, the words occasionally appear in print. They should not be confused. *Patricide* is the killer of, or the act of killing, one's father. *Matricide* bears the same definition except that it applies to one's mother. *Parricide* is a more inclusive term. It means "the act of killing one's father, mother, or other close relative" or "one who commits such an act."

patriot. See *expatriate*.

patron. In formal texts a *customer* should not be called a *patron*. A patron is a wealthy person who fosters or protects a person or an institution.

peak/peek. If one takes a "peak" at a dictionary, he will find that *peek*, meaning, "to glance quickly," is spelled *peek*. A *peak* is a projecting point, like the *peak* of a mountain.

peal. See *peel/peal*.

peculiarly enough. See *curiously enough/peculiarly enough/oddly enough*.

pedal/peddle. Note that the former is a lever ("Albert broke the right *pedal* on his tricycle"). The latter, *peddle*, is to sell from place to place. Be sure when writing these homonyms not to confuse their spelling. The word for the one who peddles has variant spellings—*peddler* and *peddlar*. The former predominates.

peel/peal. Sometimes confused. One *peels* an apple, but a bell is known for its *peal*.

peer. A person who is your *peer* is your equal, not your superior.

pendant/pendent are easily confused words because they sound alike and are spelled almost alike. *Pendant* is a noun meaning "a thing that hangs," usually an ornament ("Madame Pompadour enjoyed wearing large *pendants* that dangled below her neck"). *Pendent* is an adjective meaning "hanging down." A pennant may be *pendent* from the window of a fraternity house. In fact a *pendant* is *pendent*.

penury/penurious. Although a person in extreme poverty is said to be in a state of *penury*, that is, "destitute," its adjective form (*penurious*) has had a shift in meaning. It now means "stingy."

people/persons. "The room seated thirteen *people*." Make it *persons*. Use *persons* for an exact number of individuals. Use *people* to designate a large uncounted assembly ("The ticket collector said that about *3,000 people* attended") or an anonymous mass ("Lincoln was a man of the *people*").

per. This Latin preposition is appropriate with Latin words: *per diem, per annum*. But it sounds technical or legalistic where *a* or *an* would do. Avoid "55 miles per hour" and "a tax of $5 per head." Make it "*an* hour" and "*a* head." Rather than "We're sending the package *per* parcel post," use *by*.

percent/percentage. A proportion of the whole is conveniently referred to by *percent* or *percentage*. *Percent* means "in the hundred"; *percentage* means "a proportion of something considered in hundredths" or "an unstated proportion." *Percent*, when used in place of *percentage* ("We want a large *percent* of the take"), and *percentage*, when meaning "profit" or "advantage" ("If I stay what's my *percentage?*" "There's no *percentage* in going to summer school"), are colloquialisms best avoided in careful usage. The same advice applies to *percentage* when the intent is to mean "a few," "a small number," or "a small quantity." In "During every year a *percentage* of the students fail to return library books," *a small number* or *a few*, if that was the intended meaning, would be better. And bear in mind that a *percentage* might be any number between zero and a hundred, it need not be a small number.

perchance, meaning "possibly," since it sounds literary, is preferably replaced by *perhaps* or *maybe.*

per diem/per annum are terms accepted on every level of discourse. (See *per.*) Nevertheless, prefer the English versions of these Latin expressions—daily or a day for *per diem* and yearly or a year for *per annum.*

perfect. See *absolutes.*

perhaps. See *maybe/may be; might perhaps.*

period of. "He worked there *for a period of* twelve years" is preferably reduced to "He worked there for *twelve years.*"

period of time. Time is inherent in the word *period*. Therefore, referring to a period of time is verbiage. "A long period of time" may be reduced either to "a long period" or to "a long time." The same idea of time is conveyed in *lapse*; hence *a lapse of time* is also unnecessarily wordy. Of course, a specific period may be involved in a lapse, which means that, say, a lapse of five hours is correctly put and is not excessive.

permanent truth. See *direct quotations.*

perpetuate/perpetrate. These must be troublesome words to some people, considering how often they are misused, one for the other. To *perpetuate* is to make enduring, to make perpetual. To *perpetrate* is to commit, to do something evil or criminal. A scholarship fund may be perpetuated; a crime is perpetrated.

persecute/prosecute. Do not confuse. To *persecute* is to torment, to harass, with unjust attacks or to afflict unfairly. To *prosecute* is to follow through to an end; in law, to conduct legal proceedings against someone.

personal friend. Except when there is need to distinguish a friend with whom you are socially active from one who is involved only in, say, your professional life, a friend should be called simply a *friend*, not a *personal friend*. A person is a friend only if there is a personal relationship. Which means that the expression "a personal friend of mine" is both pointless and redundant. Distinguish between *friend* and *acquaintance*. The latter is someone you know, but with whom no close relationship has developed; a friend is someone you regard with some affection.

personally is often used unnecessarily. In *"Personally,* I think the administration is militaristic" or in *"Personally,* I believe our country has the world's best defense," *personally* is meaningless and should be omitted.

personal pronouns. See *pronoun antecedents*.

persons. See *individual*; *people/persons*.

perspective/prospective. Noun *perspective* means "point of view"; adjective *prospective* means "expected," "probable."

perspicuous/perspicacious. These words are often confused. The chief culprit is *perspicuous*, which means "lucid," "easily understood," referring to the clarity of an idea. Its misuse for *perspicacious*, which means "keen in understanding," can be embarrassing. We speak of a *perspicuous* explanation, speech, or dissertation. We speak of a person with foresight as *perspicacious*.

persuade. See *convince/persuade*.

perturb/disturb overlap in meaning to a certain extent, since both pertain to confusion and disorder. What difference there is between them is that *perturb* refers solely to mental anguish. A person made uneasy or anxious is *perturbed*. *Disturb*, which may also refer to mental agitation, is chiefly used of physical disorders. A person may be *perturbed* or *disturbed* upon hearing that war was declared, but if his hair is mussed by a passing wind or the papers on his desk are blown apart, he is *disturbed*. And so are his hair and the papers.

peruse. Use "read" unless to read carefully or with critical care is meant.

pessimistic/gloomy. Although these words connote sadness, they are not synonyms. *Gloomy* means "melancholy." A gloomy person is in low spirits. *Pessimistic* means "looking on the dark side of things." A pessimistic person expects the worst. He believes that things tend to be evil and the worth of living is questionable. *Gloom* is usually a temporary state; *pessimism*, a permanent one. A *pessimist* may live his life in gloom. (See *optimistic/pessimistic*.)

petit/petite. *Petit*, pronounced *peht*-ih, is a legal term (a *petit*, or small, jury). *Petite*, meaning "small or trim," is pronounced puh-*teet*.

phantasy. See *fantasy/phantasy*.

Pharaoh, the title given to the ancient kings of Egypt, is one of the hardest words to find in a dictionary. The reason—almost everyone looks up *pharoh* or *pharoah*, but finds no such listings. The correct spelling, of course, is *pharaoh*.

phase. See *element/factor/feature/phase*; *faze*.

phenomenon. Its plural forms are *phenomena* and *phenomenons*. Prefer the former, the Greek form. It is nonstandard to say *phenomenas*. (See *agenda*; *criterion*; *data*.)

Philippine Islands is spelled with two internal *p*'s. But *Filipinos*, the natives, is spelled with one *p*.

phobia/mania. Distinguish between these unreasoning emotional states. They are not similar. A *phobia* is an irrational fear; *mania* is a mental disorder characterized by great excitement.

physician/doctor. All physicians are doctors of medicine, but not all doctors are physicians. Doctorate degrees are awarded in many disciplines—dentistry, philosophy, education, literature, science, and law, to state some of the most prominent. A *doctor* is, according to its Latin derivation (*docere* "to teach"), a learned man, a teacher.

physiognomy. See *countenance/physiognomy*.

picaresque. See *picturesque/picaresque*.

pick/choose are interchangeable except in formal writing, where *pick* does not suggest the selectivity of *choose*. We pick a grape from a bunch or a card from a deck, but we choose a lot on which to build a house. A person who makes a pick does it somewhat casually, perhaps perfunctorily. A choice implies deliberation, the weighing of possibilities. *To pick on*, meaning "to irritate or tease with faultfinding," as in "Why does he always *pick on* me?" is an expression best confined to colloquial speech.

picturesque/picaresque sound almost alike. What is *picturesque* is like a picture. *Picaresque* is having to do with a rogue, a person full of rascality, from the Spanish *picaro*, an adventurer or rogue.

piebald is not a pie that has no crust. It refers to a combination of patches of black and white or of other colors (a *piebald* pony).

pitiable/pitiful. Easily confused. The first refers to that which is deserving of pity or to that which is lamentable or deplorable ("The children are in a *pitiable* condition." "His efforts to prove himself were *pitiable*"). The second means "exciting pity" (a *pitiful* cry) or, an unrelated meaning, "contemptible" (a *pitiful* excuse) or "meager" (a *pitiful* collection of dishes in her cupboard).

Pittsburgh. See *Cincinnati/Pittsburgh*.

pizza pie. This is a redundant mixture of Italian and English. *Pizza* is an Italian pie. The English word "pie," therefore, should be omitted.

place/put. These synonyms are interchangeable in many contexts. The essential difference between them is that *place* connotes more care, more deliberateness than *put*. Something is placed where it belongs or where it will look or serve best. Little thought is usually given to where something is put. When the basket you're carrying becomes too heavy, you simply put it down. You *put* your galoshes away, but you *place* flowers on the dining room table. (See *noplace/someplace/anyplace/everyplace*.)

plaintiff/defendant. Those who cannot recall the legal term for a person who institutes an action at law (*plaintiff*) may call him the *complainant* ("one who has a grievance"). The name of the party against whom the suit is brought is, of course, the *defendant*.

plan ahead/advance planning run neck and neck for tautological honors. Does anyone plan behind? Of course not. Planning must envision a future.

plan on/plan to. Both are idiomatic. One may *plan on* studying tonight or *plan to* study tonight. But to express intention in formal discourse, follow the verb with an infinitive (*plan to*).

playwright/playwrite. *Playwright* is the correct spelling. A *wright* is a craftsman—a shipwright, a millwright, a wheelwright. A *playwright* writes plays (and holds rights to them).

pleaded. See *pled/pleaded.*

plead innocent. An expression best avoided, since no such legal plea exists. The accepted form is "plead not guilty."

please be advised was a pompous but favorite expression during the days of high-button shoes. It certainly has no place in today's correspondence. It makes no sense to advise your correspondents anyway, especially since your advice has not been solicited. Simply tell them what you want to say.

pleased. Use pleased with *by* in the passive (*pleased by* flattery); *with* when adjectival (*pleased with* the car); *at* before gerunds (*pleased at* being chosen).

pleasurable. See *salable.*

plebeian. Often misspelled. Be careful. Note the *ei*, pronounced with an *e* sound. All the other words that have an *e* sound, except those preceded by *c* (*receive*), are spelled *ie* (*belief*).

pled/pleaded. Both these past tenses of *plead* are acceptable forms. Perhaps *pled* is more frequently heard. In any event, it has the advantage of being the shorter word.

plentiful/plenteous, meaning "an abundant amount," are interchangeable ("The apples this spring are *plentiful* or *plenteous*"). Most writers prefer *plentiful*, since *plenteous* sounds literary and somewhat full-blown.

plenty is a noun meaning "abundancy" or "sufficiency" ("He has *plenty* of money"). As given, *plenty* is followed by *of*. Without it, the expression becomes an unacceptable colloquialism in which *plenty* functions as an adjective—"He has *plenty* room"— or as an adverb—"The lawn is *plenty* large." Replace *plenty* with "enough" in the first example and "very" in the second.

plurality. The words *plurality* and *majority* should be distinguished. *Plurality* is a term that applies when three or more candidates are competing for the same office. The candidate who garners the most votes, but no more than the combined votes of the other candidates, has a plurality. For example, if Tom received 70 votes, Ralph 50, and Bill 40, Tom would have a plurality of 20, but no majority. A plurality is the difference in the count between the leader and the next candidate. A majority is more than half the votes cast. (See *majority*.)

plural nouns, choice of. The plural form *hooves* is obsolete; use *hoofs*. "Scarf" has two acceptable plurals—*scarfs* and *scarves*. The former predominates in the United States. The plural forms of "staff" are *staffs* and *staves*. Prefer *staffs*. (See *teeth*.)

plural numbers. See *spelling of plural numbers*.

plus. A preposition, meaning "with the addition of," not a conjunction. Therefore two *plus* two *is* four, not *are* four. The subject *two* is regarded as a unit; in effect *two* becomes *four* because two *added* to two *is* four. But if the subject is plural ("His *plans plus* ours are to be presented"), a plural verb must follow. Do not begin a sentence or clause with *plus*; substitute *furthermore, moreover*, or any other appropriate conjunction.

pneumonia. See *often*.

podium. See *dais/podium/lectern*.

poetess. An antiquated word. Use *poet* instead.

point in time. Swap the cliché *at this point in time* for a simple word: *now*.

point of view. See *viewpoint/point of view*.

politic. See *frolic*.

polygamy/polygyny/polyandry. *Polygamy* is having more than one spouse, whether a wife or a husband, at the same time— *polygyny* is having more than one wife; *polyandry*, more than one husband.

pore. See *spill/pour/pore*.

port/harbor. Loosely interchanged, but it is best to reserve the word *port* to mean a place where ships are loaded and unloaded and *harbor* for a place where ships are protected against the weather and can be accommodated. A *port*, therefore, primarily refers to a city of a harbor; *harbor*, to a place of shelter for ships ("We can see our *port* city and we expect to be in its *harbor* within an hour." "Shanghai is a large *port* city with an excellent *harbor*"). (See *any old port in a storm*.)

portentous. Note its spelling, not *portentious*.

port in a storm. See *any old port in a storm*.

portion. See *part/portion/share.*

position of modifiers. See *modifiers.*

possess, when ownership is considered, is a fancy word for *have.* It is better to say "He *has* a strong personality" rather than "He *possesses.*"

possessive antecedents. An antecedent of a personal pronoun cannot be a noun in the possessive case. For example, "In Dr. Johnson's *Anecdotes,* he discusses many personal incidents," *he* has no antecedent. The writer's intention was to refer to Dr. Johnson, but his name is serving as an adjective, modifying *Anecdotes.* The sentence recast might read: "In his *Anecdotes,* Dr. Johnson discusses. . . ." In "*Don's* father says he may not go out to play," *he* may refer to either *Don* or his *father.* According to governing rules, *he* should refer to *father,* yet the intended antecedent seems to be *Don.* Change to "Don's father says that *Don* may not . . .," thus bypassing the possessive antecedent and ambiguity as well.

possessive case forms, in the main, are not troublesome, since convention has firmly established rules governing their formation. A question is sometimes raised, however, concerning the placing of the sign of possession in compound nouns. The answer is that it is placed at the end (my father-in-*law's* hat, the major-*general's* medal). Be careful of a plural possessive (*fathers-in-law's*). The possessive form for organizations, buildings, etc., may be omitted where the idea of possession is clear: Drivers and Mechanics Bank; West Chester State Teachers University. (See *double possessive; mother-in-law.*)

possessive, double. See *double possessive.*

possessive pronouns. "The books are the *teacher's* and the pencils are *her's,* too." Only true nouns take apostrophes; personal pronouns do not. Make it *hers.* Indefinite pronouns are excepted from this rule; they take *'s: someone's* hat, *everyone's* responsibility, each *other's* talents. One further exception—the personal pronoun *one's* ("Religious beliefs are *one's* own business"). (See *apostrophe.*)

possibly. The sentence "The controller said that *possibly* the ship may be launched next week" contains a redundancy (*possibly may*). The sense of "possible" is inherent in *may.* Correct either by dropping *possibly* or by changing *may* to *will.* (See *likely.*)

post-. This prefix, borrowed from a Latin word meaning "behind," is commonly used in such words as *postscript*, meaning "written afterwards." Whether to follow *post* with a hyphen is simply a matter of style. Most stylists do not use a hyphen unless the word's appearance is unsightly (*postdate, postpone,* but *post-Shakespearean, post-impressionism*).

posterior to. Pretentious word best changed to *behind* or *after*.

posthumous, meaning "after death," is not pronounced so that its first syllable, *post,* sounds like "post" in "postnasal," nor is the second syllable stressed—*huhm,* making it post-*huhm*-uhs. The accent, properly, is on the first syllable, and it is pronounced *pahs*-choo-muhs.

postponed means "delayed until a future time." Hence the expression "postponed until later" is redundant. Omit *until later*.

postprandial, which means "after dinner," sounds pompous and is best ignored, even before the meal.

potatoes. See *-o*.

pour. See *spill/pour/pore*.

practicable/practical. Unless particular care is taken with these words, it is easy to misuse them, one for the other. *Practicable* implies that something is workable—that is, capable of being put into practice. *Practical* means "useful," "not theoretical." Something that is workable or manageable is practical, which makes the word somewhat synonymous with *practicable*. When *practical* is applied to persons, it means "realistic," "sensible" (*practicable* is used only with reference to things). That which is *practicable* refers to what can be done; if it was successful or profitable, it was *practical*.

practically/virtually. As a rule *practically* means "in a practical manner," which implies effectiveness and practicality. It also means "nearly" or "almost," as in "The stream is *practically* dry." In this last sense *practically* and *virtually* share the same meaning; *virtually* means "almost entirely." You may have said, "The stream is *virtually* dry" to the same effect. Some writers would prefer *nearly* or *almost* in the above examples to the lead words.

practice. See *customary practice*.

pre-, a Latin prefix, means "before" (that which precedes goes before). A question sometimes raised is whether it should be followed by a hyphen when the base word begins with an *e*. Modern stylists write the word solid if it causes no confusion (*preeminent, preempt, preelection*). (See *pre/pro-*.)

pre-/pro-. Spell compounds as one word (*prearrange, proscribe*) unless the second element is capitalized (*pre-Columbus, pro-Israel*).

precede/proceed. Probably the confusion occasioned by these words is due solely to carelessness or hasty writing. If the meaning intended is "to go before," *precede*, of course, is the word required. If the meaning is "to move forward," then *proceed* is called for. We should not say "The Secretary of State will *proceed* all the other secretaries to the dais." Make it *precede*. And note the spelling of the noun form of *proceed*: *procedure*. It has dropped one of its *e*'s.

precedence/precedents. The first means "of greater importance" and, when pronounced, its second syllable (with a long *e*) is stressed. The second means "acts that may serve as an example or authority for later similar actions." It stresses the first syllable.

precipitate/precipitous. The ancestor of these words is Latin *praeceps*, which means "headlong." Perhaps because of their common ancestry these words are occasionally interchanged. But in the best current usage they are not—and should not be. *Precipitate* means "sudden," "hasty" (a *precipitate* decision). *Precipitous* means "extremely steep," like a precipice (cliffs are *precipitous*). Remember that an angry person does not depart precipitously but precipitately ("rashly," "hastily") unless he's jumping off a cliff.

predicament. See *dilemma*.

predicate nouns. See *clauses*.

predominant/preponderant. The sense of these words is to prevail—to be stronger in power or number. Those who wonder which word to use in a sentence expressing the prevalent (the *predominant* or the *preponderant*) opinion may feel free to use either. They are interchangeable terms. Literally to *preponderate* is to be weighty; hence to exert greater force or influence.

predominate/dominate are not equivalents. A person may *dominate* (not *predominate*) a situation, but his good sense may *predominate over* folly.

prefer is generally followed by *to*, not *than* or *rather than* ("I *prefer* red *to* black"). But if *prefer* . . . *to* immediately precedes an infinitive, the difficulty is that *to* will not suit. "I prefer to swim to *to* golf" makes no sense. In such cases, *rather than* must be used ("I prefer to swim *rather than* to golf"). *Prefer*, being an absolute term, is not to be modified by *more* or *most*. In "Which does the teacher *prefer most?*" *most* should be omitted.

preferable. Something is preferable *to* something else, not *than* or *over* something else. Stress the first syllable and note that the second *r* is not doubled, as it is in *preferred* and *preferring*. Since *preferable* is a comparative, do not modify with *more* or *most*.

prejudiced toward is an easily misunderstood phrase. Although sometimes used in the sense "biased in favor of," it is usually taken to mean the very opposite—"biased against." Avoid it. The recommended idioms are "prejudiced in favor of" and "prejudiced against."

preliminary. See *preparatory/preliminary*.

premature. See *immature/premature*.

première. This word, French for "first," has been borrowed into English and is widely used as a noun ("I'm going to a *première* tonight"), as an adjective ("It is a *première* showing"), and as a verb ("The production will be *premièred* tonight"). But most authorities frown on its verbal use, as they do of its sister verb *debut*. (See *debut*.)

premises. One may own a piece of property (*property* is a singular noun), but if it is called a *premises*, the reference is to a plural noun ("These *premises* have been vacated"). *Premises* has no singular form. *Premise*, the basis for a supposition, has no connection with real estate. In Britain, the form *premiss* is used.

preparatory/preliminary. Do not use *preliminary* to refer to introductory remarks (made before a speech) that prepare the audience for what is to come. Use *preparatory*. But *preparatory* is not to be used to describe remarks before a speech that are not related to the subject of the address. Use *preliminary*.

preponderant. See *predominant/preponderant*.

preposition at end of sentence. For those dedicated to burying prepositions inside sentences, be assured that it need not always be done. A preposition is sometimes a good, sometimes even a necessary, word to end a sentence with. Make certain, however, that such placement creates no awkwardness and that its use is not unnecessary, as it is in "Where is he *at?*" or in "Let's get it over *with.*" If idiom demands a preposition at the end, you have no choice; for example, "Where did this car come from?" "The new neighbor's son has no one to play with." When Winston Churchill was chided for ending a sentence with a preposition, he mockingly retorted, "This is the type of arrant pedantry up with which I shall not put." Francis Bacon made no efforts to avoid sentence-ending prepositions. He wrote, "Houses are built to live in, and not to look on."

prescribe/proscribe. One can only ascribe the confusion between these look-alikes to carelessness. A doctor prescribes medicine. A house mother proscribes the playing of music after bedtime. To *prescribe* is to establish rules or to order a remedy for use or to advise the use of. To *proscribe* is to forbid, banish, outlaw.

present incumbent. Redundant. Drop *present*. (See *incumbent*.)

presently is a word that can be a rich source of confusion. Does it mean "now" or "soon"? The safest course to follow is to say "now" if that is what you mean and "soon" if you mean *soon*.

present perfect tense. See *past tense/present perfect tense*.

present tense. See *direct quotations*; *historical present/literary present*; *was/is*.

pressure has not been accepted as a verb by many authorities. Instead of "I feel *pressured* to sign," make it, if you wish to avoid criticism from any source, *pressed* to sign.

presumably. See *supposedly/presumably*.

presume, as in "I *presume* that's true," is colloquial for *imagine* or *suppose*. (See *assume/presume*.)

presumptuous. If you use *presumptuous*, which means "forward" or "too bold," write it that way. Not *presumptious*.

pretty, meaning "rather," "somewhat," "quite" ("It is *pretty* hard to believe he didn't know"), was an informal expression that has worked its way into acceptability on every level of usage except the most formal. Thus this adverb now ranks pretty high.

prevail. When it comes to accompanying prepositions, no word can prevail over *prevail*. Meaning "to triumph," it takes *over* or *against* ("We have finally *prevailed over* Southern Cal." "None can *prevail against* us"). When its sense is "to influence," it takes *on, upon,* or *with* ("The party *prevailed on* the governor to veto the bill"). In the sense "to have acceptance," it is followed by *through* or *throughout* ("Mormonism *prevails throughout* Utah").

prevaricate. Sometimes misspelled *pervaricate.* The word begins with a *pre-*.

prevent, when a preposition is needed, takes *from* ("David *prevented* Doris *from* leaving"). Be careful of such sentences as "The guard tried to *prevent* him leaving." Make it *his leaving* or *him from leaving. Prevent* is often followed by a gerund whose subject, if a noun or pronoun, is preferably in the possessive case.

preventative/orientate. Good words, but better still are *preventive,* meaning "serving to hinder," and *orient,* meaning "to adjust to surroundings." They are more concise and yet say it just as well.

previous means "earlier" ("The *previous* year was particularly profitable"). *Previous to* means "before," and *before* is the simpler way to say it ("The year *before* was . . ."). Rather than "*Previous to* our leaving, we will meet in the gym," make it "*Before leaving.*"

price/cost. Do not confuse the price of an object with its value. The price of a hat, for example, may be high (not costly); it is the hat, the merchandise, that is costly, even though someone else may think its price is low.

principal/principle. The confusion occasioned by these words lies in their spelling, not in their meaning. A mnemonic aid to keep them straight is to remember that a *principle* is a *rule* and that both those words end in *le.* All the other meanings take *principal.*

prior to. See *before/prior to.*

privilege. Often misspelled *priviledge* or *privilage.* Be alert. Unlike *right,* which may be followed by an infinitive (*right to vote*), *privilege* may not take an infinitive. Make it *privilege of voting.*

pro-. See *pre-/pro-.*

pro and con. Meaning "for and against," what is confusing is not *pro*—obviously "for"—but *con,* which usually means "with." In *pro and con,* however, *con* is an abbreviation of the Latin *contra,* "against."

probably. See *likely*.

proboscis, a long snout, has a silent *c*—proh-*boss*-ihs.

procedure. See *precede/proceed*.

proceed. See *precede/proceed*; *-cede/-ceed/-sede*.

proclivity. See *propensity/proclivity*.

procrustean refers to a uniformity of ideas or behavior imposed by violent or arbitrary methods. *Procrustes*, a Greek brigand, made his victims fit the exact size of a bed on which he placed them. If they were too short, he stretched them; if they were too long, he hacked off the part that extended over the bed. Procrustes obviously believed in the fitness of things.

procure. "Albert said that before going home, he would stop in at the dean's office and *procure* his diploma." If Albert were steeped in better English usage, he would have said "and *get* his diploma." *Procure*, where *get* will do, is pretentious.

prodigal. Do not believe, because of the Prodigal Son's wanderings, that *prodigal* means "roaming" or "straying about." It means "recklessly wasteful," "extravagant."

program. The prevailing pronunciation is *proh*-grahm. Note *grahm*, not *gruhm*. (See *diagram/program/kidnap*.)

prohibit. See *forbid/prohibit*.

prohibition. Although the *h* is sounded in *prohibit*, it is not in *prohibition*. Pronounce it proh-ih-*bish*-uhn.

proletariat. See *bourgeois/proletariat*.

promethean is the adjective form of Prometheus, the name of a Titan hero credited with having stolen fire from heaven for man. Because of this daring feat, *promethean* has come to describe a person who is daringly original. Prometheus was furthermore said to have created man from mud. Hence *promethean* also refers to that which is life-giving.

prone. See *prostrate/prone/supine/prostate*.

pronoun antecedents. The antecedent of a pronoun should be clearly recognizable. A failure to observe this rule can lead to serious confusion. No one can be sure what is meant in "The treasurer assured Morris that he would remain as teller if he became the vice president." Recast "The treasurer assured Morris that he would remain a teller if he, the treasurer, became the vice president" or "The treasurer told Morris, 'You will remain as teller if I become the vice president.' "

pronouns (reflexive, intensive). See *possessive antecedents*; *-self/ -selves*.

pronouns, relative. See *parenthetical phrases*.

propensity/proclivity are not exact synonyms, although each suggests a natural inclination. *Proclivity* is used of a predisposition for doing undesirable or unwholesome things, from cheating to committing violence. *Propensity* is used of harmless traits, those that are less serious, such as a leaning toward faultfinding or exaggerating.

prophecy/prophesy. Sometimes misspelled, as in "The class prophet wrote a *prophesy* that amazed everyone." *Prophecy* with a *cy* (it rhymes with *see*) is a noun, meaning "a prediction"; *prophesy* with an *sy* (rhymes with *sigh*) is a verb, meaning "to make a prediction, a prophecy." The class prophet wrote a *prophecy*, not a *prophesy*. Note that the verb is *prophesy*, not *prophesize*, and that its past tense is *prophesied*, not *prophesized*.

proportion. "Stu got a *proportion* of the winnings" does not say whether it was large or small, or even how it compared to the amount won. It is better to use *most, more*, or *a large (small) part*, or just *a portion of*.

propose should not be used to mean "intend," as in "I don't *propose* to go through with this matter." The primary senses of *propose* are "suggest" and "nominate." If you mean *intend*, say *intend*.

proscribe. See *prescribe/proscribe*.

prosecute. See *persecute/prosecute*.

prospective. See *perspective/prospective*.

prostrate/prone/supine/prostate. Both *prostrate* and *prone* mean "lying face downwards." *Prostrate*, in certain contexts, indicates "weakness" or "submissiveness." *Prone* is widely used figuratively to suggest a tendency or natural inclination. Although in many instances it's no great loss whether you use *prone* or *prostrate* in referring to position (but idiom may prefer one to the other), confusing *prone* with *supine* is another matter. *Supine* refers to one who is lying on his back, which is to say, on his spine. Clearly, a man lying on his stomach is not lying supine, though figuratively he may be—that is, inactive, passive. Also not to be confused are *prostrate* and *prostate*. A *prostate* is a muscular-glandular body organ that secretes seminal fluid.

protagonist. *The* leading actor, not *a* leading actor. There can be only one. He is not necessarily opposed by an *antagonist*; there may be none. And he may thoroughly dislike the part he is playing. The word *protagonist* is from Greek *protos*, "first" (not Latin *pro*, "for"), and *agonistes*, "actor." By extension it has come to mean the principal or the most conspicuous personage in any affair. An *antagonist* is an opponent.

protean is said of a person who is known for his variable attitudes, policies, or behavior. Proteus was a Greek sea-god who changed his form at will to elude capture.

pro tem is an abbreviation of Latin *pro tempore*, "for the time being." It is used of an official who is temporarily placed in office. The abbreviated form, with no period, is so well established that it has been accepted into formal English.

proved/proven. Either *proved* or *proven* may be used as the past participle of "prove" ("This work has *proved* [or *proven*] satisfactory"), but *proved* is to be preferred. When employed as an attributive adjective before a noun, *proven* is the commoner form (a *proven* belief, a *proven* ability). Equally acceptable are "not proven" and "not proved," although the former has an edge in usage.

proverbial. Weak clichés are further fatigued if accompanied by the word *proverbial*. Say, if you must, "He hit the roof" rather than "He hit the *proverbial* roof."

provided/providing. As conjunctions that presuppose a prior condition to be fulfilled, either word may serve. Most writers lean toward *provided* ("We will buy it *provided* our check arrives on time"). But do not forget another choice: *if* ("We'll go *if*— rather than *providing* or *provided*—it stops raining"). If *if* is appropriate, use it. It is simpler, less stodgy, and generally preferable. *Provided that* should be reserved to introduce a stipulation. Note that *provided* and *providing* are often followed by *that*. (See *if*.)

providing. See *dangling participles*; *provided/providing*.

provoke. See *aggravate*.

pseudonym. A *pseudonym* is an assumed name, often used as a pen name. And so is a *nom de plume*, a French term, now anglicized. The French have another expression meaning "pseudonym," *nom de guerre* (literally "war name"), which also has been anglicized—originally a name assumed by a soldier when entering military service.

psychiatrist/psychologist. Often confused by laymen. The distinctive difference between them is that a *psychiatrist* is a doctor of medicine who specializes in the treatment of mental illnesses. A *psychologist* is trained to study mental processes and behavior through a procedure called psychological analysis. A psychologist may be medically trained, but not necessarily so.

punctuation. See *colon*; *comma*; *punctuation, placement of*; *semicolon*.

punctuation, placement of. The American style is to place periods and commas inside closing quotation marks and colons and semicolons outside ("My country, right or wrong." " 'My country right or wrong'; there's a patriotic slogan for you"). (See *quotation marks*.)

purport. As a noun *purport* means "the main idea" ("The *purport* of the message was that the office will be closed tomorrow"). No problem there. As a verb meaning "to profess," "to claim," in the sense "is supposed to be" ("This letter *purports* to be a draft of one signed by the general"), *purport* is used only in the active, not the passive, voice. If the last example read, "This letter *is purported* to be a draft of one signed by the general," it would be improperly stated. Further, a person may not be the subject of *purport*. For example, "He *purports* to have taught as an army instructor" is not acceptable English.

purpose. See *for the purpose of*.

purposely/purposefully are not synonymous, even though occasionally seen interchanged. *Purposely* means "intentionally"; *purposefully* means "with conscious purpose." Something done on purpose—deliberately—is done purposely. Something done in a determined, deliberate manner—for a purpose—is done purposefully.

put. See *place/put*.

put in an appearance. Unacceptable for *appear* in better discourse.

put up with is accepted idiom but not *meet up with*.

puzzle/riddle. Not to be confused. *Puzzle* is a general word referring to anything or any statement that baffles or perplexes the mind ("His remarks [or his attitude, or his designs] are a *puzzle* to everyone"). It may also be a contrivance designed to test skill or to amuse. A *riddle* is a verbal problem, usually a game or pastime. Figuratively *riddle* is applied to any obscure statement or question.

Pyrrhic victory is not a hollow, meaningless triumph. It is a real victory, but won at too great a cost.

Q

quaint. See *queer/quaint/odd.*

qualified expert is redundant. A person not qualified would not be an expert.

quality, meaning "an attribute, character, or trait," should be used only as a noun, and not as an adjective. Not *quality* products, *quality* education, *quality* control. Say "It is a garment of high *quality*," and not "a *quality garment.*"

quandary, "a state of perplexity or uncertainty," is sometimes misspelled *quandry*. Note the two *a's.*

quantity. Best not used when referring to countable items. Use *number* instead. "There was a large *number* (rather than a *large quantity*) of boxes on the wharf."

quarantine, a period of enforced isolation, need not last forty days, even though the word *quarantine* is derived from an Italian term meaning "forty." Originally a *quarantine* was imposed on a diseased person to prevent him from infecting others. Today a person excluded from social companionship is said to have been ostracized, isolated, or *quarantined.*

quarter. When referring to time, the correct expression is *quarter to*, not *quarter of* ("It is a *quarter to* five"). (See *half/quarter*.)

quasi, meaning "more or less," "almost or somewhat," and pronounced *kwae-zie*, when serving as the first element in a compound noun (*a quasi patriot, a quasi argument, a quasi union*), is not hyphened. But it is in compound adjectives (*quasi-judicial, quasi-scientific, quasi-humorous*).

quay, a wharf, is pronounced *kee*, like "key."

queer/quaint/odd. *Queer* and *odd* refer to that which is out of the normal, something unexpected. One may say "Her dress looks *odd* (or *queer*)" or "His mannerisms are *queer* (or *odd*)." In this use the words are interchangeable. The sense of *quaint* is old-fashioned, something that, although out-of-date, is endearing. One may say that *queer* or *odd* leaves a person with a *queer* or *odd* feeling, but that something *quaint* is interesting and usually pleasant.

questionable/questioning. Occasionally confused. "When she heard the noise, the teacher cast a *questionable* eye at the boys in the hall." No doubt she cast a *questioning* eye.

question as to whether. In "The *question as to whether* he will make a good principal . . . ," drop *as to*. *Whether* needs no escort.

questioning. See *questionable/questioning*.

question, leading. See *leading question*.

question mark. If a direct question is a part of a sentence, a question mark may be used at the end of the question, even though it is within the sentence. "He wondered aloud, Is it possible that he did it? and then continued by answering it himself." "For those who ask, May all pupils attend? all they need do is read the bulletin board." (See *quotation marks*.)

questionnaire. You are justified in questioning the spelling accuracy of a person who writes *questionaire*. Its correct spelling calls for a double *n*.

quiche/quiescent. Although both words begin with *qui*, they are pronounced differently. The custard pie, *quiche*, is pronounced *keesh*; the word meaning "to be still or silent" is pronounced *kwie-es-unht*.

quick/quickly. "Do it *quick*." "Do it *quickly*." Grammatically, both sentences are correct. *Quick* sounds imperative. But *quickly*, because it is only an adverb (*quick* is a noun, an adjective, and an adverb), is more often found in serious writing. (See *slow/slowly*; *tight/tightly*.)

quicker is the comparative degree of adjective *quick*. Its adverb form, *quickly*, is "more quickly." Therefore, rather than "You can get to Omaha *quicker* by flying than by driving," say, at least in formal English, *more quickly*.

quid pro quo. Straight Latin for "something for something." Shopping for your neighbor on Tuesday because she shopped for you on Monday is a *quid pro quo*—an equal exchange.

quite can be quite ambiguous, for it may mean "completely" or "perfectly," which it does in strict usage, or "very" or "rather," which it does in general speech. "He was quite right" means "wholly right." "She is quite pretty" means either "*very* pretty" or "*rather* pretty." Which? In better writing avoid this colloquial sense. (See *fairly/quite/rather*.)

quite a few. See *few*.

quite all right. In "I have not been invited but it's *quite all right*," the italicized phrase is both redundant and illogical. *Quite* means "entirely" and *all* means "the whole of," which is repetitious. The phrase is usually employed to signify not that everything is fine but to offset the effects of something unpleasant. It is, in fact, far from all right. But everyone understands it, and it has become acceptable idiom.

quiz is regarded as an informal term. In formal style a proper substitute for verb *quiz* would be "interrogate" and for noun *quiz*, "inquiry" or "test."

quotation. See *quote*.

quotation marks. A comma should separate a quotation from its introductory words (Raoul said, "I will leave soon.") A question occasionally raised is whether to use a comma after a quotation that ends with a question mark or an exclamation point. The answer is, omit the comma ("Will you come tonight for dinner?" asked my uncle. "Get out of my store!" yelled the shopkeeper). Note that the question mark and the exclamation point, if part of the quotation, come before the quotation mark; otherwise, after ("Have you read 'Tonight or Never'?"). (See *punctuation, placement of*).

quote. Although *quote* as a substitute for noun *quotation* is widely accepted, and its use is approved by some authorities, in formal texts it is best avoided. Use *quotation* instead. *Quote* is a verb ("You may *quote* me").

q.v. is an abbreviation for Latin *quod vide*, which means "which see." Many writers use it to direct attention to another matter or entry, but in this handbook its English version—*which see*—is used instead.

rabbit/rarebit. Is it Welsh *rabbit* or Welsh *rarebit?* The original term was *rabbit,* but *rarebit* crept into the language and has all but superseded *rabbit.* Most menus today call this cheese dish *Welsh rarebit.* And there is no fighting it.

rack. See *nerve-racking.*

racket/racquet are interchangeable terms, but the first is to be preferred, even for the name of the bat used in tennis. When *racket* signifies an illegitimate business or operation, it sounds slangish.

raconteur. Note the ending, not *er* but *eur.* A word seldom heard, but one that should be known, is *raconteuse,* the feminine form for a storyteller.

racquet. See *racket/racquet.*

raise/rear. These words come into comparison when the bringing up of children is being discussed. Are children raised or reared? Is there a difference? The answer is that today *raise* is the standard expression in reference to children. In yester-years many people did not accept the term *raise* in this sense, insisting that only cattle were raised; children were reared. Now-adays parents may decide how to bring up their children—raise or rear them—or just let them grow up.

raise/rise. Do not follow transitive verb *raise* or intransitive *rise* with *up.* "The men will *rise,*" not *rise up.* "He will *raise* the flag," not *raise up.*

raison d'être. French for "reason for being," not just "reason."

rank/rancid. Do not confuse these words when speaking of a sour taste or smell. *Rank* pertains to a bad smell or taste (the *rank* meat, a *rank* cigar). And so does *rancid,* but it implies further that the taste or smell is stale, as butter would be that has gone bad.

rapport. See *often.*

rapt/wrapped. Everyone will understand if you write "Ernestine was deeply *wrapped* in thought," but correctly speaking she was *rapt*. *Rapt* means "seriously engrossed"; *wrapped* means "enclosed." Nevertheless, *wrapped* is accepted figuratively, as in "Matilda is all *wrapped up in* her wedding plans."

rare/scarce. Although these words have similar meanings in that they imply that something is hard to come by because it is in short supply, it is best to use them according to their distinctive meanings. That which is *rare* will always be difficult to find. The word is used of items that have particular value—those seldom found, items of unusual quality and great worth—gems, manuscripts of famous authors. *Scarce* refers to ordinary commodities or items that at the moment are not plentiful, things that have no lasting value in themselves. Bananas may be scarce because of the season, but their scarcity is temporary. They will become available again.

rarebit. See *rabbit/rarebit*.

rarefy. See *liquefy*.

rarely ever/seldom ever. In "We *rarely* (or *seldom*) *ever* go to Vineland," *ever* does not belong. *Ever* means "always" and *rarely* and *seldom* mean "almost never," and that makes the expression incongruous. But you may say, and properly so, "We *rarely* (or *seldom*) *if ever* go to Vineland" because *if ever* has the meaning "if at all." In this usage prefer *seldom* to *rarely*.

rather. One may use either *had rather* or *would rather*. Both expressions are acceptable. (See *fairly/quite/rather*; *relatively*.)

ratiocination, which refers to a process of logical reasoning, is not a common word, but it crops up occasionally in serious works. Pronounce it *rash*-ee-ahs-ih-*nae*-shuhn.

ravage/ravish/ravishing are not to be confused. To *ravage* is to commit violent destruction. To *ravish* is to carry off by force, to plunder, but it has also come to mean "to rape." *Ravishing* means "enchanting," "very delightful."

ravel/unravel have the same meaning. Although the prefix *un-* usually turns the meaning of a word in an opposite direction, it doesn't in this case. (See *loosen/unloosen*.)

ravenously hungry. Tautological. A very hungry person is ravenous, famished. *Ravenous* means "exceedingly hungry."

ravish/ravishing. See *ravage/ravish/ravishing*.

raze is to level, meaning "to destroy." To say "razed to the ground" is redundant.

re- means "again," which means that *again* should not accompany those words in which its sense is built in through an initial *re-*. For example, *regain, rebuild, recur, refill,* and *replace* seldom if ever can accommodate *again.* However, "to repeat again" is a legitimate phrase if what is meant is one more repetition. Compounds with *re-* are written as one word, even if the second element begins with *e* (*reelect, reemerge*), but note that *recollect and re-collect, recover* and *re-cover, reform* and *re-form* have different meanings, the hyphen giving *re-* the sense of "again."

re/in re. In Latin, *in re* means "in the matter of." In legalese and commercialese, *re*, by itself, is used in that sense. The expression as a replacement for "about," "in reference to," or "concerning" is inappropriate in formal writing.

reaction is a technical term that refers to "a display of some form of energy in response to a stimulus." In general usage it has come to signify any response, whether or not impulsive or instantaneous. But the word *reaction* is inappropriate if a person has had time to reflect, to consider. You should not ask someone to mail you his reaction to a proposal. Ask for an *opinion*, an *impression*, a *feeling*, or a *thought*, or merely a *reply*.

readable/legible share the meaning "capable of being read." A handwriting that is legible is readable. Although *readable* has a further meaning of "easy and pleasant to read" ("The book was *readable*; in fact, a pleasure from cover to cover"), this sense is not so widespread as its negative number, *unreadable*, which means "tedious," "boring," "not fit for reading."

real/really. Almost daily one hears adjective *real* misused as an intensive for its adverb form *really* ("He looks *real* good to me," "The road is *real* slippery," "Jane is *real* pretty"). In this sense *real* means "very." But in formal English it means "true," "actual," "genuine," and precedes a noun ("It is a *real* Bengal tiger"). *Really* means "actually," "truly," "in reality." *Real* is also sometimes mistakenly used as the equivalent of *serious*. Change "He's in *real* trouble" to "*serious* trouble." (See *regular/ real/true*; *sure/surely*.)

realize. See *know/realize*.

realtor. A member of the National Association of Real Estate Boards is a *Realtor*, always written with a capital *R*. In loose usage, any real estate agent is known as a *realtor* (lower case *r*). Inaccurate as that may be, the indiscriminate use of the term is widespread and recognized by some dictionaries. Do not pronounce it *realator*.

rear. See *raise/rear*.

reason is because. See *because*.

reason why. Redundant in "The *reason why* he did it was that. . . ." Omit *why*. (See *because*.)

rebel/extol. Be not beguiled by the spelling of the past tense (*rebelled, extolled*) and participial forms (*rebelling, extolling*) into spelling the present tense with a double *l*. Spell as given, not *rebell* and *extoll*. But note that *toll* has two *l*'s.

rebound/redound. "Such a foolish move will surely *rebound* to his discredit." The word required in the example in *redound*. To *rebound* is to recoil or spring back. Athletes often rebound when they are tripped up, when they slide, or when they slam into the side of a court. To *redound* is to contribute or add to. Something that has a beneficial effect on something else redounds to its benefit ("His good deed will *redound* to his advantage").

rebut/refute. The former means "to answer in contradiction," which, however, does not necessarily disprove; the latter, "to show to be false by counterargument or demolishing evidence." *Refute* is the stronger word. To *rebut* is merely an attempt to disprove; to *refute* is to succeed in disproving. (See *refute/ deny*.)

recant. See *retract/recant*.

receipt. Saying "We are *in receipt of* your package" is permissible in any style of English, but saying "We *have received* your package" is better.

receivable. See *spelling*.

recently. See *just recently*.

reckon/guess. These verbs in the sense "to suppose" or "to think"—a common usage in ordinary speech—are informal at best ("I *reckon* we ought to leave now." "I *guess* I should call home soon"). Both *reckon* and *guess* have standard meanings, but none apply to the forming of ideas that govern action.

recollect/remember. Often misused, one for the other. In "I *recollected* his name the moment I was asked," make it *remembered*. One *recollects* by making a conscious or expressed effort—that is, by bringing to consciousness what has been stored in memory. Recollection is a process, sometimes frustrating, that gradually works its way through. It is never instantaneous. *Remember* implies that one can bring to mind out of memory without or with little conscious effort ("I will always *remember* my scoutmaster and his back-breaking stamina").

recommend. Note the double *m*. (See *accommodate*.)

recommend/refer. "Dr. Flowers, I was *recommended* to you by my college roommate." Although this statement or one like it is far from unusual, it is incorrectly put. The patient was *referred* to Dr. Flowers. It was Dr. Flowers who was *recommended* by the college roommate.

recondite. See *erudite/recondite*.

recrimination. See *accusation/recrimination*.

recto. See *verso/recto*.

recur/reoccur. Both these words mean "to happen or occur again." They are seldom interchangeable, however, because they have slightly different meanings. *Recur*, the commoner of the two words, implies a repeated or periodical occurrence, certainly more than one ("We hope that an earthquake will not *recur* in San Francisco during our lifetime"). *Reoccur* suggests a single or one-time repetition ("Having passed the course in chemistry, Raymond relaxed knowing that another examination with test tubes and Bunsen burners would not *reoccur*").

recurrence/reoccurrence. To mean an occurrence again, a repetition, use *recurrence*. *Reoccurrrence* is obsolete.

recurring/frequent share the meaning of happening repeatedly. The distinction between them is that although both point to recurrences that come again and again, *frequent* implies that they take place at short intervals. An alcoholic may have *recurring* bouts of stomach discomforts (perhaps every week), but he is likely to have *frequent* desires for a nip (perhaps every hour).

redound. See *rebound/redound*.

redundancy is superfluity. A redundant expression is excessive in that it says more than is needed (complete master, first priority, habitual custom). *Tautology* (which see) is a useless repetition of an idea, the saying of a thing over again without adding anything to its clarity or force (modern furniture of today, visible to the eye, pair of twins, each and every). Most dictionaries regard these words as synonyms. Some grammarians find a shade of distinction between them, but the shade is hard to discern and even harder to explain.

refer. See *allude/refer*; *recommend/refer*.

refer back is a redundancy. The prefix *re-* means "back."

referee. See *umpire/referee*.

reference. See *with reference to*.

reflexive pronouns. See *-self/-selves*.

refurnish/refurbish are not exact synonyms and the words should not be used interchangeably. To *refurnish* is to furnish over again. Some dictionaries do not list this word because it is simply *furnish* prefixed by Latin *re-*, "again." To *refurbish* is to brighten, to do up anew. *Furbish* is polish; hence to *refurbish* is to polish again, but its usual sense today is "renovate."

refute/deny. These words have the same connotation—a contradiction of a statement made. To *deny* is to assert that what has been said or claimed is not true. To *refute* is to disprove. One who denies an allegation merely answers it by declaring it untrue. One who refutes it proves by evidence that it is false and groundless. (See *rebut/refute*.)

regard/regards. The plural noun expresses good will or good wishes ("Give my *regards* to Broadway"). The prepositional phrases *in regard to* and *with regard to* mean "in reference to." Do not confuse them with the plural form *regards*. *In regards to* and *with regards to* are nonstandard. If you wish to take a safe course, see whether the simpler words *in* and *about* will serve. If they do, prefer them, not merely for the sake of accuracy but because they economize. (See *consider/regard*.)

regarding/concerning/respecting. Requesting someone's opinion by asking for his comments *regarding* (or *concerning* or *respecting*) the matter is unnecessary and unwise. It is simpler and more direct to use *about*.

regardless. See *irregardless*.

regret. See *repent/regret*.

regretful/regrettable. "I think it *regretful*, or is it *regrettable*, that I am always mispronouncing your name." *Regrettable*, the word needed, means "causing regret." *Regretful* means "feeling remorse," "sorrowful." *Regrettable* implies that a happening is unfortunate ("Estelle's boorish manners at the dinner table were *regrettable*"). Perhaps if her behavior were called to her attention, she would be regretful. As a general rule use *regretful* of a person and *regrettable* of an event, occurrence, or condition.

regular/real/true. "He's a *regular* hero." When used in this sense, *regular* is informal. Make it *a real* or *a true* hero.

regular routine. By definition a *routine* is a regular method. Hence *regular* is redundant with *routine*. And so it is in *a regular weekly conference* or in *the regular monthly meeting*.

rehabilitate. The question is whether *rehabilitate*, meaning "to restore to a good position" or "to reform," is used only of people or is used also of things. Although authorities lack a consensus, the frequent use of *rehabilitate* by urban restorers of run-down areas has established the term among redevelopers of real estate. This extended meaning is now employed as often as its traditional sense, to restore a person to a position of respectability or usefulness.

reiterate/iterate. *Reiterate* means "to say again." And so does *iterate*. Which makes these words puzzling. Certainly English doesn't need both words when one will do. Reserve the use of *reiterate* for something said over and over again. Perhaps that is its only distinction from *iterate*.

relating to/relative to. Overused and pretentious, as in "I read a book *relative to* horse breeding." Make it *on* or *about*.

relation/relative. You may call your aunts, uncles, and cousins either *relations* or *relatives*. The words are synonymous and are standard English to designate persons related by blood or marriage. Some writers favor *relative* but the choice is personal, purely a matter of taste ("All my *relatives* [or *relations*] live in Wyoming"). But be careful not to say "My neighbor is no *relation to* Dr. Reynaud." Make it *"no relation of* Dr. Reynaud" or "is not *related to.* "

relative clauses. See *one of those . . . who*.

relatively should not be inserted in a sentence if there is nothing to indicate a relationship. "Buying a house now is a *relatively* wise move to make." Relative to what? Omit *relatively*. Substituting *comparatively* for *relatively* would not be helpful. That adverb is properly used only if a standard of comparison preceded. Those who say it is a *comparatively* easy game to learn are thinking of *rather* or *fairly*, for which *comparatively* is not a synonym. And neither is *relatively*. But one may rightly say, "Fifty applicants were tested, but *comparatively* few were accepted."

reluctant. See *reticent/reluctant*.

remain, like *feel* and other copulative verbs (which see), may take an adjective ("In the face of danger, we *remain calm*"). If manner is to be shown, then an adverb must follow ("We will *remain calmly* on the porch until the storm subsides"). (See *bad/badly*.)

remand back. See *revert back*.

remediable/remedial have as their key sense *remedy*. But that which is *remediable* is capable of being remedied or cured ("Poor speaking habits are *remediable*"), whereas that which is *remedial* provides the remedy. It cures or relieves ("*Remedial* reading courses have helped many children").

remember. See *recollect/remember*.

remembrance seems as though it should begin with the word *remember*. But it doesn't. It is not spelled *rememberance*—no *e* immediately after the *b*.

remind. "You may keep books out no longer than two weeks," the librarian *reminds*. To set the example straight, *reminds*, since it is a transitive verb, must be followed by an object, as, for example, "reminds the students."

reminiscence. Note the *sc* combination. Not *reminisence*, but *reminiscence*. Be careful.

remit has two basic meanings, "to send" (money) or "to transmit" and "to send back" ("The judge will *remit* the case to a lower court for retrial"). The context should make clear the meaning intended. "Peter was instructed to *remit* the fine" may mean, out of context, either that Peter should pay the fine or that he should return it to the person who paid it.

removable. See *spelling*.

renounce. See *retract/recant.*

renowned, meaning "widely celebrated," "famous," is sometimes misspelled *reknowned.* Watch it.

reoccur. See *recur/reoccur.*

reoccurrence. See *recurrence/reoccurrence.*

repairable/irreparable. Something repairable can be put in good condition—that is, mended. That which is irreparable has been damaged beyond repair. Observe that *irreparable* has no internal *i* and that its second syllable is stressed.

repeat again. See *re-.*

repel/repulse. Often interchanged, since both mean "to drive away" or "to drive back." There is no dissimilarity in sense between "The enemy was *repelled* at the city gates" and "The enemy was *repulsed*. . . ." *Repulse*, in the example, implies the presence of physical force, but it may also mean "to reject" ("Amanda *repulsed* everyone's advances at the picnic"). Only *repel* connotes aversion or disgust which may be induced by a person's offensive habits or condition (when eating he may drip food on himself or have a body odor). Of course, a person may intentionally act in such a disgusting manner as to repel anyone. He would be, we might then say, *repulsive.*

repent/regret. Although the definitions of these words overlap, there is a distinction in their application. One who regrets may also wish to repent, but this feeling does not always follow. To *regret* is to feel sorry, to be distressed about something, the same feeling that one who repents has. But *regret* suggests a lesser degree of feelings of guilt than *repent.* One who repents desires to make amends for what was not done or for what was done wrong.

repertoire/repertory. A *repertoire* is defined as "the list of plays, operas, parts, or pieces, that a company, an actor, a musician, or a singer is prepared to perform." The term *repertory* is given the same meaning. Hence you may say that the Temple University Players have a *repertoire* (or *repertory*) of at least ten plays. When reference is made specifically to the theater, *repertory* is preferred (*repertory* theater, *repertory* company).

replace has two senses, which should be differentiated. To avoid ambiguity, the context must make clear whether *replace* is being used to mean "to put back into place" ("to put in place again") or "to succeed" ("to fill or take the place of"). Saying that the mayor, after his trial, was replaced may mean he was returned to office or that someone was substituted for him. (See *substitute/ replace*.)

replaceable. See *spelling*.

replete. Authorities disagree on whether *replete* means "filled with"—that is, completely so—or simply "abundantly supplied with." It's a writer's choice, but preferably, rather than *replete*, use *full* or *filled* when it will do. Be sure, if *replete* is used, not to use it with a negative, as in "The library is *not replete* with magazines."

replica is often loosely used to stand for "copy," "counterpart," "duplicate," "imitation," "miniature," "model," or "reproduction." It is best, if one of these words is appropriate to the context, to use it instead of *replica*. In the field of art, *replica* has a narrower meaning. There it is a duplicate or copy of a work made by the original artist or made under his supervision.

reported. See *reputed/reported*.

represent does not mean "compose" or "make up." Do not say "Blacks now *represent* the majority of school students in Detroit." Make it "now constitute." To *represent* is to stand for or symbolize.

repulse. See *repel/repulse*.

reputation. See *character/reputation*.

reputed/reported. Not to be confused. *Reputed* means "generally considered," "supposed to be such" ("He is *reputed* to be an anthropology authority." "Mr. Ralston is *reputed* to be the bank's major stockholder"). *Reported* means "announced," "described," "made known" ("The accident was *reported* to the police immediately").

rescind. See *retract/recant*.

resign. Although it is correct to say "He *resigned from* his ambassadorial post," you may also correctly say "He *resigned* the ambassadorship." In the sense given, *resign* may be used as an intransitive verb (followed by *from*) or as a transitive verb (with a direct object).

resistance. See *existence/resistance*.

respectfully/respectively. The former means "full of respect" or "with respect" ("He addressed his economics professor *respectfully*"). The latter means "with respect or reference to each of several things in the order in which they were mentioned" ("John, Paul, and Alphonse married a girl from Oklahoma, New Mexico, and Wyoming, *respectively*").

respecting. See *regarding/concerning/respecting*.

respective. Omit when it adds no meaning to the sentence. In "Each diner offered his *respective* toast," *each* has already said what *respective* suggests.

restaurateur. This word has no *n*, not *restauranteur*.

restive is not a synonym for *restless*. Use *restive* of a balky animal or a fretful person. Although dictionaries define *restive* as "uneasy," "restless," it is best to discriminate between these words. A person too nervous to sleep is restless, not restive.

result. "Harmon injured his leg *as the result of* the collision." "Our plants were damaged *as the result of* the hurricane." The leg injury and the damage to the plants were, you can be sure, not the only result of the accident and the hurricane. Change the phrase "as *the* result of" to "as *a* result of."

résumé, meaning "a summary" and pronounced rae-zyoo-*mae* or *rae*-zyoo-mae, is preferably written with an acute accent over each *e* (*résumé*). Without these marks, the word might be taken for *resume*, a verb meaning "to begin again."

resume/continue. The question whether *resume* or *continue* should be used in "After the recess we will *resume* (or *continue*) our discussion" may be answered, first, by saying that either word may properly serve, and second, by adding that *resume*, with its sense of continuing after an interruption, is preferable.

resurrect. See *enthuse*.

reticent/reluctant. "Little Johnnie felt somewhat *reticent* when asked to go to the front of the room before all those people." No doubt the word intended was *reluctant*. *Reticent* means "mum" or "disinclined to speak." *Reluctant* means simply "averse" or "unwilling," and is not necessarily associated with speech.

retract/recant. Use *retract* to mean "withdraw." A statement or promise that is retracted is withdrawn, leaving matters just as they were before the statement or promise was made. Synonyms are *rescind* and *revoke*. Use *recant* when forced to go back, not only to withdraw but also to disavow—a denial of one's own words. A synonym is *renounce*.

retroactive is followed by *to*, not *from* ("All charges are *retroactive to* September").

return back. The only way a person can return. Omit *back*; it is unnecessary. *Return* means "to go back."

reveal. See *disclose/reveal.*

revenge. See *avenge/revenge.*

Reverend/Honorable. Do not follow this title of respect with the surname only. Include the first name or initials (the *Reverend* A. T. Smythe, the *Honorable* Arlin Richards).

reverend/reverent. Distinguish carefully between these words. *Reverend* means "worthy of reverence" or "entitled to great respect." *Reverent* means "feeling or showing reverence" or "deeply respectful."

reverse/revert. Be careful with these words. To *reverse* is to turn the other way or to turn upside down. To *revert* is to go back. (See *obverse/reverse*.)

revert back. Since *revert* means "to go back" (*re-*, from Latin, means "back"), what reverts can only go back. *Revert back* is therefore redundant. And so is *remand back*, and for the same reason. *Remand* means "to send back."

revolve/rotate. Often mixed up, usually *rotate* where *revolve* is called for. To *revolve* is to move in a circle, to orbit a central point, as the moon revolves around the earth or the wheels of a moving car around its axle. To *rotate* is to turn around its own center, as the earth rotates on its axis or as a top spins on its tip.

rhetorical question. A question for which no answer is expected; it is asked for its effect, not for information. In fact, there may be no logical answer ("Who among us can predict the future?").

rhyme/rime. The first is the preferred spelling. (See *nor any drop to drink.*)

rhythm. Note the spelling.

riddle. See *puzzle/riddle.*

right/rightly. *Right* is a noun (the *right* to leave), an adjective (the *right* time to leave), and an adverb (leave *right* after the game). Whether to use adverb *right* or its *-ly* form *rightly* depends on the position of the adverb in the sentence. When the adverb precedes the verb, with the sense "properly," *rightly* is called for ("Peter *rightly* refused to answer." "He *rightly* assumed that his wife had signed"). When the adverb follows the verb, *right* is the correct form ("Elaine never does anything *right*." "Write it *right*"). (See *privilege*; *sharp/sharply*.)

right along/right away enjoy idiomatic support, but in formal composition, substitute *directly, immediately,* or *at once.*

rightly. See *right/rightly.*

riled is a word not generally accepted by formalists ("Not receiving his report on time *riled* him"). Make it "annoyed" or "angered."

ring. "At the check-out counter, the cashier *rung* up the items quickly." Incorrect. The past tense of *ring* is *rang*; its participle is *rung*. "The cashier *rang* up the items quickly." (See *swim.*)

Rio Grande/Sahara/Mt. Fuji are proper names in English. The first one is a river, and the second an arid area or desert. But since in Spanish *Rio* means "river" and in Arabic *Sahara* means "desert," correct reference, to avoid redundancy, is to omit the words "river" and "desert" and say merely *Rio Grande* and *Sahara. Mt. Fuji* or *Fujiyama,* a mountain, offers a choice, but *Mt. Fujiyama* is repetitious—*yama* means "mountain."

rise/arise/get up. In formal English one *arises,* and less formally, *rises* in the morning when he awakens and leaves his bed. But most of us do it informally—we *get up.* (See *awake/wake.*)

rob/steal. To *rob* is to take property feloniously. But it must be taken from a person or place. The thing taken is not robbed, the person or place is. To *steal* is to take furtively. It may be a cookie from the jar or a kiss from your favorite aunt—or it may be possessions belonging to another person. In sum, a person or place is robbed; possessions are stolen.

robber/thief/burglar. These criminals have one thing in common; they have unlawfully taken something that didn't belong to them. A *robber* steals by using threats or violence. A *thief* steals secretly or stealthily. A *burglar* enters a premises with felonious intent. Someone who puts a gun to your ribs and then extracts your wallet is a robber. If he lifts your wallet by picking your pocket, he's a thief. If he enters your home through a window and takes a wallet from your nighttable, he's a burglar.

roman à clef, literally "a novel with a key," is a novel in which the characters represent actual persons but have been given fictitious names to conceal their identity. Oscar Wilde was caricatured in *The Green Carnation*. The *f* is not sounded in the last word, which rhymes with *may*.

Romance languages are not languages involving romantic stories. They are languages which have developed from the Roman tongue—Latin. These include French, Spanish, Italian, and Portuguese.

roman letters/russian dressing are words derived from geographical names. Since their sense is distinct from the original source, the words are written in lower case. Other words so affected are *anglicize, arabic* figures, *manila* envelope, *venetian* blinds, and *turkish* towels. But capitalize *Roman* in *Roman* numerals. There is no settled policy concerning the capitalization of these proper adjectives and others like them. Follow the suggestions in a stylebook or choose your own style.

Roman numerals. When typing or printing Roman numerals, remember that "one" is represented by I, not by the Arabic 1.

rotate. See *revolve/rotate*.

round. In such expressions as "He *turned around*" and "John *walked around* the block," *around* is preferred to *round*. But a versatile athlete is "an all-round athlete."

rout/route. A *route* is a way or course. Colloquially *rout* is given the same meaning ("My newspaper *rout* [or *route*] takes me to the edge of town"), and they are pronounced alike—*root*. Verb *route*, meaning "to set into flight" or "to defeat disastrously," is pronounced *rowt*.

R.S.V.P. The French abbreviation for "Please reply" stands for *répondez* (not *réspondez*) *s'il vous plaît*.

rumple. See *crumple/rumple*.

run/manage/operate. A not unusual statement is "He *runs* a good shop." The meaning is clear but the wording is colloquial. In writing and in better speech, use *manage* when referring to an employee in charge, and *operate* when referring to the proprietor.

run-on sentence.   See *comma splice*.

Russia/U.S.S.R.   Often confused. Russia, the former empire, is now the Union of Soviet Socialist Republics (or Soviet Union), of whose fifteen republics the largest is Russia.

russian dressing.   See *roman letters/russian dressing*.

Sabbath/Sunday are not synonyms. *Sabbath* is a day of rest. It is, according to the Ten Commandments, the seventh day of the week; hence Saturday—the day to rest and worship. Sunday is the first day of the week. Jews and Seventh-day Adventists observe the Sabbath on Saturday; Muslims, on Friday. Most Christians worship on Sunday and, since it is their day of rest, they call this day *Sabbath*.

sacrilegious. Not only the irreligious misspell this word. Although *sacrilegious* pertains to religion (more specifically, to disrespect of what is sacred), it does not come from the same ancestor. *Sacrilegious* is simply the adjective form of *sacrilege*. Note the *rile* in *sacrilegious*. Pronounce it sak-rih-*lee*-juhs.

Sahara Desert. See *Rio Grande/Sahara/Mt. Fuji.*

said has several suitable substitutes—*replied, answered,* even *whispered.* But not words that indicate facial expressions. Not "Men are like children," she laughed, or "Woodworking is therapy for me," he smiled.

salable. Preferably spelled as given. Note that the *l* is not immediately followed by *e*. Many words drop a terminal *e* when adding *-able*: *excusable, likable, lovable, pleasurable, sizable, usable.* (See *spelling.*)

salvageable. See *spelling.*

same/similar are not alike in meaning and are therefore not to be interchanged "He jogged two miles yesterday and the *same* (not a *similar*) distance today." *Same* means precisely alike, identical. The likeness of that which is *similar* is not exactly the same as the object to which it is being compared. It may be said that something that is the same has an absolute resemblance; something similar has a partial resemblance. You may use *similar* with a copulative verb ("This fabric *is similar* to that"). But with a finite verb, its adverb form is required ("This machine *works similarly* to that").

same identical. "It's the *same identical* pattern my sister selected" is double talk. Use either *same* or *identical*.

sample. See *example/sample*.

sanatorium/sanitarium are listed in some dictionaries as synonymous terms. But strictly speaking, a *sanatorium* is an institution for the treatment of diseases, a place for healing. The word derives from Latin *sanare*, "to heal." A *sanitarium* is a health resort. This word comes from Latin *sanitas*, "health." Note the *ato* in the spelling of *sanatorium* and the *ita* in *sanitarium*.

sanction. Noun *sanction* means "approval" and, quite oppositely, "disapproval or punishment." This latter sense is used especially of embargoes to punish a nation. The context must resolve its ambiguity.

sanguinary/sanguine. "He's so cheerful that everyone says he's blessed with a *sanguinary* disposition." The word needed is *sanguine*, which means "naturally cheerful and hopeful." *Sanguinary* means "bloody" or "bloodthirsty" (a *sanguinary* battle). Be careful not to confuse.

sarcasm/irony. Do not mix up these words; they are not interchangeable. *Sarcasm* consists of bitter remarks designed to give pain. *Irony* is saying the opposite of what is meant. "It was *sarcasm* when he called me a big baboon, but it was *irony* when he referred to my unemployed brother as a big success."

sarsaparilla, a soft drink, may be pronounced *sas-pah-rih-luh*, but when written, it needs an *r* in the first syllable. And note the second *a* and double *l*.

satiric/satirical. These adjectives have the same meaning, "sarcastic," and are therefore interchangeable. Formal usage prefers *satirical* ("His *satirical* remarks stunned everyone"). Note that *satyric*, meaning "lecherous," is derived from *Satyr*, a Greek woodland god known for his revelry with maidens.

savant/savoir. A *savant*, not a *savoir* (a French verb meaning "to know," "to be knowledgeable"), is "a wise or learned man." From *savoir* has come the expression *savoir faire*, the French equivalent of "poise."

save. In "All *save* the captain were drowned," *except* would be better than *save*. In the sense used, *save* sounds affected.

savings, as in "His savings *were* (not *was*) considerable," is a mass noun treated as a plural. But in "Becoming a teetotaler meant *a savings* of $10 a week," the "a" indicates that a singular noun must follow, which *savings* is not. Make it *a saving*. Of course, the sentence could be restructured: "Becoming a teetotaler meant *saving* $10 a week," but there *saving* is not a noun. Incidentally, time that is one hour ahead of standard time is termed *daylight saving time*, not *daylight savings time*. In that phrase *saving* has no terminal *s*.

savoir. See *savant/savoir*.

saw where, as in "I *saw where* the papers said a depression is imminent" or "I could *see where* anyone might believe it," is substandard. Do not use *where* for *that* to introduce a noun clause.

scan. "I scanned it" does not say whether you glanced at it or scrutinized it. Originally a reference to the metrical structure of poetry ("By *scanning* Shakespeare's sonnets, one learns that the poet favored iambic pentameter"), *scan* has acquired in current ordinary usage two diametrically opposed meanings, "to look hastily" (to skim newspaper headlines) and "to examine minutely" (to pore over a map). One scanner is casual; the other, thorough. The context must make clear the sense intended.

scarce. See *rare/scarce*.

scarcely. See *double negatives*; *hardly/scarcely*.

scared. See *frightened/scared*.

scarify is not related to the word *scare*. To *scarify* is to make scratches or cuts, as on skin. Figuratively it means to criticize severely. Pronounce it like *scar(ab)*.

scent. See *smell/stench/scent*.

schism, meaning "division," is pronounced *sihz'*m, the *ch* is silent.

scissors. For those troubled by the grammatical number to ascribe to this noun, be assured that some authorities consider it a singular (the scissors *is*) and others, a plural (the scissors *are*). More writers lean toward the latter form (the scissors *are*).

score. In Lincoln's memorable *Gettysburg Address*, the opening statement "Four score and seven years ago" adds up to 87 years. A *score* is the equivalent of twenty years.

Scotch/Scots/Scotsman. Residents of Scotland prefer to be called *Scots* or *Scotsmen*, not *Scotch* or, and even less, *Scotchmen*. No one objects to such terms as *Scotch whiskey* and *Scotch tape*. In Britain, "Scotch" means whiskey.

scrip/script. Far too often one hears *script* used for *scrip*. Be careful. *Script*, as in *manuscript*, refers to something written; *scrip* is a certificate representing money or other fiscal documents, often issued by a government in time of emergency.

scrupulous. See *meticulous/scrupulous.*

scrutinize. "He scrutinized the catalog closely" contains a superfluous adverb. To *scrutinize* is "to examine or search closely." One who scrutinizes always gives careful attention. Hence *closely* in the example should be excised.

sculpt/sculpture. A question sometimes raised is which of these verbs is preferred in formal writing. The answer is that they both may be used in any style of writing, for they are equally acceptable. Those writers who prefer *sculpture* to *sculpt* ("It took two months to *sculpture* that hand" rather than "two months to *sculpt* that hand") believe that *sculpture* sounds more dignified then *sculpt.*

seasonable/seasonal. Use *seasonable* to mean that which is appropriate to the season of the year. Snow in Boston is seasonable in January, since it comes at the expected time of the year. It would not be in July. Reserve *seasonal* to refer to that which pertains to, or is connected with, a season: seasonal employment, seasonal business activity, the seasonal migration of birds.

seasons, capitalization of. Do not capitalize the seasons of the year—*spring, summer, fall, winter*—unless personified (Old Man Winter).

second/third. Most stylebooks recommend 2*d* and 3*d* as ordinal figures rather than 2*nd* and 3*rd*. And note the hyphen in "a second mate is *second-rate.*" *Second-best* and *second-class* are also hyphened. But *secondhand* is written solid.

secondhanded is not a word in the English language. Use *secondhand*. However, *underhanded* is acceptable.

-sede. Only *supersede* (from Latin *super*, "above," and *sedere*, "to sit") takes *-sede*. (See *-cede/-ceed/-sede*.)

seeing as how. See *being.*

seem. A copulative, or linking, verb. It takes adjectives, not adverbs ("He *seemed* happy." "He *seemed* good"). (See *can't seem to.*)

seeming paradox. Omit *seeming*. A *paradox* is a seemingly contradictory statement that may nonetheless be well founded.

seize. See *siege/seize.*

seldom ever. See *rarely ever/seldom ever.*

select/selected. A *select* course of study is a program of courses chosen from a larger number; a *selected* course of study is a program of higher grade or quality than the ordinary.

-self/-selves. Pronouns with these endings are either reflexive ("I cut *myself*"), which turns the action back on the doer, or intensive ("I *myself* did it"), which emphasizes the doer. But not "Send it to George or *myself*" (objective case *me* is required). And do not use a *-self* form after *between*—not *between you and myself*, for example, but *between you and me* (*me* is the object of preposition *between*). "My wife and *myself* invite you to tea" also needs recasting, "My wife and I," since *I*, as a subject of the sentence, must be in the nominative case. (See *between you and I.*)

self-confessed. He did it the only way possible (who else can confess for you?) *Self* here is redundant.

self-deprecate/-depreciate. See *deprecate/depreciate.*

semi-. The guide laid down by most style manuals is to spell *semi-* compounds solid (*semifinal, semiannual, semiofficial*) but to hyphen when the second element is capitalized or begins with *i* (*semi-Hispanic, semi-independent*). (See *bi-/semi-.*)

semicolon. A troublesome mark of punctuation to many people. Yet it should not be, for a semicolon has only two common uses. The first is to separate main clauses not joined by a conjunction ("Edmund studied hard; his brother loafed") or joined by a conjunctive adverb ("He spent years in prison; *however*, he was unreformed"). The second is to demarcate parts of a series ("Ronald had five pencils, all red; Susan had six, three red and three blue; Arthur had two, both blue"). And note that the word *semicolon* is not hyphened. (See *punctuation, placement of.*)

semimonthly. See *bi/semi.*

señor/señora. See *accent marks*.

sensual/sensuous. Since both words denote an appeal to the senses, confusing them is an easy matter. *Sensual*, which has an unfavorable connotation, refers to physical pleasures—to bodily appetites—especially sexual pleasures that, so to speak, gratify the flesh. (As a mnemonic aid note that both *sensual* and *sexual* end in *ual*.) *Sensuous*, on the other hand, pertains to intellectual pleasures, aesthetic pursuits, the beauty that emanates from art, music, literature, fine food, and the like—those experienced through all the senses.

sentence fragments. Those disturbed by sentence fragments should know that they have been used, and effectively, by many respected writers. Try one. And see. Like this one. But don't overwork them because then they become less effective.

sentence structure. "The teacher asked for six tall and one short *boys*" sounds awkward. Switching *boys* to *boy*, which is often the case because of the attraction of the singular "one," does not add up—six and one make more than *one boy*. The sensible solution is to recast—for example, "The teacher asked for six tall boys and one short one."

Sentences containing two or more subjects that pertain to one idea are considered a unity and are construed as a singular construction. Hence they take a singular verb (ham and cheese *is*, a horse and buggy *is*, love and affection *is*, the long and short of it *is*). (See *collective elements*.)

Be alert to the placement of modifiers that look in two directions, that can modify the word before it or the one after it. These modifiers, called *squinting modifiers*, make for ambiguity. "The speaker whom the audience greeted enthusiastically bowed three times" may mean "the audience greeted enthusiastically" or "the speaker enthusiastically bowed three times." In "The athletes I know will warmly welcome the new coach," *I know* may refer to the "athletes" (those whom I know) or indicate a belief that there will be a warm reception. (See *parallel structure; word arrangements*.)

sequence of tenses in direct quotations. See *direct quotations*.

sergeant/earnest. Two commonly misspelled words. *Sergeant*, although pronounced with *ar*, is spelled with *er*. It does not have an *a* in its first syllable, but it does in its second. *Earnest* is pronounced with *er*, but it has an *a* (a mute *a*) in its first syllable. It therefore is spelled *earnest*. Just remember that someone in earnest has his *ear* attuned.

serial comma. Much has been written about the desirability of using or omitting a comma before the connective *and* where three or more elements are mentioned. Should one write *red, white, and blue* or *red, white and blue*? Newspapers usually omit the comma before *and* in a series. But scholarly writing requires it. The best course to follow is to use the comma to avoid possible confusion. Certainly the presence of the serial comma is not bothersome, yet its absence could cause ambiguity. "I like brown, purple, orange and red" might mean that I like three colors, the third being a combination of orange and red, or that I like four colors, the third being orange and the fourth red.

serious crisis. Have you ever known of, or been in, a crisis that wasn't?

set/sit. In ordinary usage, *set*, meaning "to place" or "to adjust," is a transitive verb requiring a direct object ("*set* the plates on the table," "*set* the clock," "*set* the record straight"). *Sit*, meaning "to take a position" or "to be seated," is largely intransitive ("he *sits* down," "the town *sits* on a hill," "we'll *sit* outside"). But these principles have exceptions—the sun *sets* (intransitive); a man *sits* himself down (transitive). Further, in a few constructions either *sit* or *set* is acceptable: the hen *sits* or *sets* on eggs; the jacket *sits* (or *sets*) well on his shoulders.

sewage/sewerage. *Sewage* is waste material, refuse matter, the contents of the sewer. *Sewerage* is the system of sewers through which waste is removed. Therefore, it is the *sewage* (not the *sewerage*) that contaminates the stream.

shall/will. Controversial auxiliaries. Most authorities agree as follows: use *shall* in the first person to express simple futurity—that is, that something will happen—and *will* in the second and third persons. To express determination, obligation, promise, willingness, or permission, reverse the formula—use *will* in the first person and *shall* in the second and third persons. This is the practice in better writing. Which means that MacArthur's often repeated declaration—"I shall return" (determination)—is, according to these principles, a grammatical blunder, as is Martin Luther King's "We shall overcome" (same reason).

In spite of the rules propounded through the years by respected grammarians, in general speech and in informal writing, in fact in the usage of most people including the educated, *will* has taken over and is used with all persons. *Shall* has just about disappeared. (See *shall be/am*.)

shall be/am. Expressing present time when a future tense is called for is unwarranted. This common error often appears when an invitation is extended. The invitee says "I *shall be* pleased to accept." What he means is "I *am* pleased to accept." He may of course add, "I shall be pleased to come," a pleasure he expects to have when he comes. But at this moment his only pleasure is in accepting the invitation.

shambles. Originally a designation for stalls where meat was sold, and then a place to slaughter animals, *shambles* has by extension come to signify any scene of carnage. In popular usage its sense has been further broadened to apply to a mere state of chaos or disorder, without reference to bloodshed ("The playroom was a *shambles*"). Many authorities deprecate this current extension.

shape is commonly but inaccurately used for "condition" in a sentence such as "He's in bad *shape* to play tennis today."

share. See *part/portion/share*.

sharp/sharply. A word that can serve as an adjective and an adverb is generally not used by formalists adverbially if it has a distinctive form of adverb. *Sharp* and *sharply* is a case in point. Adverb *sharply* is preferred except where abruptness or vigilance is involved ("He made a *sharp* left." "The time set was five o'clock *sharp*." "Look *sharp*"). (See *right/rightly*; *slow/slowly*.)

she should be used instead of *her* in "If you were *her*, would you go?" The verb *to be* always takes the same case after it as the one before it. Since *you* is in the nominative case, *she*, which also is in the nominative case, must follow. This also applies to *I*, *he*, *we*, and *they*.

ship/boat. Even educated speakers and writers mix these terms. What they should do, if in doubt, is use general terms instead, like *vessel* or *craft*. A *ship* is a large sea-going vessel. A *boat*, propelled by oars, sails, or an outboard motor, is relatively small. All ships carry boats, lifeboats that is. Some boats do not fully fit this description. Ferry boats, for example, are not small, but they do not travel the sea lanes.

short. See *brief/short.*

short-lived. See *long-lived.*

shortened words. Many clipped words have been accepted into formal English. Their original forms may be unknown, even by the educated. The full name of a *bus*, for example, is *omnibus* (the dative case of Latin *omnes*), meaning "for all." A *fanatic* is a religious zealot. Shorten the word and get a sports enthusiast, a *fan.* The word *mob* is an abbreviation of *mobile vulgus*, "the fickle crowd," and *taxi* is from the elongated *taximeter-cabriolet* (Latin *taxare*, "to charge," French *metre*, "to measure," *cabriolet*, a French two-wheeled carriage).

should/would. In general usage follow the rules applicable to *shall* and *will.* In indirect discourse, when quoting what someone has said or written (which is always in a dependent clause), replace *shall* in the original statement with *should, will* with *would.* "I *will* send you a copy of my book" (direct quotation). "He said that he *would* send a copy of his book" (indirect quotation). (See *ought/should.*)

Strict grammarians use *should* as an auxiliary in preference to *would* after a first person pronoun (*I, we*). To be absolutely correct, one should say, "I *should* like to go," rather than " I *would* like to go." In less formal usage *would* predominates, even among educated people. The decline in the use of *should* parallels that of *shall* in *shall/will* constructions. (See *shall/will.*)

should not/ought not to. See *hadn't ought to*; *ought/should.*

should of is a nonstandard expression for *should have* ("Seymour *should have* [not *should of*] telephoned earlier"). It is sometimes seen even in educated writing, but it shouldn't be. Equally undesirable are *could of* for "could have," *might of* for "might have," and *must of* for "must have."

show up. "He should *show up* soon" informally means "he should make an appearance" or "arrive" soon. In formal usage prefer one of the latter substitutes or recast the sentence.

shrink/sink. These verbs follow a similar pattern in that they have two forms for the past tense—*shrank, shrunk* and *sank, sunk.* The first named is commoner. The past participle of *shrink* is either *shrunk* or *shrunken* (when used adjectivally [an ancient *shrunken* head], the form *shrunken* predominates). *Sink* offers no choice. Its past participle is *sunk*. To rhyme with *shrunken,* you have to switch to the adjective *sunken* (a *sunken* ship).

shut. See *close/shut.*

shy/shy of. See *modest/shy.*

sic. Everyone should know that Latin *sic* meaning "so" is used to signal an inaccuracy in the original material, usually a misspelling ("Ronald Regan [*sic*] was born in Illinois"). The *sic* indicates that the quotation was printed exactly as it had been written.

siege/seize. "The *seige* lasted two days; then the general was *siezed.*" Of course *seige* is correctly spelled *siege,* and *siezed* should be spelled *seized.* These misspellings are far from uncommon.

Sierra Nevada mountains is an expression that is technically wrong because in Spanish *Sierra Nevada* means "snowy mountains." In strictly formal English, be sure to omit *mountains,* but in general writing and in speech, adding *mountains* is a peccadillo.

sight/site/spectacle. "What a *sight* for sore eyes. It is a perfect *site* to build on." These words should not be confused. *Sight* means vision or something seen or to be seen. *Site* is a place or piece of land. *Spectacle* is synonymous with *sight* except that a *spectacle* is a display, a striking sight, something unusual. Both *sight* and *spectacle* can be used derogatorily ("In that hideous purple dress, she is a *sight.* In fact she's making a *spectacle* of herself").

signature/autograph. A name written by a person on a check is his *signature.* If an actor signs his name under his picture, it is more appropriately called an *autograph.*

similar is sometimes misspelled *similiar.* Do not insert a third *i.* (See *same/similar.*)

similar to. Consider *like* as a substitute. It gets to the point more quickly and saves a word besides. "It was an experience *similar to* the one we had last year" (*like* the one).

simile. See *metaphor/simile.*

simplistic/simplified. These adjectives share the meaning "made plainer" or "made less complicated." To indicate that something is no longer complex, you may say it has been simplified or made simplistic. Be careful of *simplistic*, however. It has acquired in the minds of many people the sense of "greatly simplified" or "oversimplified." To say that someone's explanation is simplistic is to imply that it is so plainly understandable that anyone should grasp it with no further explanation. And note that *simplistic* is not a synonym for *simple*.

simply meaning "really" or "absolutely" is colloquial (*simply* great, *simply* wonderful, *simply* priceless). Avoid in serious writing.

simulate/dissimulate. To *simulate* is to put on a false appearance, like a person feigning illness. To *dissimulate* is to hide under a pretense, to dissemble, as does a person who conceals his dishonesty with charitable gifts.

since. "We lived here *since* 1948" needs correcting. When *since*, expressing time, is preceded by a verb, it should be in a perfect tense, not in the past tense ("We *have lived* here *since* 1948"). (See *ago/since*.)

sine die in Latin means "without a day." In the United States it is used by groups to indicate that, although their business has not been concluded and they will be reconvening to continue their work, they are adjourning without setting a new meeting date.

sine qua non, Latin for "without which nothing," refers to an essential thing or condition, which means it is indispensable. In popular usage the phrase has been extended to include persons, who are often more indispensable than anything else. (See the dedication page in *The Story Behind the Word*.)

sink. See *shrink/sink*.

sip. See *brief outline/little sip*.

sister-in-law is pluralized by adding an *s* to *sister—sisters-in-law*. (See *possessive case forms*.)

sit. See *set/sit*.

site. See *sight/site/spectacle*.

sizable. See *salable*.

size. "They owned a small-*size* (or small-*sized*) farm in Iowa." Either the noun or the adjective may form a compound adjective and be properly used in this construction. Of course, the example cited could be simplified by saying "They owned a small farm in Iowa," omitting *size* entirely. When *size* is used strictly as a noun, it is incorrect to omit the *of* in these expressions: "this *size of* picture tube" or "that *size of* box."

size up is commonly used to mean "appraise" or "make a judgment about" ("He walked into the room and *sized up* the situation almost immediately." "I tried to *size up* my sister's new boyfriend"). Avoid this expression in formal language.

skillful should not be spelled *skilfull* or *skillfull*, even though *fulfill* is spelled with one internal *l* and, preferably, with two terminal *l*'s—*fulfill*.

slacks. See *pair of.*

slander. See *libel/slander.*

slang. See *English, levels of.*

slightly obvious. Don't permit *slightly* to intrude as a deceptive modifier, destroying the effect of the intended meaning. *Obvious* means "easily seen or understood," which makes no sense with *slightly.*

slogan/motto. These words do more than overlap in meaning. In some respects they are exact synonyms. The *slogan* of a company, fraternity, or other organization is an inspiring catch phrase. It could just as well be called a *motto.* In other uses, however, a *motto* expresses an ideal, a moral aim, or a spiritual objective; the word *slogan* would not serve so well. For example, a well-known American *motto* is "E pluribus Unum." Another is "In God We Trust."

slovenly, in "Christine dresses *slovenly*," doesn't belong. *Slovenly* is an adjective ("Angela's *slovenly* closets irritated her husband"). Its adverb sense needs a phrase, as in "Christine dresses in a *slovenly* manner." Obviously, it is impermissible to add a *-ly* ending to a word that already has one.

slow/slowly. Those concerned with the proper usage of these words (highway signs warn motorists to drive slow, and *slow* is often used, as in "He walked *slow* but he got there") may relax in the knowledge that both words are adverbs. Therefore, "to go *slow*" is just as correct as "to go *slowly*," even conceding that *slowly* is the traditional adverbial form. True, in formal discourse *slowly* is to be preferred because it is only an adverb; *slow* is equally an adverb and an adjective. (See *quick/quickly*; *right/ rightly*; *sharp/sharply*; *tight/tightly*.)

small businessman/small-business man. Understandably some writers are troubled by these expressions, not certain which is correct. They both are. A *small businessman* is a businessman whose physical stature is small. A *small-business man* is one whose business is small. Although the word *businessman* normally is spelled solid, if the latter meaning is intended, clarity requires that a hyphen be inserted between *small* and *business* to tie those words together and that *businessman* be divided into *business* and *man.*

small in size is a common redundancy. Reduce its size by omitting *in size.* All that is needed is *small.*

smear. Verb *smear* means "to cover or stain with anything sticky, greasy, or dirty." Figuratively *smear* has come to mean "to disparage," "to soil," "to defame"—to smear a person's good reputation by unproved accusations and innuendos.

smell/stench/scent. The distinction in the meanings of these words should be carefully noted. *Smell* is a neutral word in that it refers to what the olfactory organ detects, with no implication of pleasantness or unpleasantness, like its synonym *odor.* A *stench,* too, is a smell, but an extremely unpleasant one. It is, it might be said, malodorous, so repellent as to burn the nostrils or make one nauseated. Its synonym is *stink.* The word *scent,* on the other hand, suggests a delicate odor, possibly one that emanates from flowers or perfume. Its synonym is *aroma,* which is always a pleasant scent.

Like all copulative verbs, *smell,* meaning "to give out an odor," is followed by an adjective, not an adverb ("The flowers *smell* sweet," not *sweetly.* "The room *smells* bad," not *badly*). But it is not unusual to hear someone say, "It *smells* horribly" or "It *smells* disgustingly." Good usage does not tolerate *horribly* or *disgustingly* in those instances, but people, by and large, do— and so do some usage critics.

Smithsonian Institution. Note the correct name, *Institution,* not *Institute.*

so/that are not synonymous for "very." "It is *not so* cold in Montana this week" should be reworded "not very cold" or "not extremely cold." "It is *not that* warm today" should be recast "not very warm today." Must these words be used in tandem when *so* serves as a conjunction or may *so* go it alone, as in "He changed jobs *so* (*that*) he could have more free time"? In formal English couple *so* with *that*.

so as. Usually deserving of excision. "Murray left early *so as* to be home before the children arrived." Delete *so as*. See *as ... as/so ... as*.

so-called, as in a *so-called* mechanic, means "called by this term." Sometimes the expression implies doubt or sarcasm ("I've been wondering about this *so-called* chef; let's take him with a grain of salt"). *So-called* is hyphened when it precedes a noun (his *so-called* friends), but not when it follows one (his friends *so called*). Do not place quotation marks around the noun that is so-called, not "the so-called 'friend.'"

so far as ... is concerned, as in "*So far as* farmers *are concerned,* they would like frequent rainy periods,*" is reducible to "Farmers would like frequent rainy periods." For the sake of economy, try to avoid using this unnecessary phrase.

solder. See *often*.

solicitor. See *lawyer*.

solid/stolid. A person who shows no emotion is *stolid* or expressionless, but a person who is dependable, *solid*, is a man of substance. (See *impassable/impassible*.)

soliloquy. See *monologue*.

sombreros. See *-o*.

some is best not used to modify a numeral adjective. Prefer *about*. In "*Some* ten or fifteen men were hired today," change to "*About* ten or fifteen. . . ." Avoid using *some* to mean "worthy of notice"—for example, "That was *some* party."

somebody. See *someone/somebody*.

somebody else's. Logically this phrase should read *somebody's else*, which, incidentally, was the prescribed way many years ago. But idiom has changed the form. And so with *anybody's else*, now *anybody else's*, and *everyone's else*, now *everyone else's*.

someday/some day. See *sometime/some time*.

someone/somebody. This sentence, "*Someone* left *their* cap on the shelf," or one like it, is not infrequently heard. The error is in failing to realize that *someone* and *somebody* are singular and that referent pronouns must also be singular. Make it "his" (if a man's cap).

someplace is informal for "somewhere." Say "We parked *somewhere* (not *someplace*) near the evergreen trees." Written as two words (adjective *some* and noun *place*), *some place* is standard English ("We had to find *some place* to park our car"). (See *noplace/someplace/anyplace/everyplace*.)

something/somewhat of a. In a sentence such as "In his town he is *somewhat of a* hero," preferably *something* should replace *somewhat—something of a* hero. But *something*, meaning "very," "to some extent," or "in some degree," as in "The earthquake's rumble was *something* awful," is substandard.

sometime/some time. In "My grandmother said she would see me *some time* soon," the word called for, instead of *some time*, is *sometime*, an adverb meaning "an indefinite time" and written as one word. *Some time*, two words, referring to a specific time or day, consists of an adjective and a noun ("Please pick *some time* suitable to you"). Ordinarily if the sense of the sentence without this expression is not seriously affected, the word wanted is one-word *sometime* ("I will arrive [*sometime*] after five"). In no case can two-word *some time* be omitted from a sentence without confusing its sense. These guidelines also apply to *someday* and *some day*.

someway for *somehow* is considered standard English by a number of writers, but others regard it as colloquial ("We have to solve this problem *someway* [or *somehow*] today"). *Somehow* sounds better.

someways. See *anyway*.

somewheres is a nonstandard variant of *somewhere*.

son-in-law. Its plural form is *sons-in-law*. (See *possessive case forms*.)

sooner, the comparative form of *soon*, takes *than*, not *when* ("No sooner had I locked the car door *than* [not *when*] I realized I had left the key inside").

sophomore. Note the three *o*'s. Not "He's a high school *sophmore*."

sort. See *these kind/those sort*; *kind of*; *sort of/sort of a*.

sort of/sort of a. "I felt *sort of* ill" should be reworded "I felt *rather* (or *somewhat*) ill." Although informally *sort of a* is a common expression ("He is *sort of a* hero in his community"), do not in any speech, and certainly not in writing, say *a sort of a*. (See *half; kind of; these kind/those sort; type.*

sotto voce, meaning "very softly," "in an undertone," is often mispronounced. The second element is pronounced *vo*-chay.

source. *Source* refers to where something comes from. Therefore, "His only *source* of business was *from* his uncle" is redundant. Delete *from.*

south. See *compass directions.*

souvenir is sometimes misspelled *souvenier* and sometimes *suvenir*. Be careful.

Soviet Union. See *Russia/U.S.S.R.*

spaghetti. See *graffiti/spaghetti.*

speak/talk. The preposition that follows these words—*to* or *with*—nails down the sense of the sentence. To speak or talk *with* a person is to engage in a conversation, each person making a contribution. To speak or talk *to* a person is to address him, perhaps to redress him. It may be even a monologue, which the listener might be happy to hear the end of.

speaking of. See *dangling participles.*

special. See *especial/special.*

specie/species. "Of all the birds we saw at the zoo, the most beautiful *specie* was the cardinal." Make it *species*. *Specie* is hard currency, coins; *species* refers to a distinct class or category in which the individuals possess common attributes. *Specie* has no plural form; *species* is singular or plural.

spectacle. See *sight/site/spectacle.*

spelling. There is no reliable rule to determine when a final *e* is dropped before the suffix *-able*. If not sure whether to retain the *e*, consult a dictionary (*salable* but *salvageable; removable* but *manageable; likable* but *unknowledgeable; receivable* but *replaceable.* (See *diagram/program/kidnap; roman letters/russian dressing.*)

spelling of plural numbers avoids problems if the following guide is followed: Use an apostrophe with a plural figure—1's, 2's, and so on. Use no apostrophe when the numerals are spelled out—ones, twos, and so on.

spell out. Be careful of this valuable expression. It is hard to live without it, but it must be protected against the intrusion of redundancies. Since "to spell out" is to present the details, do not say "The surveyor *spelled out the details* of this plan." He may, however, spell out his plan or give the details.

spill/pour/pore. The word *spill*, in reference to a liquid, confuses no one. A glass of milk that was spilled was overturned accidentally. If the milk had been poured, it would have been done so purposely—to *pour* means "to cause to flow." The caveat is not to use *pour* mistakenly for *pore*. *Pore* means "to read intently," in the way one reads a book or document. "The archeologist spent two years preparing for his expedition by *poring* (not *pouring*) over all available records."

spiral means "to curve around a fixed point." It does not indicate an upward direction; it may go up, down, or sideways.

spit/expectorate. *Expectorate* is a euphemism for *spit*. Yet the words are not precisely synonymous. To *spit* is to expel saliva. To *expectorate* is to cough up phlegm from the lungs. This latter word comes from Latin *ex*, "from," and *pectus*, "chest." Either *spit* or *spat* may serve as the past tense and participle of *spit*. The preferred form has been *spit*, but the use of *spat* is increasing.

spitting image, when referring to a resemblance between parent and child, is properly phrased *spit and image*.

split infinitive. Those troubled by the idea of a split infinitive—an adverb placed between *to* and the verb—should be assured that it is a pedantic bogey. This is not to say that infinitives should be needlessly split. The ordinary position of a modifier is before the word it modifies. But if placing the adverb somewhere other than immediately after *to* causes clumsiness, unnaturalness, or ambiguity, do not hesitate to split— and join the best literary company. The following splits eliminate an otherwise awkward or ambiguous phrase—"to openly admit," "to at least notify," "to strongly criticize," "to really believe." Let your ear be your guide. No rule book can help.

splutter/sputter. *Splutter* is a blend word, a coalescing of the front end of *splash* and the back end of *sputter*. Which of these words, meaning "to talk in a hasty, confused manner," is preferable? They are equally desirable and equally acceptable on any level of English. *Sputter* is preferred to describe either a person talking so hastily and confusedly that the words seem spat out or an engine that appears to be on the verge of conking out.

spoonerism. See *malapropism/spoonerism.*

spoonfuls. See *-ful.*

sprain/strain. Often confused. A *sprain* is defined as "an injury to the ligaments or muscles of a joint caused by a sudden twist or wrench." Usually sprains occur in an ankle or wrist. A *strain* is an injury caused by too much effort or by stretching, a forcing beyond normal limits (a runner may strain a leg; a domestic, her back while scrubbing floors).

spring. See *seasons, capitalization of.*

sputter. See *splutter/sputter.*

square. Never modify with *more* or *most*, but you may say "more nearly square." (See *absolutes.*)

squinting modifiers. See *sentence structure.*

Sr. See *Jr./Sr.*

stalactite/stalagmite. These terms refer to deposits of lime formed by dripping water that congeal and resemble icicles. To distinguish them from each other, remember that *stalactite* has a *c* in it. A *stalactite* comes down from the *ceiling. Stalagmite* has a *g.* A *stalagmite* rises from the *ground.*

stall. All one gains by *stalling* is time, which makes "He's *stalling* for time" redundant.

stanch/staunch. The original meaning of *stanch* was "to stop the flow of blood," as from a wound. *Staunch* meant "firm and steadfast," as of a trusted friend. Time has shaded their meanings so that the words now are interchangeable. Nevertheless, prefer *stanch* when speaking of a flow of blood and *staunch* when speaking of a reliable associate, colleague, or relative.

stand is colloquial for "bear" or "endure" in "I can't *stand* him."

standard English. See *English, levels of.*

stanza. See *verse/stanza.*

start. See *begin/commence/start; start off.*

start off, as in "To *start off* the day right, exercise," has an unnecessary word—*off.* Excise it. (See *begin/commence/start.*)

start up. See *up.*

state. Lowercase the word *state* when referring to a state of the United States ("The United States consists of fifty *states*." "Wisconsin is the dairy *state*"). Verb *state* for *say* is pretentious. To *state* is to declare formally. But rather than "He made a statement saying," use *stated*.

stationary/stationery. Often confused because they're pronounced alike. *Stationery* is writing material. A mnemonic aid is to remember that both "letter" and "envelope" are spelled with *e*'s—hence *stationery* with its final *e*. *Stationary* is an adjective meaning "remaining in one place or position," "fixed."

status, meaning "social or professional standing," may be pronounced *stae*-tuhs or *staht*-uhs. Either pronunciation is acceptable.

status quo/status quo ante. Although some people employ these terms interchangeably, it is better to use *status quo* to mean "as things are" and *status quo ante*, "as things were."

staunch. See *stanch/staunch*.

stay/stop. To be avoided is "We *stayed* in San Francisco, *stopping* at the Fairmont Hotel." *Stay* means "to remain for a time"; *stop*, "to cease moving." Hence "We *stopped* in San Francisco and *stayed* at the Fairmont Hotel."

steal. See *rob/steal*.

stench. See *smell/stench/scent*.

stepfather. Spell it as one word. All *step-* words are written solid—*stepchild, stepbrother, stepparent*.

stet in Latin means "let it stand." It is a way of instructing a printer that the original is the approved copy and to ignore the corrections.

stevedore. See *longshoreman/stevedore*.

stigmatize, meaning "to brand," is followed by *as*. Not "He was stigmatized a cheat," but "He was stigmatized *as* a cheat."

still is redundant in "The problem *still continues*," as it is in "The problem *still persists*" and in "No matter how many sports capture the imagination, baseball *still remains* the national sport." *Still* is not used redundantly when it represents *nevertheless*. (See *modifiers*; *yet*.)

still and all. This phrase seldom if ever has any meaning. Avoid. *Still* alone will do.

stimulant/stimulus. Sometimes mistakenly used, one for the other. A *stimulant* is anything that excites to action. Common stimulants are coffee and alcohol. A *stimulus,* especially an incentive, also is something that rouses action. It may be a bonus or an extra week's vacation. A *stimulant* quickens your bodily action or mental process; a *stimulus* urges you on.

stink. If the stink of sauerkraut is still in the nostrils, should one say the sauerkraut *stank* or *stunk?* Both forms are correct. The past participle is *stunk.* (See *smell/stench/scent.*)

stolid. See *solid/stolid.*

stop. See *stay/stop.*

straight/strait. To keep these words straight, bear in mind that a person in serious trouble is in sad or desperate *straits,* not *straights.* And if his trouble unbalances him, he might be placed in a *straitjacket,* not a *straightjacket.* Adjective *straight* means "direct," "uncurved" ("The path is *straight*"); noun *strait* (usually in the plural) is a narrow water passage—the Straits of Magellan—or a position of difficulty (also usually in the plural)—"The treasurer found himself in dire *straits.*" Adverb *straight* means "honestly" ("Tell it to me *straight*") and "directly" ("Go *straight* to the store").

strain. See *sprain/strain.*

straitjacket. See *straight/strait.*

straits. See *straight/straits.*

strangle means "to kill by squeezing the throat to stop breathing." Adding "to death" (*strangle* to death) is redundant.

strata ("layers of material" or "social levels") is the plural of *stratum,* and these words, at least in formal composition, should be so used. *Strata* is sometimes construed as a singular in common language and *stratas* as its plural form. Although one may refer to an *agenda,* it is incorrect to refer to a *strata.* (See *agenda*; *data*; *phenomenon.*)

strategy/tactics. The former has to do with an overall plan; the latter with the specific means by which the plan is implemented. "General Brown's *strategy* is superb; equally laudable are the *tactics* of his staff." As a subject or a science *tactics* is treated as a singular noun ("*Tactics is* a difficult course to master"); it becomes a plural when referring to the implementations themselves. *Stratagem* has two *a*'s; *strategy,* one.

stratum. See *strata*.

stretched wordings. If we remember that conciseness makes for good writing, we will avoid such locutions as *to come to the realization* and *to reach an agreement* when *to realize* and *to agree* will say it more briefly. One who is *in violation of* the law has, in simple language, *violated* the law; a person who *has the capability of* lifting a 250-pound dumbbell *can lift*; one *in possession of* a 24-inch lawn mower *has* a 24-inch lawn mower. In writing, terseness is a virtue; wordiness, a common fault.

stupid. See *ignorant/stupid*.

stupid idiot. See *tautology*.

suasible. Those disturbed when hearing this word need not be. It is a perfectly acceptable adjective meaning "capable of being persuaded." But since it is uncommon, it should be used sparingly.

sub-. Spell compounds as one word (*subnormal, subcommittee, subdivision*.)

subconscious. See *unconscious/subconscious*.

subject to. See *addicted to/subject to*.

subjunctive. See *was/were*.

subsequent/consequent are sometimes mistakenly interchanged. *Subsequent* means "coming after," "succeeding," "later" ("*Subsequent* study proved he was wrong"). That which is *consequent* follows as a natural result or effect ("Because he mistreated his secretary, her *consequent* resignation came as no surprise").

subsequent to is bound to lead to wordiness. Use *after* if it will do. "The accident occurred five days *subsequent to* the time of his retirement" is reducible to "five days *after* his retirement," a saving of four words.

subsist/exist both pertain to life. To *subsist* is to support life; to *exist* is to have life.

substitute/replace. Do not regard these words as synonymous, even though a substitution and a replacement wind up with the same result. *Substitute* means "to put in the place of"; *replace* means "to take the place of." Thus if a red book is removed from the desk and a brown one is put in its place, the brown book is substituted for the red one and the red one is replaced by the brown. One source of trouble with these words is that each takes its own preposition. "The forester wanted to *substitute* long hikes up the mountain *with* shorter ones on flat terrain." Incorrect. *Substitute* is followed only by *for*. If you prefer to use *by* or *with*, use *replace*.

succeed. See *-cede/-ceed/-sede.*

successive. See *consecutive/successive.*

succinct/concise are synonyms in that both refer to what is stated in few words. *Succinct* emphasizes the absence of window-dressing, the omission of elaboration. *Concise*, from Latin *caedere*, "to cut," suggests brevity, that what is stated contains no unnecessary words.

such/this. Not to be regarded as synonyms. "*Such* a person" means "this kind of person." " *This* person" means "the one just mentioned."

such a tends to lead to errors that border on illiteracy. Commonly one hears this kind of sentence, "The pharmacist is *such a nice* person," when what is meant and should have been said is *a very* (or *an exceptionally* or *unusually*) *nice* person. *Such a* in formal English should be used as an intensive only when followed by a *that* clause, implying a result or consequence ("The pharmacist is *such* a nice person *that* his customers enjoy talking with him").

When *such a* or *such an* modifies a compound subject, the verb required is singular ("*Such an explosion and fire* at our plant *points* to the work of sabateurs").

such as. Place immediately after the word it qualifies. It is incorrect to say, "Some citrus fruits are hard to peel, *such as* grapefruit." Make it "Some citrus fruits *such as* grapefruit are. . . ." Depending on the construction of the sentence, and considering rhythm, *such as* may or may not be preceded by a comma, but it should never be followed by one. In "House tools, such as, hammers, saws, and awls," omit the comma after *as.*

suffer. Idiomatically a person suffers *from*, not *with* indigestion. One suffers *with* a classmate if they are both being punished at the same time. (See *from.*)

sufficient/enough. Synonyms meaning "equal to the required amount." Therefore do not use these words together, as in "The food was *sufficient enough* to tide us over." It is just as though one says "sufficient sufficient" or "enough enough." (See *enough*.)

suit/suite. Everyone knows that a suit is a set of clothes worn together or a grouping of cards from one of the four sets in a deck. And everyone knows that *suit* is pronounced *syoot*. But *suite*, which is a matched set of furniture or rooms, is not pronounced properly by everyone. It should be *sweet*, but often one hears *syoot*, the way *suit* is sounded.

summer. See *seasons*.

Sunday. See *Sabbath/Sunday*.

superior to. See *inferior to/superior to*.

superlative. See *double superlative*.

supersede/consensus. Probably these two words vie for mis-spelling honors. More often than not, one will see them written *supercede* and *concensus*. To avoid these blunders, try to remember that *supersede* is a distinctive word; it alone among the "seed words—*intercede, precede*—ends in "sede" and that *consensus* has to do with "sense," not with a *census*. If these guidelines don't help, look the words up in a dictionary before using them. (See *-cede/-ceed/-sede*; *surpass/supersede*.)

supine. See *prostrate/prone/supine/prostate*.

supplement/complement. The first means "something ad-ditional"; the second, "something that completes." A *supplement* to a book adds new material or updates the old. A *complement* makes something whole. A man's necktie, carefully selected, will complement his attire. (See *complement/compliment*.)

suppose/supposed/supposing. Do not use *suppose* where *sup-posed* is called for. "He was *suppose* to show up at 9 sharp" needs *supposed*. (Do not forget the *d*, even though it is usually not clearly pronounced.) And do not use *supposing* where *suppose* is called for ("*Suppose* we all left right now," and not "*Supposing* we all left right now").

supposedly/presumably. *Supposedly*, which means "in a way assumed to be actual, real, or genuine," implies uncertainty. It negates any assumption that what is said is fact. "Ted is *sup-posedly* planning a trip to the Orient" means that the information has not yet been verified. *Presumably* means "probably," and therefore, if it replaced *supposedly*, would make the arrangements seem more likely. That which is presumably true is probably so; that which is supposedly true is possibly so, but questionable.

supposing. See *suppose/supposed/supposing*.

sure/surely. *Sure* is an adjective; *surely*, an adverb. However, in relaxed conversation *sure* is often used adverbially, as in "He *sure* looks good" or in "We *sure* had a fine time." Educated people know that both in speech and in writing, *surely* is required (*they surely do*, not *they sure do*). (See *real/really*.)

sure and is colloquial for *sure to*. Not "Be *sure and* go tonight," but "Be *sure to*. . . ." (See *try and*.)

surely. See *sure/surely*.

surly. "He looked surly," but "He acted surlily." *Surly* is an adjective; *surlily* is its adverb form. "He acted in a *surly* manner" sounds better, however, because it avoids the prolonged liquid sound of *surlily*.

surpass/supersede. To *surpass* is to excel, to exceed, to transcend. One who surpasses his classmates does better than the others. To *supersede* is to replace. *Supersede* is sometimes mistakenly used for *surpass*, possibly on the theory that someone who supersedes is regarded as being better than his predecessor. This, of course, is mere conjecture. The predecessor might not be inferior but, on the contrary, superior to his replacement. (See *supersede/consensus*.)

surprise. What may surprise some people is to learn that the key word is sometime misspelled *suprise*, as in "Last night he *suprised* me by coming home early." Possibly the *r* is dropped in the first syllable by those who do not sound it in speech—and then write it that way.

surrounded in "They were *surrounded* on three sides" is sheer rubbish. Saying they were surrounded on all sides is equally disastrous. To *surround* is to encircle completely, which means "to inclose on all sides." When *surround* takes a preposition, it is *by*. "We are surrounded *by* evergreens," not *with* evergreens.

suspended modifiers should preferably take commas to establish the relationship of the elements ("I am interested in, and concerned about, Joseph." "Blanton lives near, yet three miles from, Smithfield"). What is particularly important is not to omit the first preposition, as in "I am interested and concerned about Joseph" (interested *in*), and, if commas are used, not to omit the second one. Of course such sentences can be restructured and the suspended modifiers eliminated. (See *commas*.)

suspicion should not be used as a verb. Not "We *suspicioned* that Gary was involved in the theft," but we *suspected*. Use *suspicion* as a noun only.

sustain, as in "He *sustained* a broken leg," is decried by some writers because *sustain* means "to bear" or "to endure," which is hardly applicable. Some dictionaries equate *sustain* with *suffer*, the word that the objecting writers would prefer.

swim.   No one has trouble with its past tense, *swam*. Its past participle is another matter. In "She *had swam* so long that she was exhausted," *swum* is required. Possibly the reason for this misusage is that *had swum* is an ugly combination of sounds, but it is the correct form nonetheless.

sympathy.   One has *sympathy with* a cause with which he is in agreement, but *sympathy for* or *toward* a person who is suffering.

systemize/systematize.   For those who wonder which is correct, the answer is both are. For those who wonder which word is preferred, the answer is the latter(*systematize* the filing cabinets). This preference runs counter to other words that offer a choice. Usually the shorter form is preferred. But not here. (See *preventative/orientate*.)

table d'hôte/à la carte. These terms suggest the price one may expect to pay for a restaurant meal. The first, *table d'hôte*, refers to a meal with a fixed price; the second, *à la carte*, refers to a menu on which items are individually priced.

tablespoonfuls/tablespoonsful. See *-ful*.

tactics. See *strategy/tactics*.

take. See *bring/take*.

take in/take on are informal expressions. The first is used to mean "mislead" or "visit." In formal discourse it should be rendered "I was *misled* (not *taken in*) by what he said." "In Washington we *visited* (not *took in*) the art museums." To *take on*, colloquially, is to show excessive emotion. "She *took on* terribly when she heard about her dog's death" in formal composition should be amended to read "She was *exceedingly upset* when. . . ."

take it easy. As used here, *easy* is an adverb. The expression is informal and should be restricted to spoken English. "One may *do* something *easily*," but in general speech we say "He *takes it easy*."

take place. See *occur/happen/take place*.

take sick, as in "My cousin *took sick* last Tuesday," is nonstandard. Make it *became sick* or *ill*.

take stock in meaning "to trust in" ("Don't *take stock in* what a dismissed employee has to say") is a colloquialism.

talisman, a charm, an object thought to have magical powers, is clearly a singular form. Its plural may be confusing. It is *talismans*, not *talismen*.

talk. See *speak/talk*.

tantalize/harass. Do not use *tantalize* when you mean *harass*. To *harass* is to trouble by repeated attacks. To *tantalize* is to tease by arousing desires that are not fulfilled. (See *harass*.)

target. A vogue word best avoided not only because it is tiresome but also because it is often misused. One reads that the target for this year's sales is being lowered or that the target for this year will beat or pass last year's. Targets, according to current usage, are set, raised, increased, exceeded, or achieved. The fact is that a target is not involved in any of those things. A target is a stationary object that, if aimed at accurately, is hit.

taste is a copulative verb and is therefore followed by an adjective, not an adverb. "It *tastes good* (*sweet*)," not "It *tastes well* (*sweetly*)." When preceded by a personal subject, *taste* may be qualified by an adverb ("He *tasted* it *hesitantly*"). (See *copulative verbs*.)

tasteful/tasty. The first means "having good taste" or, of objects, "done in good taste." *Tasty* is a colloquial term meaning "savory," which, by the way, together with "appetizing," is an appropriate replacement.

tasteless. See *distasteful/tasteless*.

tautology, a synonym for wordiness, is the useless repetition of an idea in different words. There is no limit to the number of absurd tautologies that can be, and are, invented. A list of those that come readily to mind would fill pages. The caution is to read twice what has been written to be certain that the same idea has not been said twice. For example, *complete and unabridged* or *consequent result* are patently repetitious, as are *hastily improvised, flat plateau*, and *exactly identical*. All this is a *tiny inkling* of what anyone but a *stupid idiot* should do to see that his tautologies are kept to an *irreducible minimum*. Which by now should be *obviously evident*. (See *redundancy*.)

taxi. See *shortened words*.

teaspoonfuls/teaspoonsful. The first is the correct plural form. The pluralizing *s* is simply added to the end of the word. Adding it to the second element (*spoon*) is incorrect. (See *-ful*.)

teeth. For those disturbed by the fact that they brush their teeth with a toothbrush, let them rest comfortably in the arms of idiom, which needs no logic to shore up its strength. How this oddity developed no one knows. It came and has stayed. Pluralizing the first element of a noun united to another to form a compound is proscribed by custom (*footstool*, not *feetstool*, *man-hater*, not *men-hater*). And so *toothbrush*, not *teethbrush*.

temerarious. Often misused in the sense of "timid" (it means "recklessly daring," "rash") and often misspelled, too. Note the middle *erar*.

temerity/timidity. Sometimes confused. *Temerity* means "boldness" or "rashness"; *timidity* means "shyness" or "cowardice." (See *temerarious*.)

temperament is sometimes misspelled *temperment* by those who, in all probability, fail to pronounce the *a*—*tehm*-perh-*ah*-mehnt. Its adjective form, *temperamental*, it should be noted, has five syllables, the middle one being *a*, which needs to be sounded.

temperature. See *fever/temperature*.

temporarily. See *momentarily/temporarily*.

tend to. Instead of "Albertson will *tend to* our financial problems," in better writing change to *attend to*. *Tend to* in the sense "look after" is informal.

tenses. See *direct quotations*; *since*.

terribly. Everyone knows, or might guess, that this word means "in a manner that strikes terror." But in general speech, it is almost never used that way. Instead it has acquired the meaning of "very" ("I was made *terribly* unhappy." "Yesterday was *terribly* warm"). Do not use *terribly* in this sense in formal composition.

testimony. See *evidence/testimony*.

than. Possibly no English construction stumps more people than the one involving *than* in a sentence like "Gertrude criticizes Herbert *more than* I/me." Strictly speaking, *than* is a conjunction and therefore the case of a following pronoun must be the same as that of its antecedent. The simplest way to resolve the problem is to use the form of pronoun that would be required if the clause in question were spelled out. This means that either *I* or *me* would be correct, depending on the meaning intended. Make it *more than I* if Gertrude criticizes Herbert more *than I do*. Make it *me* if Gertrude criticizes Herbert more *than she criticizes me*. (See *as*.)

than any/than anyone. See *anyone else*.

than what. "We did more *than what* we had planned." Omit *what*.

that. See *which/that*.

that (as a conjunction). Whether to say "I believe that our team will win" or "I believe our team will win" depends partly on which construction sounds better and partly on idiom. Including *that* is never an error. But it is unnecessary after verbs like *say* or *think* ("He *said* you're just grand"). Many writers in highly formal usage always retain *that* ("He *said that* . . ."). But when an element of time follows a verb such as *say, tell, inform,* or *announce, that* in any usage is needed to avoid ambiguity. There you have no choice. For example, "Captain Smythe announced today guerillas had been seen in the valley" might mean either that the captain made an announcement today or that guerillas had been spotted today. Insert *that* after *today* if his announcement was made today. (See *because*; *whether/if/that.*)

that (as a pronoun, conjunction). *That* may function as a pronoun or as a conjunction. In "The peddler *that* rings his bell the loudest gets the most attention," *that* is a pronoun (*peddler* is its antecedent), and it serves as the subject of the following clause. When a conjunction introduces a clause, it does not serve as a subject and can therefore be omitted without harming the sense of the sentence ("Since my grandmother hears no bells, she thinks *that* the peddler is gone" or "Since my grandmother hears no bells, she thinks (no *that*) the peddler . . ."). (See *so/that.*)

that (as an adverb). Do not use *that* as an adverb. Usually the word wanted is *so*: "He swam only *that* far"; "Things are not *that* bad"; "We're not *that* busy today." In each instance, replace *that* with *so*.

that/which. Three basic rules. First, use *that* of persons, animals, or things; *which*, only of animals or things. Second, use *that* in restrictive clauses, those that limit or define the meaning of its antecedent ("A student *that* studies hard is bound to succeed")—the *that* clause, which limits *student* to one who studies hard, is essential to the sense of the sentence. Third, use *which* to introduce a parenthetical clause, a new thought that is informative but unnecessary to the sense of the sentence ("The brown house, *which* is the third one on the street, has been put up for sale"). One simple guideline, which does not always work, is to use *which* if the clause is to be set off by commas; otherwise, to use *that*.

that/who. Since both relative pronouns may be used of persons, a question arises, "How do you choose one over the other?" Many particular users of English prefer *who* when the antecedent is a proper noun or a personal pronoun ("It was *Tom Reynaud who* said . . ."; "It was *he who* said . . .") and *that* when the antecedent is a general noun, a generic person ("The *athletes that* train regularly suffer few injuries").

that is. See *i.e./e.g.*

that . . . that. In "People think *that* if everyone leaves for the shore on Friday *that* the roads will be clear on Saturday," the second *that* does not belong. The governing rule is that any *that* not required for sense or smooth transition should be omitted. This means that *that* should not be repeated when it introduces a single clause, even though interrupted by a long phrase, but should be repeated when it introduces more than one clause ("We believe *that* we should go and *that* we should arrive by nightfall").

that there. See *here.*

that which. See *what.*

the. The article *the* is sometimes troublesome when two nouns are linked by *and*. If the nouns are thought of in conjunction, as in "*The* sons and daughters (meaning the children) of the mayor visited him yesterday" or in "*The* King and Queen attended," *the* should not be repeated before the second noun. It also should not be repeated when two nouns are considered a combined quality ("We greatly admire *the* strength and courage of Israel's pioneers"). But note that although in "*The* secretary and treasurer" the reference is to one person, in "The secretary and *the* treasurer," it is to two. The presence or absence of *the* also distinguishes these ideas: "schools for *the* boys and girls"; "schools for *the* boys and for *the* girls." Ordinarily use the article *the* before each coordinate noun: "*The* teachers, *the* supervisors, *the* administrators—all will be there."

the/a. When a possessive form immediately precedes the title of a book or newspaper that begins with *A* or *The*, it is good style to omit the *A* or *The*. "I'm reading *his New York Times*," rather than "I'm reading *his The New York Times*." And so with "Here's Shakespeare's *Tempest*" rather than "Shakespeare's *The Tempest*."

theater/theatre. One may feel free to use either of these variant spellings. But *theater* is the commoner spelling in the United States; *theatre* seems affected. And so with other words ending in *-re—center, centre; meter, metre.*

the fact that. See *fact.*

their's. "He thinks it is the Beckmans' house, but we know it is not *their's.*" Be not beguiled by a previous apostrophized possessive into inserting an apostrophe in the possessive pronoun *theirs.* It never takes an apostrophe. Not *their's.*

theism. See *deism/theism.*

then. May one, with propriety, say, when referring to a specific period, "I knew *the then* chairman"? Unfortunately not all authorities can be pleased no matter what the answer is. Some approve; others disapprove. But even though *the then chairman* sounds awkward, it is nevertheless used by many respected writers, perhaps because it is more economical than *the chairman at the time.*

thence. See *hence/thence/whence.*

the other. "We returned one book yesterday and *the other* four today" is more accurately given "*and the four others* today." Saying "the other four" implies a previous four. (See *another.*)

there/it. Avoid introducing a sentence with these words where possible. "There are many who think that. . . ." Change to "Many think that. . . ." "It is the understanding of many people. . . ." Change to "Many people understand. . . ."

thereafter is a good, old English word, but it sounds old-fashioned. Rather than "We will spend three days in Vermont, *thereafter* head for Maine," make it "*then* head for Maine" or, if preferred, *after that.*

there are. See *there is/there are.*

the reason is. See *because.*

therefor/therefore. The first is seldom used except as a legalism. It means "for that" or "for it," as in "The punishment *therefor* is banishment." *Therefore* means "for that reason" or "because of" ("He is not here on time; *therefore*, he has forfeited his deposit").

therefrom. See *there- words.*

therein. See *there- words.*

there is/there are are expletives often criticized by some authorities as inept introductions to sentences written by lazy thinkers. True as all this might be, it is also true that expletives are a useful device to direct attention to a forthcoming explanation, particularly in expository writing. Furthermore, expletives have appeared in the works of many distinguished authors and should therefore not be condemned out of hand. The practical problem, since *there* is a false subject, is to identify the true subject, to be sure the verb agrees with it. Clearly, a sentence such as "*There are* nine players on a baseball team" presents no difficulties, but how about "*There is* a boy next door and a girl down the street who took top honors"? Some usage critics would plump for the plural (*are*). Others approve of the singular *is* because of the attraction of the singular *boy*, which is part of a compound subject. With such divided opinion, all a person can do is to decide for himself. (See *here is/here are*; *it is/it was*.)

there- words. A group of words that begin with *there* sound pompous, smack of legalese, and are old-fashioned. Among these words are *therefrom*, which replaces the natural-sounding *from it*; *therein*, a heavy-handed word for *in it*; *thereof*, the lawyer's *of it*; *thereon*, ditto for *on it*; *thereto*, a mark of the legal mind for *to it*. Then there is *theretofore* for *up to then*; *thereunto* for *to it*; *thereupon* for *on it* or *then*; and *therewith* for *with it*. One might say "Now there's a group of unnecessary words."

thesaurus, a specialized dictionary, is a word derived from a Greek word meaning "treasury." A *thesaurus* is a compilation of synonyms and antonyms.

these kind/those sort. In better speech and in writing, *kind* and *sort*, singular nouns, must be modified by singular adjectives. Make it *this kind*, *that sort*, and so on.

the way/just as. In strictly formal English *the way*, as in "Tell it *the way* I told you," "Throw the ball *the way* I showed you," should be replaced by the subordinate conjunction *as*. But note that *as* should not be accompanied by *just*: "I conducted the business *as* my father did before me," not "*just as* my father did before me."

they. "If anyone is ready to leave, *they* should raise *their* hand" mixes a singular subject—*anyone*—with plural referents—*they, their*. This type of error arises because English has no singular pronoun with a common gender. Saying "If anyone is ready to leave, let *him* or *her* raise *his* or *her* hand" is awkward. One solution is to use *him* and *his*, the masculine gender representing both sexes. Or recast with a plural subject, "Will *those* who are ready to leave raise *their* hands?" (See *everybody/everyone*.)

thief. See *robber/thief/burglar*.

thing is such a broad all-purpose word that its meaning often is indistinct. Rather than "The *thing* about Jane that annoys us most is her boorishness," change to *characteristic, trait, idiosyncrasy, peculiarity*, or some other more specific word.

think. "I *think that* we ought to leave soon." After *think*, *that* is unnecessary. Omit ("I think we . . ."). (See *don't think; believe/feel/think*.)

third. See *second/third*.

this here. See *here*.

those sort. See *these kind/those sort*.

though/although. These concessive conjunctions are interchangeable where either will fit. *Although* is thought to be stronger than *though*. When *though* serves as an adverb meaning "nevertheless" ("I trust him, *though*"), it may end a sentence; *although* may not do so. *Though* is also sometimes used to approximate the meaning of *but* ("This matter needs further study, *though* we cannot pursue it now").

thousands. The rule governing the use of *million* applies. When a number precedes *thousand* (*two thousand* books were distributed), it is written without a final *s*. But *thousand* becomes *thousands* (with a final *s*) if no number is given ("We saw *thousands* of soldiers marching"). (See *million/millions*.)

thresh/thrash. Remember that grain is threshed and a person is thrashed. To *thresh* is to separate grain; to *thrash* is to flog.

through. "I will be *through* with dinner in five minutes." In this sense—that is, "completed" or "finished," *through* is colloquial in the opinion of many authorities. (See *finished*.)

throughout does not need the company of "whole" or "entire." The meanings of those words are inherent in *throughout*. "The coach paced back and forth *throughout the whole* game." Omit "whole." "He stared at the chairman *throughout the entire* meeting." Omit "entire."

thru for *through* is not a recommended spelling, even in informal writing.

thus/thusly. *Thusly* is a deviant form of *thus* that belongs in no one's writings. *Thus*, meaning "in this way" or "as follows," is already an adverb—so *thusly* can offer nothing useful. Further, since *thus* sometimes sounds stuffy, you can imagine how *thusly* must sound.

tight/tightly. *Tight* is an adjective. It also is an adverb. You may say "Turn the faucet off *tight*" or "Turn the faucet off *tightly*" and be correct in either case. *Tight*, with instructions or commands, is more effective, but formal English favors *tightly*. (See *slow/slowly*; *quick/quickly*.)

till/until. The choice between these words is yours to make. Either one is acceptable in formal usage, although generally *until* is preferred. But perform no surgery on these words. Neither *'til* nor *'till* deserves even clinical attention. The shortened form *'til* for *until* is undesirable, and *'till* is nonstandard.

timber/timbre. These homophones are sometimes misused for each other. Be careful. *Timber* is wood; *timbre* is resonance. Obviously, it is not the *timber* of someone's voice that could be disturbing; it is the *timbre*. *Tim*-ber is a correct pronunciation for both words, but *timbre* has a variant, *tam*-ber.

time. In formal writing, *time* is expressed in words: two o'clock in the afternoon; almost three-thirty in the morning. In less formal writing, figures are customary: 2 p.m.; 3:30 a.m. Saying 2 p.m. in the afternoon or 3:30 a.m. in the morning is redundant. Omit *in the afternoon* and *in the morning*. "What time are we to meet?" is standard English, but in strict formal writing, make it, "At what time. . . ?"

time card/time clock/timepiece Timepiece is one word—*time card* and *time clock* need two words.

timidity. See *temerity/timidity*.

tinged/tinted are synonymous in that each connotes a light coloring. But idiom has established some particular uses. For example, "Her voice was *tinged* (not *tinted*) with envy." We speak of a sky *tinged* in purple but sunglasses *tinted* gray. *Tinted* here indicates a darkening (window panes are *tinted*, windshields are *tinted*). A water tumbler may be *tinged* in yellow (a slight trace of color) at the rim but have a *tint* (a faint, delicate coloration) at its base. The meanings of *tinged* and *tinted* so often overlap that they are, in fact, only a mere shade apart.

'tis/'twas. Unless you are writing poetry or being humorous, do not use these contracted forms for *it is* and *it was*.

titled. See *entitled/titled*.

titles. Capitalize all principal words but not articles, conjunctions, and prepositions unless they begin or end the title (*Stop the World, I Want To Get Off*). Internal prepositions consisting of five or more letters are capitalized (*Nothing Comes Between Us*), and so is *To* when it is a sign of the infinitive. Be careful in written communications not to repeat a person's title in another form. Omit the second title in Dr. T. H. Browne, M.D. and in Attorney L. M. Seyfert, Esq. But Professor William Sanger, M.D. is correct as given, since the second title is different from, and does not repeat, the first title.

to is used unnecessarily, as in "We're wondering where John went *to*" and in "Where did the boys go *to*?" *To* should be omitted after *where*. (See *preposition at end of sentence*.) *To* is not the preferred preposition when used with the name of a place visited. Use *in* ("We have been *in* [not *to*] Chicago twice").

to/through. An advertisement of a sale from Monday *to* Friday is misleading. Does the sale end Thursday at store closing? Or on Friday? A person told to count *to* ten should stop at nine, but almost everyone would include ten in the count. To avoid the risk of ambiguity, use *through* for *to* or add *inclusive*.

together is superfluous in "connect *together*" and "cooperate *together*." (See *join together/gather together*.)

together with/along with. "The Chicago architect, *together with* two colleagues, were seen walking in New York" is incorrectly put. *Together with* introduces a parenthetical element, a descriptive phrase, which does not create a grammatical plural. The verb must agree with the simple subject. Make it *was seen*. "It is the English teacher, *along with* some advanced students, who decide what play to use." Since *along with*, like *together with*, has no bearing on the number of the verb, change *decide* to *decides*. (See *as well as*; *in addition to*.)

to infinitive. In a series of infinitives, use *to* before each infinitive. Not "I wanted *to* go, see, and enjoy" but "I wanted *to* go, *to* see, and *to* enjoy."

tomorrow/yesterday. Why should *yesterday* not receive the same idiomatic treatment as *tomorrow*? After all, we have had the benefit of yesterday, and none of us can be sure that there'll be a tomorrow. Yet we may say "*Tomorrow is* payday or *tomorrow is* Saturday." Logically one should say "will be" instead of "is," but idiom supersedes logic. With *yesterday*, you must use *was*. Saying "*Yesterday is* Saturday" makes no sense.

to my knowledge/to the best of my knowledge. Is there a difference between these expressions? The answer is yes. The first one suggests that the speaker is knowledgeable about the subject he's discussing. The second says that the speaker cannot vouch that he has much knowledge, but whatever it is, whether faulty or deficient, he's willing to expose it.

too. "Bob is tall *too*" implies that, in addition to whatever else was said about him, he also is tall, or that, like his friends, he is also tall. "He is *too* tall" implies that his height does not comply with a given standard. *Too* may modify a participle that serves as an adjective ("He was *too bewildered* to find his way"), but not if the participle has retained its verbal force. "He was *too occupied*," for example, needs *too much*. When used as an intensive meaning "in excess," *too* should be preceded by *only* ("We were *only too* delighted to accept"). (See *overly; very*.)

Many writers no longer set off *too* with commas ("They *too* wish they were going").

took sick, an everyday expression ("My secretary *took sick* yesterday"), is best changed to *became sick*.

toothbrush. See *teeth*.

tort. See *tortuous/torturous/tortious*.

tortuous/torturous/tortious. Although the first two are derived from the Latin word *torquere*, "to twist," their current meanings are entirely different. *Tortuous* means "winding," "twisting," as is a pathway that bends and curves. Figuratively it means "crooked," "not straightforward," as might be a devious plan or a deceitful scheme. *Torturous* means "inflicting torture," "causing pain." *Tortious* is a legal term, meaning "constituting or involving a civil wrong," which in law is called a *tort*.

total. "*A total* of 96 men was annihilated during this past week by the Viet Cong" is wrongly put. The phrase *a total* takes a plural verb (*were*); *the total,* a singular ("*The total* of fatalities *was* 96 men"). But do not compound errors with redundancies. In "Of the 96 men who faced *total* annihilation, 14 were Americans," delete *total.* Returning to the first sentence, it would read better if written "Ninety-six men were. . . ," omitting *a total of,* which is almost always superfluous. If you prefer not to begin a sentence with a number, then use the introductory phrase in the example. You have to do this anyway if using a figure, since beginning a sentence with a figure is considered an objectionable practice. (See *absolutes*; *number, the* [*a*].)

totally. Be careful not to use *totally* to modify a verb whose sense is absolute—for example, *demolished* (see *destroyed*), or to use it to mean "very," as in "Evelyn had a *totally* exhilarating trip."

to the best of my knowledge. See *to my knowledge/to the best of my knowledge.*

to the contrary in strictly formal English should be rendered *to the contrary notwithstanding. Despite* is an economical substitute.

to the manner born, not *to the manor born,* was Hamlet's reply to Horatio. That is, Hamlet was explaining that trumpets were sounded whenever the king drank a flagon of wine. His words were "Ay, marry, it is:/But to my mind, though I am native here/And to the manner born, it is a custom/More honored in the breach than the observance." (See *misquotations*.)

toward/towards. A writer with a preference for one of these forms should feel free to use it. Either is acceptable on any level of usage but *toward* is somewhat more prevalent.

traffic. See *frolic.*

trans-. Compounds are spelled as one word; hyphen only if the second element is capitalized: *transship, transoceanic, transatlantic,* but *trans-Siberian.*

translate/transliterate are not synonyms and so are not to be interchanged. To *translate* is to reproduce meaning—that is, "to turn something expressed from one language into another" ("Our class *translated* a portion of *Caesar's Gallic Wars*"). To *transliterate* is to reproduce sounds in a different alphabet—that is, "to substitute words of one language from those of another" ("We were able to pronounce the words on the Russian sign by *transliterating* the Cyrillic letters").

translucent/transparent. Sometimes confused, possibly because the essence of both words is "allowing light through." *Translucent* means diffusing light so that images beyond are not clearly visible (frosted glass). *Transparent* means transmitting light so that images beyond are clearly visible (clear glass).

transpire. The meanings "occur," "happen," and "take place" have been applied to *transpire* so often that some authorities consider *transpire* in those senses as standard English. But actually *transpire* does not mean any of those things. It means "to come to light," "to emerge from secrecy," "to become known by degrees" ("From the investigation, it *transpired* that the mayor was involved with underworld figures." "It *transpired* that our neighbor had left his money to the university"). Even when used correctly, *transpire* sounds pretentious. Prefer *became known*.

travel. See *l* endings.

treble. See *triple/treble*.

tri-. Compounds are spelled as one word: *trisemester, tricolor*.

trigger. A good verb with a particularly crisp sound, used of anything that initiates or sets off something. But it should not be overused. Consider *begin, cause, initiate, produce, signal*, or *start*.

triple/treble. These words, meaning "threefold" or "three times as much or as many," are equally acceptable. *Triple* is the predominant form (except in music), but lawyers still talk of treble damages.

triumphant/triumphal. Although this pair is related to *triumph*, their usages have developed distinct patterns. *Triumphant* means "victorious or successful" ("The *triumphant* team was besieged by well-wishers"). *Triumphal* pertains to the celebration of a victory (a *triumphal* procession, a *triumphal* reception); it is not applied to persons but to events.

trooper/trouper. A *trooper* is a cavalryman or a policeman. A *trouper* is a professional actor. A person who because of fortitude or experience, or both, can confront a vicissitude and handle it competently is said to be a good *trouper* (not *trooper*), but if things go wrong he may "swear like a trooper."

truculent. Only purists insist that this word must still be used in its literal sense of "fierce, cruel, deadly." Realists recognize its current usage, in which it means "disagreeably pugnacious" or "aggressively assertive." Although you may not wish such a person as a dinner partner, do not make him out to be barbarous or ferocious.

true. See *regular/real/true.*

true facts. See *fact.*

trustee/trusty. A *trustee* (a person appointed to administer the affairs of an organization or holding the title for the benefit of another) may become a *trusty* if the trust in him has been misplaced. A *trusty* is a prison inmate in whom the warden places trust. The plural of *trustee* is *trustees.* The plural of *trusty* is *trusties.*

truth. See *veracity/truth.*

try and for "try to" occurs often in speech, but most authorities condemn it on the ground that only one action is being called for, whereas *and* implies two. Therefore, "Let's *try to* learn," not "Let's *try and* learn." But some arbiters of usage insist that *and* reinforces the idea so that greater determination is thereby expressed, as in "*Try and* stop me." In formal writing, nevertheless, *try and* should be avoided. (See *nice and.*)

Tuesday is properly pronounced *tiuz*-dih; but it is commonly, and acceptably, pronounced *tooz*-dih.

tumult/turmoil seem as though they have the same meaning—namely, a commotion or disturbance. They both do imply commotion or disorder but of somewhat different kinds. To be precise, *tumult* should be used when a large group is noisy or uproarious, such as a victorious ball team celebrating in the locker room. A *turmoil* is a state of agitation that may or may not be accompanied by noise. And it need not involve many people. In fact, it may apply to only one person. With *turmoil* it is the mental disturbance, not the number, that counts.

turbid/turgid. These look-alikes should be differentiated. *Turbid* means "not clear," "cloudy," "muddy," as is a creek that has had its bottom stirred up. Figuratively it means "confused." *Turgid* means "swollen," "distended," "bloated." It is often applied to a pretentious style of speaking or writing in the sense of "inflated" or "pompous." *Bombastic* is a good synonym.

turmoil. See *tumult/turmoil.*

'twas. See *'tis/'twas.*

tweezers is a plural form ("These *tweezers don't* work right"). To use it with a singular verb, recast as in "This *pair of tweezers is* rusty." (See *pair of*.)

twins. Those fortunate enough to have *twins* should call them just that, not "a pair of twins." *Twins* are two offspring. *Pair* means "two." Two plus two adds up to four. Two at a time is enough for most people.

two first. See *first two/last two*.

twos. See *spelling of plural numbers*.

type, a noun, should be followed by *of* before another noun. ("It is the *type of* hat everyone likes"). Saying "It is the *type* hat . . ." is substandard, since *type* is not an adjective. Although *type, kind,* and *sort* are regarded as synonyms, *type* is preferred when the category is well defined. When the reference is more general, use *kind* or *sort* ("This is the *kind* [or *sort*] of official we can trust"). (See *group*; *kind*; *manner*.)

typescript. See *manuscript/typescript*.

typhoon. See *hurricane/typhoon*.

$\mathcal{U}$

ultra-. Compounds beginning with *ultra-* are spelled as one word (*ultramodern, ultraconservative*) unless the prefix precedes a vowel (*ultra-ambitious, ultra-exclusive*).

umbrella, "a shade, screen, or guard," is not to be spelled *umberella,* as some people mispronounce it.

umpire/referee. For those wondering whether there is any difference between the functions of an *umpire* and a *referee,* the answer is no. Each is responsible for enforcing regulations and for ruling on contested plays, movements, and so on. In sports an *umpire* and a *referee* serve as judges, but in different sports— a referee in boxing, an umpire in baseball. Football has both a referee and an umpire.

un-. This prefix, meaning "not," is attached to the following element (*unaided, unabated, unaware*) unless the second element is capitalized (*un-American*).

unable/incapable are synonymous adjectives. They mean "lacking ability or power." It is correct, therefore, to say "She was *unable* to attend because her mother was ill" and "She was not promoted because she was *incapable* of handling the work." The difference in usage between the words is that *incapable* suggests a longstanding, if not a permanent, unfitness, whereas *unable* is usually applied to a specific, but temporary, condition. A person with a speech defect is *incapable of* expressing himself clearly. A person struck on the head by a baseball is *unable to* move until his senses return. Note the different prepositions each takes—*unable to, incapable of.*

unabridged/expurgated. Something *unabridged,* such as a dictionary, is comprehensive in that it has not been reduced by condensing or omitting. That which has been *expurgated* has been reduced, cut, because passages thought obscene or otherwise objectionable have been removed. To that extent the ma-

272

terial has been shortened. The antonym of *unabridged* is not *expurgated* but *abridged*.

unanimous. See *absolute*.

unapt/inapt/inept. *Inapt* and *inept* share the sense "not apt," "unsuitable." More often, however, a person who is clumsy at his job is said to be *inept*. "*Unapt* also means "unsuitable" but the meaning "not likely to" predominates ("A brave soldier is *unapt* to weep"). *Inept* is generally defined as "without aptitude or capacity."

una voce, "with one voice," is pronounced *oona voh*-chay. (See *sotto voce*.)

unaware/unawares. One who confuses these words makes an adjective serve as an adverb or vice versa. Adjective *unaware* means "not aware of," "ignorant," "not knowing" ("She was *unaware* of her husband's impending bankruptcy"). Adverb *unawares* means "unexpectedly," "without preparation," "by surprise" ("The squall caught the fishermen *unawares*." "Baldness creeps up on many men *unawares*"). *Unawares* modifies a verb. *Unaware* is followed by *of*.

unbeknownst, which means "unknown," is a pompous substitute for *unbeknown*.

unbeliever. See *disbeliever/unbeliever*.

uncomparable/incomparable. Easily confused because they share the meaning "incapable of being compared" and are distinguished idiomatically only by their prefixes, both of which mean "not." *Incomparable* also means "matchless" in the sense "exclusive." ("Einstein's genius was said to be *incomparable*." "Bowling and cricket are *uncomparable*.") "Absolutes" (which see) are *uncomparable*.

unconscious/subconscious. The former is sometimes loosely used to mean the latter, as in "*Unconsciously*, Dave was thinking that he should install a security system." The sense there is that Dave was not wholly conscious of his thoughts. *Subconsciously* would be a more appropriate term, since *subconscious* refers to mental activity of which a conscious person is unaware. To be *unconscious*, in medical usage, is to be "unaware, with no conscious control," like someone in a deep sleep or in a coma. In general usage *unconscious* is taken to mean that a person either is unaware of something (perhaps he did not perceive it) or did something unintentionally.

under-. Spell compounds as one word—*underweight, underestimate, undercapitalize.*

under. When dealing with collective quantity, some authorities approve of *under* in the sense of "less than" ("Murray made *under* $50 last week." "Oscar spent *under* five minutes on that project"). In better writing, certainly in formal writing, prefer *less than* to *under.* With distinguishable units, *under* would not serve in any kind of writing. Use *fewer than.* ("*Fewer than* thirty dogs were entered in the show"). (See *fewer/less*; *more than/over.*)

undergraduate student. *Student* is superfluous. Omit. Say "He's an *undergraduate.*"

underlining. See *italics.*

under separate cover was a standard phrase years ago. But now it is preferable to be more specific. For example, "We're sending you the catalog by parcel post" (or by "Federal Express" or by "Air Mail"). If the plan was to send the catalog by one of these means or one like it, but the carrier had not been selected when the letter was written, say "the catalog is being sent separately."

under way/under weigh. Although historically a ship moving ahead is said to be under weigh (which means the anchor has been weighed or lifted), the accepted idiom today is "under way." That phrase now applies to anything that has started, whether a ship or a charity drive.

undeterred. See *deter.*

undiscriminating. See *indiscriminate/indiscriminating.*

undisposed. See *indisposed/undisposed.*

undoubtedly/doubtlessly, adverbs meaning "beyond question," "assuredly," "indisputably," are interchangeable. The commoner word is *undoubtedly.* A bookish synonym is *indubitably.* (See *doubtlessly.*)

undue/unduly. "Despite the ominous signs of war, there is no need for *undue* alarm." "Regardless of recent bank failures, we should not be *unduly* pessimistic about the future of our economy." Tautological. The first sentence says in effect that there is no need for more alarm than there is need for. The second, that we should not be more pessimistic than we should be. Avoid the double negative. Excise *undue* and *unduly*.

uneatable/inedible. Something that is *inedible* can normally be eaten but at the moment is unpalatable because improperly prepared (undercooked spaghetti) or unripened. Something that is *uneatable* cannot be eaten under any circumstances because it is not a foodstuff—cloth, metal, wood. However, *inedible* is sometimes used in the latter sense, especially since *uneatable* does not appear in some dictionaries.

unequivocally is sometimes misspelled *unequivocably*, probably by those who pronounce it that way.

unexceptional/unexceptionable. *Unexceptional* means "not exceptional," "ordinary," "routine" ("Although Bill was an excellent language student, in mathematics his grades were *unexceptional*"). *Unexceptionable* means "beyond criticism," something that is wholly acceptable without change ("His record of attendance was *unexceptionable*"). (See *exceptional/exceptionable*.)

unfrequent/infrequent. Although these adjectives are synonymous (both mean "not regular or habitual," "occurring occasionally"), *infrequent* is heard and seen more often ("Arlene's visits are *infrequent*," preferred to *unfrequent*). But in the sense "not regularly visited," "unpatronized," *unfrequented* alone is correct ("This area is *unfrequented* [not *infrequented*] during the winter months").

unhuman/inhuman. A man who abuses his children may be said to be *inhuman* (not have the traits of civilized human beings—sympathy, pity, warmth, or compassion) but not *unhuman*. That which is unhuman is not a human being.

unidentified. See *unknown/unidentified*.

uninhabitable. See *habitable/inhabitable*.

uninterested. See *disinterested/uninterested*.

unique means "the only one of its kind"; consequently, it cannot be compared. Something cannot be more unique than something that is without an equal. Although most adjectives admit of degrees, and can therefore be modified by *very, more, less*, or *most*, this is not so with "absolutes," of which *unique* is one. There is a little latitude, however, offered to those who must reduce *unique*'s absolute sense of oneness. It is permissible to qualify *unique* with "almost" or "nearly." But this does not go so far as to condone "rather unique" or "very unique." One may say, however, that a style is *more unusual* than another. (See *absolutes*.)

United Kingdom.   See *Great Britain/United Kingdom*.

United States is treated as a singular ("the United States *has*," "The United States *is*"). The names of other countries with plural forms are regarded as plurals and treated accordingly ("The Netherlands *have*," "The Hebrides *are*").

universally.   An "absolute" meaning "without exception." Hence not to be modified by adverbs that imply degree, like *very* or *more*. Saying "His actions were *universally* condemned *by all*" says the same thing twice.

university/college.   A *college* awards degrees for undergraduate study. A *university* awards masters' and doctoral degrees as well. A university may have (and most of them have had up to present times) a graduate school devoted to professional training in law, medicine, dentistry, and so forth. Today a college offering graduate work, even if limited to a master's degree, calls itself a *university*.

unjust/injustice.   The adjective and noun take different negative prefixes—*un-* and *in-*.

unkempt.   Confine the use of the word *unkempt* to mean "uncombed."

unknowledgeable.   See *spelling*.

unknown/unidentified.   Be particularly careful of the word *unknown*. We may say that the future is unknown. But since, with the possible exception of a hermit living on top of a mountain everyone is known to someone, do not say the coroner examined the body of an unknown man. Make it an *unidentified* man.

unless and until.   Why burden the reader with a wordy phrase, and a cliché at that, when either word will do.

unloosen.   See *loosen/unloosen*.

unmistakable means "clear" in the sense that it cannot be misunderstood. Adding a negative, as in the "The teacher addressed the class in *no unmistakable* language," which is intended to be an intensive to make the thought particularly clear, actually has an opposite effect. The double negative means "mistakable." And it certainly was not the teacher's intention to use mistakable language. The best assemblage of words would be "The teacher addressed the class in language that was *not mistakable*."

unmoral. See *amoral/immoral/unmoral*.

unorganized/disorganized imply a lack of systematized structure. But their implications are different. That which is unorganized lacks system or unity because it has never been systematized. That which is disorganized no longer enjoys the system or organization it once had. Something has disrupted its organization.

unravel. See *ravel/unravel*.

unreadable. See *illegible/unreadable*.

unrenowned. Sometimes misspelled *unreknowned*.

unresponsible/irresponsible. When the meaning is "not responsible," as may be someone who ignores his debts or duties or is careless in handling other people's property, the word to describe that person is *irresponsible*, not *unresponsible*.

unsatisfied/dissatisfied. One who is unsatisfied is unhappy or displeased about something, as is one who is dissatisfied. However, the words, despite their similarity, have different applications and are not ordinarily interchangeable. A person is unsatisfied if he receives or experiences less than expected—for example, if, when seeking information, he is given evasive answers ("Your analysis leaves me *unsatisfied*"). *Dissatisfied* connotes active discontent or displeasure by a person who has not received what he thinks he has a right to expect. ("The foreman was *dissatisfied* with his Christmas bonus"). In terms of food, an unsatisfied diner has left the table with his craving for food not satisfied. He's still hungry. A dissatisfied diner simply did not enjoy the food. If he's exceedingly dissatisfied, resentful, then he's *disgruntled*.

unsocial/unsociable. Although these words overlap in meaning, they have a fine line of distinction between them. An *unsocial* person dislikes social activities and social life. He may boldly say so or indicate it by his behavior. If this attitude is deeply embedded, it may be lifelong. An *unsociable* person is disinclined to engage in friendly social relations. Of course, that failing is equally true of an "unsocial" person, but the behavior of an "unsociable" person may simply be a matter of a passing mood.

unthinkable. See *indescribable*.

until. See *till/until*.

unwieldy, meaning "hard to handle or operate because of its size or shape," is spelled as given, and not, as is sometimes seen, *unwieldly*, with an extra *l*.

up. Used appropriately as standard English in many combinations, but also unnecessarily in others. For example, in "We should *start up* early so that our friends won't have to *wait up* for us," the *up*'s are unnecessary. In formal discourse, say "What's the secretary planning" rather than "What's the secretary *up to*."

upon. See *on/upon*.

up to date means "abreast of the times." Those concerned with its hyphenation may follow this convention. Hyphenate when the expression is used attributively ("It is an *up-to-date* system"). But note, "This brings my payments *up to date*" (no hyphens).

upward/upwards. The adjective has only one form *upward* (an *upward* movement); the adverb has two, *upward* and *upwards*, but *upward* is generally preferred ("The balloon flew *upward* very quickly"). Euphony is the deciding factor. But do not use *upwards* in the sense "more than," as in "*Upwards* of 200 people were there," except as a colloquialism.

urban/urbane. Sometimes confused because of their similar look. The first means "pertaining to a city" or "to the characteristics of a city" ("*Urban* life is hectic compared with country life"). *Urbane* means "sophisticated" or "polished," attributes supposedly acquired by those living an urban life ("His *urbane* manner impressed everyone"). *Urban* is accented on the first syllable; *urbane*, on the second.

us/we. See *appositives*.

usable. See *salable*.

usage/mileage. Note that *usage* has no internal *e* but that *mileage* has one.

usage/use. These words are not to be interchanged, since they enjoy distinct meanings. *Usage* refers to a manner of handling something (rough usage). Or, as it relates to language, a practice that, by reason of its long-time use, creates a standard, particularly regarding the meaning of words. *Use* is "the act of employing or putting into service."

use/utilize. In many, if not in most, instances in which *utilize* is employed, it could sensibly be replaced by *use*. Certainly *use* is called for in "He *utilized* all the items his father sent him." Perhaps *utilize* is preferred by those who believe it sounds more elegant than simple *use*. *Utilize* has a narrow sense of "to put to a useful purpose or to profitably use," as by expanding productivity by finding new uses for something already in service. Waste material now being converted into a useful product is said to be utilized. Unless the word fits, pass it up.

used to. See *use to/used to*.

useless numbers should be excised from better writing. For example, "I am sending you the Underwood and the Smith-Corona, *two* antiques that should command a good price." The correspondent would have reached the conclusion easily that only two typewriters were involved; adding *two* was unnecessary. "I would like you to meet my *four* granddaughters Lauren Rose, Arin, Jill, and Cara." Delete *four*.

use to/used to. There is no valid reason to misuse *used to*, in the sense of "accustomed," if such illiteracies are avoided as "I *used to could* do it," which correctly rendered is "I *used to be able to do* it." (Be sure to preserve the *d* in *used to*, not *use to*.) Negative sentences, however, not only cause trouble but also are tongue-twisters. The correct form, at least the one preferred by many writers, is *used not to* ("We *used not to* mind sitting in the sun all day"). An alternative employs *did not use to* ("We *did not use* [not "used"] *to* mind. . . .").

U.S.S.R. See *Russia/U.S.S.R.*

usually may be placed immediately before or after the verb, as rhythm dictates. Either "He *usually* is late for dinner" or "He is *usually* late for dinner." The latter sentence has a pleasanter beat. (See *commonly/generally/frequently/usually*.)

utilize. See *use/utilize*.

utter. Note its disparate meanings. As a verb, *utter* means "to express audibly"; as an adjective, "complete." Verb *utter* should be distinguished from *say*. To *say* is to speak; to *utter*, to make a sound. We say, "He didn't *utter* a sound," which means that he didn't even grunt. Adjective *utter* should preferably be used in an unfavorable sense. We do not speak of "*utter* love," meaning "a love that's complete," but we do speak of *utter* nonsense. *Utter* is the comparative of obsolete *ut*; its superlative is either *uttermost* or *utmost*. The latter form is preferred.

uxorious, a good word because it tells so much. But be certain the context makes clear which of its two meanings is intended—"foolishly fond of, or extremely submissive to, one's wife." (Of course, the first may lead to the second.)

vacant/empty. Although these words apply to anything that contains nothing, their applications in general usage are different. Consider a house. A *vacant* house has no one living in it, but temporarily so. Perhaps it is vacant because the occupants are away on vacation. An *empty* house has no furnishings. It will so remain until something is brought into it. Which may not be for a long time—or ever. A position that is unfilled is *vacant*, not *empty*. The vacancy, it is expected, will be temporary.

vaccinate/inoculate. These words frequently show up together because to *vaccinate* is to *inoculate* against smallpox. Note that *vaccinate* (from Latin *vacca*, "a cow") has two *c*'s. *Inoculate* has only one. (See *innocuous/inoculate*.)

vacillate/fluctuate. These synonyms mean "to change continually," "to vary," "to waver." The difference in their usage is that *fluctuate* applies to both things and persons, but *vacillate*, only to persons. We say the temperature fluctuated drastically over the weekend and that a friend's emotions fluctuated between cheerfulness and moroseness. As to *vacillate*, we say a bachelor vacillates so much between the "singles" route and marriage that his life is in a quandary.

vacillation. See *ambivalence/vacillation*.

valuable/valued. Everyone knows that something *valuable* has great monetary value. It is costly because it is particularly useful or rare. Although something valued may also be valuable, most often *valued* refers to that which is esteemed, highly regarded. A person's services may be highly valued, yet not valuable. Valued friends are not valuable. A picture of one's father may be valued, but it is hardly valuable.

valuable asset is accepted idiom and may be used on any level of English, even though it seems redundant. Every asset is valuable to an extent, but the phrase is well established.

value should be preceded by *of* when used with the verb *to be* ("*Of* what *value* can this possibly be?"—not, "What value can this possibly be?" "After WWI German marks were *of* no *value*").

valued. See *valuable/valued*.

value judgment is almost always a redundancy. It is a rare case in which *value* serves any purpose in that phrase.

valueless. See *invaluable*.

varied. See *various/varied*.

variety. The number of the verb following *variety* depends on the article preceding it. *A variety* takes a plural verb ("*A variety* of birds *were* in the park today"); *the variety*, a singular ("*The variety* of orchids in the greenhouse *was* small"). (See *number*; *total*.)

various/varied. *Various*, meaning "more than one," is best not used as a pronoun, as in "*Various* of the students gathered round the teacher's desk," even though some usage authorities approve of it. Use *various* as an adjective only, implying different kinds, and do not follow it with *of* ("*Various* flowers are now blooming"). *Varied* means "changed" or "marked by variety." A person may have a varied background which has given him an interest in *various* (not *varied*) cultures.

various and sundry. This phrase has two strikes against it. It is redundant and a cliché. Pitch another one and strike it out.

vary/at variance. "The classrooms *vary from* one another *in* size." "The styles of clothing *vary with* the seasons." *At variance* takes *with*, never *from* ("These two sets of figures are *at variance with* each other").

vehicle/vehicular. Authorities do not agree on the pronunciation of this word. Some approve of vee-*hih*-k'l, in which the stressed second syllable has an *h* sound, but others, and they predominate, recommend *vee*-ih-k'l. But note that *vehicular*, meaning "of a vehicle," is pronounced with a strong *h* sound—vee-*hihk*-yoo-lahr.

venal/venial. These look-alikes and sound-alikes are sometimes puzzling. *Venal* means "capable of being bribed." A venal act is a corrupt one. *Venial* means "excusable," "pardonable." A venial sin is so slight as to be forgivable.

venetian blinds. See *roman letters/russian dressing.*

venial. See *venal/venial.*

veracity/truth. Often wrongly interchanged. *Truth* refers to that which is true—for example, a fact is a statement of what is true. *Veracity* means "truthfulness." A habitually truthful person is admired for his veracity. He is, to use a five-dollar word, *veracious.*

verbal. See *oral/verbal.*

verbal nouns. See *-ing words.*

verify/corroborate should not be loosely used for each other, for they have distinct meanings. To *verify* is to prove something is true ("The detective *verified* the prisoner's alibi"). To *corroborate* is to confirm or to supply further evidence of the truth of something ("The accountant *corroborated* the testimony of the witness regarding the amount of the embezzled funds").

veritable, meaning "being truly so," is preferably not used when *real* will do.

vernacular. See *dialect/idiom/jargon/vernacular.*

verse/stanza. Although given many meanings, a *verse* actually is a single line of a poem. It is not to be confused with *stanza,* which is a group of lines that form a division of a poem. The first *verse* in Gray's memorable *Elegy Written in a Country Churchyard* is "The curfew tolls the knell of parting day." It appears in the first *stanza.*

verso/recto. Printers' jargon is confusing to the layman, but the key words have filtered into general usage. *Verso* is the left-hand page of a book; *recto* is the right-hand page.

versus. Except in citations of legal cases, do not abbreviate *versus:* cotton *versus* polyester, not cotton *vs.* polyester.

very. "The druggist was *very distressed.*" Many grammarians would disapprove of that sentence because participle *distressed* is an active verb and is therefore not permissibly modified by *very,* an adverb of degree. *Very* needs an adverb to modify. Nevertheless, *very* may modify a participle if—and only if—the participle has lost its verbal function and is now regarded as an adjective—"very worn," "very upset," "very tired." But with *distressed,* since it has retained its verbal status, the modifier must be *much, greatly, deeply,* or some other such suitable adverb

("The druggist was *greatly* distressed"). If *very* is used, follow it with *much* ("The druggist was *very much* distressed"). (See *much*.)

very badly. See *worst way*.

via means "by way of" ("Michael went to Mexico *via* Puerto Rico"). It should not be used to refer to a method of transport in the sense "by means of" or "through the agency of," as in "We're shipping the package *via* air freight," at least not in formal discourse. Use only for the route. Pronounce it *vie*-uh.

viable means "capable of living," a definition that does not often fit current usage, especially as seen in print—for example, "There is no *viable* market in the United States for cars made in China." Whatever *viable* means there, it has nothing to do with living. Extending its meaning to accommodate present-day thinking is not to be criticized, of course, if the enlarged sense bears some relationship to "life." But it makes no sense to equate *viable* with "effective," "practicable," or "workable." Preferably use those words instead.

vice-. A question often asked is whether to use a hyphen between *vice* and the following noun. The preferred style is to omit the hyphen (*vice president, vice chancellor*). But in other forms of these words, the hyphen is retained (*vice-presidency, vice-chancellorship*). If the reference is to the Vice President of the United States, the words are capitalized.

vichyssoise, a leek soup, is properly ordered if pronounced vih-shee-*swahz*, the final *s* sounding like *z*.

vicinity. See *in the immediate vicinity of*.

victuals. Prounce it *vittles*.

vie takes preposition *with*, not *against*.

viewpoint/point of view. For those writers who hesitate to use *viewpoint* as a replacement for *point of view*, the advice is to feel free to do so. Although *viewpoint* had been criticized by some linguists who steadfastly resisted its entry into better English, many of them have now been won over by its widespread usage. Probably in the strictest formal discourse, the more suitable choice would be *point of view*.

violently, as in "The Republicans *violently* opposed the Democrats' proposal," should be changed to *strongly*. Inherent in *violently* is action not only strong but physically harmful or damaging.

virgule is the name of the typographical mark (sometimes called a *slash*) that is used in this book to separate headwords. Also called *solidus* or *diagonal*.

virtually/actually. These words should be treated distinctively. If something is virtually so, it is not actually so. And vice versa. *Virtually* means "in essence" or "to all intents and purposes," but not "in fact." When your agent acts for you, you're virtually (that is, in effect) acting yourself, even though you are not actually present. Colloquially, *virtually* means "almost" or "very nearly" ("We were *virtually* numb from the cold when we spotted an all-night restaurant"). (See *practically/virtually*.)

vis-à-vis, French for "face-to-face," is most often unnecessarily used as a preposition where *about, against, compared to, as opposed to*, or another word would be more suitable ("The President will consult Congressional leaders *vis-à-vis* [*about*] the budget." "His bushes looked skimpy and desolate *vis-à-vis* [*in comparison with*] his neighbor's plantings").

visit/visitation. Some people might not believe that these words are bothersome, since their meanings are clear. Not so. Occasionally one hears in speech and even sees in print the word *visitation* where *visit* belongs. Formal visits are visitations— those by a committee delegation from a state, those by the Pope to a foreign country. Going to a friend's house for an evening is a *visit*.

viz., an abbreviation for Latin *videlicet*, stands for *namely*, a more suitable term in ordinary writing. Whether the abbreviated form or *namely* is used, it should be preceded by a comma or semicolon ("There are four seasons; namely, spring, summer, fall, and winter." "The school has two assistant deans, *viz.*, A. J. Richardson and T. S. Elliot." Note that some stylebooks recommend that neither *namely* nor *viz.* be followed by a comma.

vocal cords. See *cords*.

vociferous, meaning "loud and noisy," is a perfectly good word, but sometimes unfortunately misused to mean "voracious"— shades of Mrs. Malaprop. In "My son Edward is a *vociferous* reader of murder mysteries," the word required is *voracious*, which means "to devour" but has figuratively come to mean "very eager," "unable to be satisfied."

voice.   See *active voice/passive voice*.

voracious.   See *vociferous*.

vulgar English.   See *English, levels of*.

$\mathcal{W}$

wages. Although a *salary* is a stipend paid for services rendered, which is equally true of *wages*, *salary* is a singular noun and *wages* a plural. "His wages *is* bound to make him rich" should be changed to *wages are*. Caveat: Some writers accept *wages* as a singular noun.

wait on/wait for. It is not uncommon to hear someone say *wait on* in the sense "wait for" ("I'm *waiting on* the delivery boy who is due in five minutes"). The expression is dialectal and does not belong in better discourse. "To wait on," as in "to wait on a customer," is to serve him.

wait up. See *up*.

wake. See *awake/wake*.

wane. See *wax/wane*.

want. See *wish/want*.

want to is colloquial for *ought* or *should*. Not "You *want to* be careful when moving around in a rowboat," but "You *should be*. . . ."

War Between the States. See *Civil War*.

-ward is a suffix meaning "in the direction of." Hence *skyward* is in the direction of or toward the sky. This means that *-ward* should not be preceded by "to the," since that sense is inherent in it. Saying "The statue is located somewhat *to the southward* of City Hall" is tautological. Make it "to the south of City Hall" or delete *to the*.

warm/warmly. The issue raised in the sentence "We know that Paul does feel *warmly* toward his school" is whether, since *feel* is a copulative verb, adjective *warm* should have been used instead of adverb *warmly*. Ordinarily a copula is followed by an adjective, but in this instance idiom prescribes otherwise for the sake of clarity. The thought in "to feel warmly" is to regard with affection. To "feel warm" is to have an elevation in temperature.

was/is. "Armstrong declared that space *is* infinite." That statement is a permanent truth, since the fact concerning space is unchanging. Hence the present tense *is*. Normally the tense in a dependent clause is the same as that in the main clause ("David *said* he *lived* in Hicksville," not *lives*, even though he still lives there). (See *historical present/literary present*.)

was/were. Do you prefer "If I *was* President" or "If I *were* President"? In terms of usage both expressions are heard, but in careful writing, only *were* is correct. The reason for *were*, with its plural connotation, governed by a singular pronoun, *I*, is that this construction is in the subjunctive mood. Although fast disappearing from the English language, this mood has retained one deeply embedded use (and it seems to be here to stay)— to indicate a condition contrary to fact, as in this example, for obviously "I" am not the President.

was a former is redundant. Someone either *was* an employee or *is* a *former* employee. Drop *former* or change *was* to *is*.

wax/wane. "His anger reminds me of the moon. First it *waxes* and then it *wanes*." The problem here is that *wax*, which means "to grow bigger," needs a modifier, which, incidentally, since *wax* is a copulative verb, must be an adjective, not an adverb (*wax loud*, not *loudly*; *waxed strong*, not *strongly*). Without a modifier, *to wax* is to polish—furniture, jewelry, automobiles. *Wane*, meaning "to decrease," "to become smaller," needs no qualifying word to support it ("The moon *wanes* after it has become full").

way, shape, or form is a common expression that serves as well if *shape and form* is excised. In "Harry's accountant said he would help him in any *way, shape, or form*," a period should follow *way*.

way/ways/away. Be careful of the common colloquial use of these words. Instead of "The lake is *way* ahead of the valley," make it "*away* ahead." And do not use *way* as an adverb for *away* ("He is *away* behind [not *way* behind] in his schedule"). Instead of "The lake is a long *ways* from here," make it "a long *way* from here"; *ways*, when preceded by *a*, is always incorrect for *way*.

we/us. See *appositives*.

wedding/marriage overlap in meaning when they refer to the uniting of a couple in matrimony ("We watched their *marriage* from the front lawn, since we hadn't been invited to the *wedding*"). *Wedding* points to the ceremony. *Marriage* does too, but it also refers to the continuance of the marital state. We say "They had a five-minute *wedding* but a fifty-year *marriage*."

weigh as a nautical term means to hoist the anchor. But when the ship begins to move, it is *under way*. (See *under way/under weigh*.)

well.   See *better/well*; *good/well*; *less/well*.

welsh/welch.   When the meaning is to renege on a debt, prefer *welch* to *welsh*. The latter term, even though in lower case, may allude to the inhabitants of Wales, who are not known to avoid their obligations any more so than the inhabitants of other lands.

west.   See *compass directions*.

what.   Understandably many speakers and writers are troubled when they use *what* in such a sentence as "We discovered that *what* we have is enough." The question is whether in formal discourse *what* should be replaced by *that which*. Take another example. Must *what* in "To avoid *what* is considered a waste . . ." be recast "To avoid that which is considered a waste"? Although there is no consensus, *what* for *that which* is sanctioned by many reputable authorities, and everyone should feel free to go along with them. Whether the verb *to be* used with *what* should be singular or plural is another question. It is generally agreed that when *what* is the equivalent of "that which," it is singular; when it stands for "those which" or "things that," it is plural ("As to our supply of sand, *what* we have *is* sufficient." "As to the number of dictionaries in the library, *what* we have *are* sufficient").

what all is dialectal in "*What all* are you looking for?" Possibly *all* is intended to intensify, but that is not reason enough. Omit *all*. (See *you all*.)

whatever.   "Jackson used *whatever* books that were available." Delete *that*. *Whatever* means "any . . . that." Combining *whatever* and *that* is tautological. (See *ever*; *-ever*.)

what for, meaning "why," is substandard in "*What* did the teacher do that *for*?" Make it "Why did the teacher do that?"

when. See *is when/is where.*

when, as, and if. This expression is commercialese for *when* or *if*, either of which conveys the same idea. (See *if and when*.)

whence. See *hence/thence/whence*.

whenever. See *ever; -ever*.

where should not be followed by *at* or *to*. Not "*Where* is he *at?*" but "*Where* is he?" Not "*Where* did he go *to?*" but "*Where* did he go?" (See *is when/is where; preposition at end of sentence*.)

whereabouts. Although opinion is divided on whether a singular or plural verb should follow, certainly in formal writing the singular verb is to be preferred ("His *whereabouts is* unknown"). Only if the whereabouts of several people are in question is a plural verb appropriate ("The brothers all scattered, and their *whereabouts are* unknown").

wherever. See *ever; -ever*.

wherewithal, meaning "necessary means," is a good word, but use it sparingly and in an appropriate context. It sounds too quaint for ordinary use. And note that although the final syllable is pronounced *all*, it ends in *al*.

whether. See *as to whether*.

whether/if/that. In many instances any of these words may introduce a clause ("I doubt *whether* he will come." "I doubt *if* he will come." "I doubt *that* he will come"). *If* has a shade of informality; some careful writers would prefer *whether*. *That* is required in negative sentences ("I do not doubt *that* he will come"). Be sure to avoid such ambiguous constructions as "Let me know *if* John intends to play tonight," which may mean either you are to inform me in any case or you are to inform me only if John intends to play tonight. "Tell us *if* you sent the box" may mean either to tell us *whether* you sent the box or to tell us *only* if the box was sent. (See *if*.)

whether or not. "*Whether* he was truthful *or not* is the question." The question that the example really raises is whether *or not* should be dropped. The answer is yes, and that answer applies to most cases where "or not" follows *whether*. Only when a construction with *whether* sets out alternatives, each to be given equal stress, is *or not* required. One cannot sensibly say "We shall go *whether* it rains." It must be "*whether or not* it rains."

The guideline suggested by some authorities is to substitute *if* for *whether*. If the substitution does not affect the meaning of the sentence, use *whether* alone. If it does, as it would in "We shall go *if* it rains," add *or not*.

which/that. Use *which* when the clause it introduces would take commas ("The brownstone house, *which* I lived in for five years, is to be torn down") and *that* when no commas are called for ("Soccer is the sport *that* I like best"). The *which* clause is a commenting clause; if deleted, the sentence would stand. The *that* clause is a defining or limiting clause. Without it the sentence would collapse. (See *comma*; *that/which*.)

while, when used as a conjunction of duration, is not a problem word. But it can be when used loosely to mean *although*. Whereas the meaning of this sentence is clear, "*While* I know that you dislike writing, I shall expect a letter from you in a day or two," consider "*While* she had her first baby in Kansas, she had her second in Missouri." Use *although*. (See *awhile*.)

while away is used correctly in "I will *while away* the time," not *wile away*.

whisky/whiskey. Except in particular uses, prefer *whisky* to *whiskey*.

who/whom. Choosing between these two words is possibly more difficult than the making of any other choice in English. *Whom* is used as the object either of a preposition ("Give the scarf *to whom* you please") or of a finite verb ("He is the man *whom* I designated"). It also is the subject of an infinitive, since the subject of an infinitive is always in the objective case ("He is the person *whom* we selected to be chairman"). Otherwise, use *who*.

Many authorities believe that, with few exceptions, *who* will eventually obsolete *whom*. Certainly "*Who* did you give it to?" sounds more natural than "*Whom* did you give it to?" Of course *whom* is the right word as can be seen by turning the sentence around—no matter how awkward it sounds—"You did give it to *whom*." Or consider "*Who* do you take me for?" which is seldom if ever properly rendered with a *whom*. But be careful of overcorrectness. In "She is a person *whom* I believe will succeed," *who* is required because "I believe" is parenthetical and *who* is not its object but the subject of "will succeed." If

"I believe" is omitted, the need for *who* becomes obvious. No one would say "She is a person *whom* will succeed." (See *parenthetical phrases*.)

whoever/whomever. What perplexes some writers when faced with a choice of one of these words is the presence of a preceding preposition that heads up a clause. Take as an example "These studies were prepared *for whomever* is attending the intermediate grades." *Whomever* might seem right because it follows the preposition *for* and is its object. But that is not so. The entire clause beginning with *for* is the object. That means further that *whoever* should replace *whomever* and become the subject of the verb *is attending* ("These studies were prepared for *whoever*. . . ."). (See *ever*; *-ever*.)

whom. See *who/whom*.

whomever. See *whoever/whomever*.

whooping cough needs its *w* sounded, not "hooping."

who's/whose. *Who's* is a contraction of "who is" ("*Who's* responsible?") or "who has" (*Who's* forgotten the umbrella?"). *Whose* is the possessive form of *who*, as in "Here's a man *whose* pride is in his home."

whose. See *of which/whose*; *who's/whose*.

widow woman is a not uncommon expression but a faulty one. Within *widow* is the sense of *woman*. Drop *woman*. *Widow* alone will do.

will. See *shall/will*.

winter. See *seasons, capitalization of*.

-wise, as a suffix, means "in the manner of" (*clockwise, lengthwise*) or "wise in the subject of" (a *worldlywise* traveler, a *court-wise* tennis player). The caveat that should be observed is not to use suffix *-wise* indiscriminately, adding it to nouns to make preposterous words. "Teamwise we are in good shape because pitcherwise we are well staffed." Wordwise, that sentence doesn't read well. It is abominable English, languagewise. (See *leastways/leastwise*.)

wish/want. "We *wish* to leave." "We *wish* a second helping." Should *want* replace *wish* in those sentences? even though both key words mean "to desire." Opinion among critics is divided. The belief is that *wish* sounds softer and that *want* sounds demanding. Perhaps, but *want* ordinarily is to be preferred except in formal writing, where *wish* is regarded as more appropriate. Be sure, however, to avoid a construction such as "She *wanted for* us to leave." The unnecessary *for* makes the sentence substandard. (See *would like for*.)

with/and. Should one say "The captain *with* his players *were* surrounded by fans" or "The captain *with* his players *was* . . ."? Certainly the nominative *captain* is singular. The question is whether the objective case *players* combines with it, thus requiring a plural verb. Since a consensus is lacking, it becomes a writer's choice. To clearly justify a singular verb, surround the *with* words with commas—"The Captain, *with his players*, was surrounded by fans." Or, if a plural sense is preferred, use *and* for *with* ("The captain *and* his players *were* . . ."). (See *as well as*; *in addition to*; *together with/along with*.

withhold. Note the double *h*.

without saying. See *needless to say*.

with reference to, as well as *in reference to*, is usually reducible to *on* or *about* ("*With reference to* [*About*] this matter, we have a divided opinion"). *Have reference to* can economically be changed to *mean*. "What we *have reference to* is that the security guard is half asleep" needs only "What we *mean* is."

with regards to. See *regard/regards*.

with the exception of. Consider a shortened version like *except* or *except for* ("All the scouts left the camp *with the exception of* Donald"). Make it *except*.

witness should not be used as a synonym for *see* or *observe*. It is a more formal word best used when describing official or dramatic events. One witnesses an inauguration or an accident. In these cases *see* would be inappropriate. You see an acrobat walk a tightrope but you witness his fall to his death.

woman/lady. Which of these terms is favored in American usage is a difficult question to answer. The names of some respected organizations include the word *women*, or a form of it; others equally respected use *ladies*. A belief persists that the term *ladies* in some uses connotes refinement; *women* suggests commonness. Be that as it may, *woman* and *women* are general words best employed in ordinary discourse. Those who frown on those terms mistakenly believe they connote disparagement.

word arrangements. If unsure of the proper order of two or more adjectives modifying the same noun or pronoun, just remember that they are best placed from short to long. Say "He is the best, the smartest, and the most capable of all our managers." (See *and/but*; *sentence structure*.)

wordiness. See *stretched wordings*.

worst. See *if worst comes to worst*.

worst of two. See *better/best*.

worst way, as in "The school needs English teachers *in the worst way*," is as undesirable a colloquialism as its sister expression "very badly" ("The school needs English teachers *very badly*"). Say instead, "The school is in *great need* of English teachers" or some other equivalent wording. Rather than "Elaine dislikes the weather in Montana *in the worst way*," make it "Elaine *extremely* dislikes" or "dislikes the weather *very much*."

would. See *should/would*.

would have ... would have. Do not repeat *would have* in a conditional statement. Replace the first *would have* with *had*, as should have been done in "If our star pitcher *would have* (*had*) shown up, we *would have* won this game."

would like for is a colloquial expression in such a sentence as "The office *would like for* me to represent the firm in Kansas." A better statement is "The office *wants* me. . . ." (See *wish/want*.)

would of is substandard for *would have*. Not "We *would of* bid on the painting if we had been at the auction," but " *We would have*." (See *could of*; *might of*; *should of*.)

wrack. See *nerve-racking*.

wrapped. See *rapt/wrapped*.

wrong/wrongly. *Wrong* is both an adjective, as in "That was the *wrong* road to take" and an adverb, with the sense "incorrectly" or "in a wrong manner," as in "Everything goes *wrong* the moment the boss walks in" (note that *wrong* follows the verb). When placed before the verb, the proper qualifier is *wrongly* ("The quotation was *wrongly* excerpted." "It was *wrongly* handled").

wrought. "The typhoon *wrought* havoc in the Philippines." The misuse of *wrought* for *wreaked*, the word required in the example, is far from uncommon. *Wrought* is not the past tense and participle of *wreak*, but of *work*. Except for its use in reference to the fashioning of metals (*wrought* iron), *wrought* is obsolete.

xerox. Although it is technically wrong to equate the word *xerox* with photograph or duplicate, usage is fast establishing it as a common verb ("We expect to *xerox* these papers this afternoon"). Those who object to this usage will find that trying to reverse the trend makes as little sense as reverting to carbon copies.

𝒴

yclept. For those wondering what this obsolete English word means, the answer is "called" or "named." Nowadays it is used only by those who think they're being humorous.

ye. If you use this archaic word (*Ye* Old Bucket Shoppe), it is good to know that it means "the" and should be pronounced *the*, not *yee*.

yes/no. In a construction containing one of these words, the *yes* or *no* should be written in lower case and with no punctuation ("Murray said yes when I asked whether he wanted to go"), and with no underlining, as in the example. The plural of *yes* is *yeses*; the plural of *no* is *noes*.

yesterday. See *tomorrow/yesterday*.

yet. In "The teacher gave me a book, but I did not open it *yet*" and in "The architect did not call *yet*," change to *but I have not opened it yet* and *has not called yet*. Negative contructions in which *yet* as a temporal adverb means "up to now" take a perfect tense verb. In "Caldwell has not *as yet* made his plans," omit *as*. Do not use *as yet* where *yet* alone will suffice. As an adverb of time, *yet* may overlap the meaning of *still*. "Are the Gerbrons here *yet*?" may be interpreted to mean "Have they arrived *yet*?" or "Are they *still* here?" Restructure to avoid ambiguity. (See *still*.)

Yiddish. For those who are under the impression that this language is identical with Hebrew, be assured that the languages are unrelated, although they use the same script. *Yiddish* may contain some Hebrew words, but basically it is of German origin and most of its vocabulary stems from German. Yiddish became a popular medium of expression among Eastern Jews, many of whom migrated to other countries, taking their language with them.

you all, when referring to one person, is a regionalism, best avoided in all regions. If more than one person is meant, rather than *you all* (grammatically correct though it be), prefer *all of you*. It sounds better (*"All of you* should now follow me"). (See *what all.*)

your/you're.   *Your*, meaning "belonging to," is a possessive adjective ("This is *your* coat"). But be careful not to write, *"Your* going to meet your father on Wednesday." The intended word was *you're*, the contracted form of *you are.* And also be careful not to spell *yours* with an apostrophe; there's no such word as *your's.* By the same token, be sure to add the apostrophe when using the contracted form for *you are* (*you're*).

yourself/yourselves.   *You* is either the nominative or the objective form of a personal pronoun. *Yourself* and *yourselves* are either reflexive or intensive pronouns. These different forms are not interchangeable, but they are sometimes confused. Do not say "I hope your wife and *yourself* can join us for dinner because my wife and *myself* would like to have you." Make it "your wife and *you.*" *Yourself* may not permissibly replace *you.* And of course "I" is needed in place of *myself.* (See *-self/-selves.*)

$$\mathcal{Z}$$

zany/zombie. These words are not synonyms. Using one or the other might be not only embarrassing but also misinformative. In "My uncle ran all over town on a buying spree like a *zombie*," probably the word wanted was *zany*. Zombies do not run; they walk slowly as though they were the living dead. The term *zany* refers to a silly person because that was what a clown in an Italian comedy was called. *Zany* is a Venetian form of Giovanni, the equivalent of John in English. A *zombie* is a corpse, reanimated through voodoo ceremonies. Hence an apathetic person, as might be expected of someone brought back from another world.

zenith/nadir. The first refers to the heavenly point directly overhead; the second to the ground immediately below a person's feet. By extension, *zenith* has come to mean "summit" and *nadir* "the bottom" or "the pit."

zero. Its plural form is preferably spelled *zeros*, without an *e* immediately before the *s*. Most style manuals recommend that unnecessary zeros be omitted ("I owe Joe $*10*" rather than $*10.00*. "We'll meet at *3 p.m.*" instead of *3:00 p.m.*). (See *naught/aught*.)

zip at one time stood for "zero," a widely used informal term. Today *zip* has an even more common usage because of the ZIP codes established by the Postal Service. ZIP is the acronym for Zone Improvement Program.

zombie. See *zany/zombie*.

zoom is used in aeronautics to mean "an upward movement at a sharp angle"; it may therefore not be used to describe a downward movement. Do not say the raven zoomed down on its prey; it swooped. And, remembering the definition of *zoom*, do not say the kite *zoomed upward*. Say simply, "The kite *zoomed*."